RAMBLERS

RAMBLERS

LOYOLA CHICAGO 1963–THE TEAM THAT CHANGED THE COLOR OF COLLEGE BASKETBALL

MICHAEL LENEHAN

MIDWAY

AN AGATE IMPRINT

CHICAGO

Printed in the United States of America.

Library of Congress Cataloging-in-Publication Data

Lenehan, Michael.
Ramblers : Loyola Chicago 1963 --the team that changed the color of college basketball / Michael Lenehan.
    p. cm.
Includes bibliographical references and index.
Summary: "The story of the 1963 NCAA national champion Loyola University Chicago Ramblers basketball team"--Provided by publisher.
ISBN-13: 978-1-57284-140-6 (pbk.)
ISBN-10: 1-57284-140-0 (pbk.)
1. Loyola University of Chicago--Basketball--History. 2. Basketball--Illinois--Chicago--History. I. Title.
GV885.43.L67L46 2013
796.323'630977311--dc23

2012042513

10 9 8 7 6 5 4

Midway Books is an imprint of Agate Publishing. Agate books are available in bulk at discount prices. For more information, go to agatepublishing.com.

"When Negroes and whites meet on the athletic fields on a basis of complete equality, it is only natural that this sense of equality carries into the daily living of these people."
—Georgia state senator Leon Butts, 1957

To my father and mother, Dan and Eve

To my son and daughter, Jack and Rose

To my wife and partner, Mary Williams

TABLE OF CONTENTS

FOREWORD...**13**

PRELUDE: **Louisville, March 23, 1963** / 15 Down...**17**

PART ONE: BEGINNINGS

CHAPTER 1: **Chicago** / Coach on a Flagpole...**23**

CHAPTER 2: **Mississippi** / We were led
to believe there were no Negroes....**31**

CHAPTER 3: **Cincinnati** / The Best Basketball Player
in the World...**35**

CHAPTER 4: **Chicago** / Out-of-Town Talent...**41**

CHAPTER 5: **New York-Chicago** / Hungry Young Men...**49**

CHAPTER 6: **Mississippi** / A Big-Time Major Mistake...**61**

CHAPTER 7: **Chicago** / Stranger in the Heartland...**65**

CHAPTER 8: **Cincinnati** / Life Without Oscar...**71**

CHAPTER 9: **Nashville-Chicago** / Fast Break Basketball...**79**

CHAPTER 10: **Chicago** / Four Fab Freshmen...**95**

CHAPTER 11: **Cincinnati** / Jucker's Surprise...**111**

CHAPTER 12: **Mississippi** / Is there anything wrong
with five white boys winning the national championship?...**117**

INTERLUDE: **Louisville, March 23, 1963** / Keep Shooting...**123**

PART TWO: COLLISION COURSE

CHAPTER 13: **Chicago** / Off-Court Adjustments...**131**

CHAPTER 14: **Cincinnati** / Defending National Champions...**137**

CHAPTER 15: **Chicago** / Racial Peace Prevails...**145**

CHAPTER 16: **Cincinnati** / Two Flukes in a Row...**157**

CHAPTER 17: **Mississippi** / Civil War Redux...**161**

CHAPTER 18: **Chicago** / Collision Course...**175**

CHAPTER 19: **Chicago** / Four Blacks and an Albino...**185**

CHAPTER 20: **Mississippi** / Come Hell or High Water...**193**

CHAPTER 21: **Chicago** / The Greatest Fast-Break Team Ever...**205**

CHAPTER 22: **Mississippi** / Cloak and Dagger...**211**

CHAPTER 23: **East Lansing** / This is history....**217**

CHAPTER 24: **Louisville** / The Final Four...**227**

OVERTIME: **Louisville, March 23, 1963**...**233**

PART THREE: POSTGAME

CHAPTER 25: **Dancing in the Streets**...**239**

CHAPTER 26: **The Future of Basketball**...**243**

CHAPTER 27: **The Man**...**253**

CHAPTER 28: **Afterward**...**265**

ACKNOWLEDGMENTS...**279**

NOTES AND SOURCES...**283**

INDEX...**291**

FOREWORD

——

I'm looking at the cover of *The Young Sportsman's Guide to Basketball* by George A. Cella, published by Thomas Nelson & Sons in 1962. The photo—two basketball teams poised for a jump ball—reminds me of an old family portrait: I see a resemblance to a game I know, but some of the details are wrong. The players' pants are impossibly short and tight, almost constrictive. Their shoes are Converse Chuck Taylors, which we know today not as basketball shoes but as fashion statements.

These are the things you notice on close inspection. But what you see first, what tells you in an instant that this picture is not from our world, is that all the players are white.

Was there really a time when such a picture was considered realistic, or even plausible?

Was there a time when it was against the rules to dunk? When a coach would bench a player for taking a jump shot? When a major college game could be decided by a score of 23–16?

Was there a time when it was considered daring or provocative to have three black players on the floor at the same time? Or when blacks were threatened, spit on, and showered with garbage as they walked onto the court?

Was there a time when civil rights protesters could be attacked by a club-wielding mob while police officers stood by? When the president of the United States had to mobilize 30,000 federal troops to put down an armed insurrection prompted by the enrollment of a single black man at a state university?

There was. I saw some of it on black-and-white TV, and in magazines that no longer exist. But my memories are vague and scant. I was just becoming a teenager. The generation that remembers it better, more directly, has started to pass. And my kids' generation knows it only from history class, if at all. I'm afraid they find it impossible to believe.

So here's a story about the integration and evolution of college basketball, set against the backdrop of the civil rights movement, one of the most convulsive periods of our nation's history. I tell it through the exploits, and sometimes the voices, of three teams that played in the NCAA tournament of 1963.

First and foremost are the Loyola Ramblers of Chicago, who then represented the future of basketball: they were one of the first major college teams with four black starters, and they played in a fast, athletic style that presaged the high-flying game we know today.

Their opponents in the final were the Cincinnati Bearcats, the Goliaths of the game, playing for the fifth straight year in what today we call the "final four." Though they had three black starters (and had four the previous year), they played a slow, deliberate game that was on its way out of style.

The third team, the Bulldogs of Mississippi State University, also played in the older style, but they represented the past in a more fundamental way. Not only were they (and the school they represented) all white, they had never even played against a black man, due to an informal state policy of athletic segregation. They had to sneak out of Mississippi in order to compete in the tournament.

The story of basketball's integration and evolution could be, and has been, told in other ways, through other teams. I don't really believe that the Loyola Ramblers singlehandedly "changed the color of college basketball," any more than I think the Texas Western–Kentucky game in 1966 "changed America forever" (Don Haskins, *Glory Road*), or that the Magic Johnson–Larry Bird championship of 1979 "transformed basketball" (Seth Davis, *When March Went Mad*), or that North Carolina's 1957 victory over Wilt Chamberlain and Kansas "revolutionized college basketball" (Adam Lucas, *The Best Game Ever*). A book like this is obliged to make such a claim on its cover, but we all know better: basketball, never mind America, is not transformed by a single game or team or season.

Still, each of these claims is built on a bit of truth; each represents a moment or a milestone in a long, involved history made up of many incidents and influenced by many heroes and villains. Fifty years ago basketball was played mostly on the floor, black players' opportunities were severely limited, and our country was reeling with racial conflict. Today basketball is played largely in the air, black players dominate, and our country is...well, still conflicted, but at least a little steadier on its feet. My aim here is to persuade you that a pivotal moment in that transition was the improbable championship of the Loyola Ramblers, a black-and-white team that opened a lot of eyes and stirred a lot of hearts. I hope you buy the argument, but more than that I hope you enjoy the story.

PRELUDE: LOUISVILLE, MARCH 23, 1963

15 Down

―――

Jerry Harkness thought it was ordained somehow. It had to be. Too much luck and coincidence were involved, too many dramatic twists. Like it all pointed to this moment. A poor kid raised in a fatherless home in Harlem starts playing high school basketball in his senior year. A struggling coach who has seen him play just once—on a bad day—offers him a scholarship to a college he knows nothing about in a place he's never been, a Jesuit commuter school in Chicago. Four years later he's an All American on national TV, the captain and leading scorer of the third-ranked college basketball team in the country—the Loyola Ramblers, underdogs but contenders in the 1963 NCAA championship.

It couldn't have happened if the dorm at Texas Southern hadn't burned down just before Harkness was to enroll.

It couldn't have happened if his teammate Jack Egan hadn't been snubbed by the University of Iowa.

Or if forward Vic Rouse hadn't overcome his childhood polio, defying doctors who said he'd probably be gimpy for life.

It couldn't have happened if coach George Ireland hadn't flouted the conventions of the day by starting four black players night in and night out.

Harkness would tell these stories for years, refining them till he learned to hold the punchlines for dramatic effect. For example, he played playground basketball but didn't think he was good enough to make his high school team. And then one day a guy walked up to him at the Harlem Y and told him, you know, you're pretty good. You could get a scholarship for that, go to college. And that guy was...

Jackie Robinson.

Here's another one: Loyola center Leslie Hunter wanted to go to college with his high school friend and teammate Vic Rouse. Hunter, 6-4 in high school, had ability but little polish. He was shorter than Rouse by a couple of inches and not as mature emotionally or athletically; in their junior year of high school he was Rouse's backup. But George Ireland was willing to take them as a twosome. And in the fall of 1960, when they arrived on the Loyola campus, Hunter was...

6-7.

So as Jerry Harkness stood at center court in Louisville's Freedom Hall, awaiting the opening tip of the NCAA final, he figured he'd been led there by fate. He knew how this story was supposed to end.

And then he ran into Tom Thacker.

Thacker too was an All American, and unlike Harkness he had been here before. His team, the University of Cincinnati Bearcats, was playing for a place in history, to become the first team ever to win three NCAA titles in a row. They were the Goliaths of college basketball, with three starters who would later play in the NBA. They were ranked first in defense among major college teams, allowing their opponents an average of only 52.6 points per game. They played a patient, deliberate game, moving and passing as long as it took to produce close-in, easy shots. If they didn't score much they didn't care, as long as their opponents scored less.

Loyola was almost the exact opposite. Competing in the tournament for the first time ever, the Ramblers were the highest-scoring team in the country, with an average of 92.9 points per game. They scored many of their points on the fast break. Their big men could run and Harkness, a cross-country star in high school, could run for hours. They were quick with their hands and feet. They played a harassing full-court defense and turned it into transition offense, stealing the ball and intercepting passes, scoring easy baskets on the turnovers. If their opponents scored a lot of points they didn't care; Loyola's aim was to score more.

Thacker introduced himself to Harkness about 30 seconds after the tip, on Loyola's first possession. Harkness took a pass on the right side of the court about 18 feet from the basket. Immediately he turned to drive around Thacker. "I knew he was guarding me way to my left," Harkness recalled many years later. "I'm left-handed, and I go to my left a lot. I was gonna fool him and start off going to my right." Dribbling with his right hand he quickly gained a step on Thacker—or so he thought. "When I took that first couple of dribbles, I felt, ooh, I'm on my way in, I fooled him. I got him. I'm in front. And I'm getting ready to go up…"

As Harkness drove toward the basket, Thacker was behind him off his left shoulder. Yet somehow Thacker managed to reach his right hand all the way around Harkness's back and smack the ball away before Harkness could put it up.

"I was shocked," Harkness said. "That never happened. I had him."

Thacker had learned the move on the playground. A kid named Les Scott used it on him repeatedly. "He was a white boy. One hell of a ball-player. He taught me that trick, and ever since I did it on my opponents. I let him think he's past me, but I stay close to him, because I know my arms are long enough to reach around him. As he gets past me, boom, I'm around him like this and the ball's gone."

"That really got me," Harkness said. "He's right in my head, right away. Early in the game, he was letting me know: It ain't gonna be easy."

And it wasn't. With Thacker on his every move, Harkness could do nothing right. He rushed shots, changed the angle of his arm, pushed off the wrong foot—anything to keep the ball away from Thacker or get off a shot before Thacker could close in. The leading scorer on the highest-scoring team in the country did not get a point in the first half. When he made his first field goal there would be fewer than five minutes left in the game.

As Harkness went, so went Loyola. They missed 13 of their first 14 shots from the field. In the first eight minutes they scored four points. At halftime they had a mere 21. They had made only 8 baskets in 34 at-tempts. Their defense wasn't bad, and Cincinnati wasn't playing all that well either. They had only 29 at the half. But the Bearcats were getting the rebounds and Loyola's fast break was stymied. Cincinnati's big man,

*6-8 George Wilson, was killing them. "This was shocking," Harkness re-
membered. "I've never seen a guy out-jump Hunter and Rouse like that."*

*In the second half Cincinnati built their lead. In one stretch they
sank five shots out of six; in another, their sharpshooter Ron Bonham hit
three in a row. With 12:29 to go in the game, they led by 15 points, 45–30.
Harkness thought of his mother watching at home in the Bronx. He
thought of his high school teammates and his playground buddies, most
of whom were watching him on TV for the first time. The neighborhood
celebrity, "stinking up the joint."*

*He thought about the night before: Having slaughtered Duke in the
semi on Friday night, he and his teammates had celebrated past 2:00 AM,
running up and down the hall in their hotel, pounding each other on the
chest and smacking each other with pillows, psyching each other up for the
final game, telling themselves over and over "We're playing for the national
title! We gotta win! We gotta win!" Had they blown it by staying up too late?
Or had they simply met their match? Either way, Harkness found himself
in a different story from the one he'd imagined. He was embarrassed. He
saw it slipping away. All he wanted now was to make it respectable, get the
lead down to single digits. "Oh, gosh, let's just make it close."*

*His teammate Jack Egan was also embarrassed. And afraid. In 1963,
15 points was a big hole to climb out of. There was no three-point shot in
college basketball then; worse, there was no shot clock. A team with a lead
could pass and dribble and play keepaway as long as their skills allowed,
and at Cincinnati the skills were practiced diligently. The Bearcats had
perfected the stall. Egan, a cocky kid from the Southwest Side of Chicago,
was not the type to get discouraged, but he did not see a way Loyola could
win. "It's a shock for us to have 30 points at this point in the game. You
know, we're used to scoring 90-some points a game. And then there's the
fear, at least in the back of my mind, that all of a sudden, in another
couple of minutes, they're just gonna take the air out of the ball and we're
gonna be playing the cat-and-mouse game. We've only scored 30 in all this
time, and they're gonna hold the ball now. Can you get 15 more points
with them getting zero? That's what the fear is in my mind: we can't catch
up if they hold the ball—and they do it every game."*

Time out Loyola.

PART ONE:
BEGINNINGS

CHAPTER 1: CHICAGO
Coach on a Flagpole

As Judy Ireland recalled it, she was still a student at Loyola when she heard about her father's hanging. It was probably 1958 or '59. Her mother Gert phoned with the news; she wanted Judy to hear from a family member that George, or at least an effigy representing him, was swinging from a flagpole outside the union building. He was not having a good year.

Loyola was a small player in the world of intercollegiate athletics. Founded by the Jesuits in 1870 as St. Ignatius College on Chicago's West Side, by 1958 it had nearly 9,000 students spread out over three far-flung campuses, including a law school in downtown Chicago and a medical center on the West Side. But the main undergraduate campus still felt like a small urban college. Located in the far-north neighborhood called Rogers Park, it was squeezed between the shore of Lake Michigan on one side (an amenity to be sure) and Sheridan Road and the Howard Street El line on the other. It served about a thousand students and had just one dorm, for men only, which hadn't been open long. At most, counting all of its campuses, there was an undergraduate student body of roughly 3,600 full-time students, of whom all but about 400 were commuters.

Still, the basketball coach was expected to produce. Loyola had been competing in basketball since 1913 and had done pretty well at

it. The program was established primarily by Lenny Sachs, a manically active athlete who earned 11 varsity letters in high school, played
basketball in the Navy during World War I, and coached high school
basketball and football while attending the American College of
Physical Education in Chicago. He took the Loyola job in 1923 but
for a few years continued moonlighting as a player for the Chicago
Cardinals and other teams in the early NFL. He coached basketball
and football at Loyola, served as athletic director, and on the side
coached football for Wendell Phillips High, the South Side black
school that supplied the nucleus of the first Harlem Globetrotters
team.[1] In his spare time he earned a bachelor of philosophy degree
from Loyola and converted from Judaism to Catholicism.

Sachs is seen as a pioneer of college basketball, one of 85 coaches
(men's and women's, college and pro, as of summer 2012) in the Naismith Memorial Basketball Hall of Fame. He took his 1938–39 team
to the finals of the National Intercollegiate Invitation Tournament, or
NIT, which was then in its second year. (Played then as now in Madison Square Garden, the NIT overshadowed the NCAA tournament
for years.) He died of a heart attack in 1942, just before a big Phillips
High football game against rival DuSable. He was 45. The blow,
combined with the displacements of World War II, led Loyola to
suspend basketball for a couple of years. When the program resumed,
so did the success. In 1949 the Ramblers[2] returned to the NIT, under
coach Tom Haggerty, and again finished in second place.

George Ireland took over in 1951. Before that he coached for 15
years at Marmion Military Academy, a Catholic boys' high school
in Aurora, Illinois, where he won more than three-fourths of his
349 games. Before that he was an All American at Notre Dame, a
playmaking guard with a good two-handed set shot. When he was a
senior, in 1936, the team was named national champion. On gradu-

---

1   The Globetrotters were based in Chicago. The "Harlem" in the name was owner Abe
Saperstein's way of branding the team as all black.

2   The name "Ramblers," a sportswriter's nickname that stuck, was originally applied
to Loyola's football team, supposedly because it traveled extensively for the time. In 1925 a
contest sponsored by the football coach and the student newspaper had produced the name
"Grandees," a nod to the Spanish origins of Saint Ignatius of Loyola, the founder of the Jesuit
order. For some reason Grandees failed to catch on.

ating he was reportedly offered a job as John Wooden's assistant at Central High School in South Bend, but he took the Marmion job because it paid $10 a month more.

In those days college basketball was a small world. Catholic college basketball was smaller. At Notre Dame Ireland played with another All American, Paul Nowak, whose sister Gertrude became Ireland's wife. He also played with a whole roster of future coaches, including Edward "Moose" Krause, who later coached at Notre Dame, and Ray Meyer, the longtime and much beloved coach at Loyola's Chicago rival, DePaul University, which is located a short El ride south of Loyola's Rogers Park campus. As a senior, Ireland ran the basketball team's peanut concession at Notre Dame football games; Meyer, who was a couple of years younger, had the job of stuffing the peanuts into paper bags.

Another teammate was Johnny Jordan, who preceded Ireland as coach at Loyola. According to at least one version of events, Jordan took the Loyola job in 1950 after Ireland turned it down. Ireland turned it down because he had been waiting for the Notre Dame job, which at the time was held by his teammate Moose Krause. Just a year after Ireland turned down the Loyola job because he was waiting for the Notre Dame job, Moose Krause left the Notre Dame job to focus on his duties as Notre Dame's athletic director. To replace Krause as basketball coach, Notre Dame hired not his old teammate Ireland but his old teammate Jordan, who then left Loyola after coaching there only a year, whereupon Ireland ruefully took the job that Jordan had vacated. At least this is the story as told by Ireland's son Mike. Years later, having become famous and sought-after as Loyola's coach, Ireland claimed he wouldn't accept the Notre Dame job if they gave him all the buildings on campus. But Mike attended and played basketball for Notre Dame, where his father always wanted him to go.

Ireland's starting salary at Loyola was $6,000 a year plus a room in the corner of Alumni Gym. Mike, who was starting high school that year, lived with a family in Evanston while his mother and sisters stayed in Aurora waiting for their house to sell. In the spring the family reunited in Skokie, a suburb just north of Chicago. Ireland's first year went well. He inherited a strong team of seniors led by a

Greek kid named Nick Kladis, and they went 17–8. But then Kladis and his fellow starters graduated. The following year Loyola was 8–15, finishing the season with an ugly streak of eight straight defeats. The year after that, 1953–54, they whittled the string of season-ending losses down to six, but again finished 8–15. Then they surged to 13–11. Then they fell back to 10–14. Ireland was getting ulcers. A surgeon removed four-fifths of his stomach. At the end of his fifth season, with one year left on his second contract, he had a record of 56–63, a winning percentage of just .470. His predecessor Tom Haggerty had left Loyola with a .730 record. Lenny Sachs finished his career at .634. Both had gone to the NIT. Ireland was going nowhere, except to the top of a campus flagpole. He needed help. Even a dummy could see that.

———————————

According to Arthur Ashe's book *A Hard Road to Glory*, the history of blacks playing basketball for predominantly white colleges goes back at least as far as 1904, when Samuel Ransom, a four-sport athlete from Chicago, starred for Beloit College in southern Wisconsin. Over the next 40 years, however, the list is short and studded with the names of exceptional figures like Paul Robeson (Rutgers, 1915–1918), Ralph Bunche (UCLA, 1921–22), and Jackie Robinson (UCLA, 1939–1941). As with so many aspects of modern American life, the big changes began at the end of World War II, when military service prompted blacks to seek their due in mainstream society.

Loyola's first black player was Ben Bluitt, a Chicagoan who enrolled out of the Army Air Force in 1946. He later coached as an assistant at the University of Detroit, another Jesuit institution, and was the first black head coach at Cornell.

Chicago's black newspaper, the *Defender*, watched closely as Bluitt and Loyola stumbled through unfamiliar territory. Early in Bluitt's first season, when he was the second-string center, the paper announced a misstep: "Loyola Coach Meekly Bows to Texas Jim Crow," the headline charged. Coach Tom Haggerty had decided to leave

Bluitt home as the team made a three-game swing through Texas. Earlier the *Defender* had cheered the University of Nevada for better dealing with a similar problem. Before a football game that Nevada had scheduled at Mississippi State College, Mississippi State's athletic director, C.R. "Dudy" Noble, wrote to Nevada suggesting that they might want to travel without two of their star players, both veterans of the war who happened to be black. Their presence in his state would "cause unfortunate commotion," Noble explained. Nevada rebuffed the suggestion and canceled the game.

Just a few days later, a similar controversy killed a football game between Penn State and the University of Miami. The *Defender* reported that this game had been arranged about a year before, after several years of trying by Miami officials. But when they realized that Penn State's roster would include two blacks, they objected that it would be "difficult to carry out arrangements." Penn State's dean of athletics advised Miami that the two players were "regular members of the Penn State football squad" and would not be left home. Instead, Penn State canceled the game.

Compared to these righteous acts, the *Defender* found Loyola's treatment of Ben Bluitt wanting. Haggerty tried to soften the insult by insisting that Bluitt would play when the Texas teams came to Chicago later in the season, but the *Defender* wasn't satisfied. "Loyola had a chance to stand out and prove to the world that it stood for equality of opportunity and equality of justice. It failed." When the Texas teams came north, a *Defender* headline jeered "Hurrah! Haggerty Uses Ben Bluitt Against Crackers." Unfortunately, having defeated SMU in Texas without Bluitt, Loyola lost on their home court with him.

In 1947 Bluitt was joined on the Loyola roster by Art White, who had played at all-black St. Elizabeth High School, a basketball powerhouse on Chicago's South Side. Bluitt and White, who both went to the NIT finals on the 1949 team, were presumably recruited by Haggerty, as was Warren Inniss, a backup center who played for Ireland from 1951 to 1954. The first black player Ireland himself recruited—at

least the first who stuck long enough to make the team photo—was
Art McZier, who arrived as a freshman in 1954.

McZier grew up in Evanston, in a mostly black neighborhood
across the street from Evanston Township High School. His mother
was a housecleaner. His father was gone. Two of McZier's boyhood
friends had fathers who worked as janitors at the high school, so
McZier got to play in the big gym as a little kid. He remembered that
Northwestern University played home games in that gym—that's
when they brought out the new glass backboards.

McZier grew to about 6-4 and played baseball, football, and
basketball for Evanston. In basketball he was a Suburban League
all star, but his college options were limited. Les Brownlee, the first
black reporter at the *Chicago Daily News*, had played football at the
University of Wisconsin and took McZier there to meet the basketball coach. "It was a cold environment," McZier recalled. "He had
never had a black player and he didn't seem too enthusiastic, you
know what I mean?" McZier considered the southern all-black colleges, particularly Tennessee State, which had an excellent basketball
program, but then one of George Ireland's spies saw him playing
in a summer league. "Coach Ireland approached me—approached
my mother—and my mother was very impressed, because his whole
thing was that he would guarantee me to get an education."

Recruiting was more casual then. A lot of it was done via personal
connections: a player might hear an encouraging pitch from an older
friend or former teammate who attended the school in question; he
(or his high school coach) would usually receive a written expression
of interest and an invitation to visit the campus. During the visit, he
would meet the head coach and maybe work out informally with a
few members of the team. Ireland himself did it this way with many
of his white players. But with the blacks he was the maestro of the
kitchen table. He didn't recruit players—he recruited moms.

McZier played varsity three years for Loyola. (Before 1972, freshmen were generally not allowed to play with the upperclassmen.)
In his senior year Ireland named him cocaptain of the team. He is
probably best remembered for his role in a stunning upset of Adolph

Rupp's Kentucky team in a Chicago Stadium doubleheader attended by more than 14,000. Kentucky, a perennial basketball power, was then ranked 12th in the nation by the Associated Press and had humiliated Loyola by 33 points earlier in the season. The game at the Stadium was much closer, the lead changing four times in the last 90 seconds. With 15 seconds to go, Loyola had the ball and a one-point advantage, 55–54. The game was all but won if they could just hold on to the ball, but they couldn't. Kentucky took possession and called time out. Their inbounds pass went to Vern Hatton, who swished a 15-footer to put Kentucky ahead by one. Now Loyola called time out. According to a story later told by George Ireland, Rupp walked over to the scorer's table to ask exactly how much time was left. Told there was one second, Ireland said, Rupp "pulled together his double-breasted suit, which was out of style then, and said, 'Well, that should do it.'"

Frank Hogan, who would later coach Loyola's most famous freshman team, threw the ball in at half court. Here's how McZier remembered it: "Actually, what was supposed to happen, I was to pick for Paul Sheedy. Paul Sheedy had this nice little two-handed set shot. Frank Hogan was taking the ball out of bounds at half court. First alternative was I pick for Sheedy, to get him free. And then I turn around just in case, the second option. Well, as soon as I ran up to set the pick Hogan threw me the ball. Right away I said the best thing to do is just throw it." The *Chicago Tribune*'s Richard Dozer called it a "blind, desperation hook shot"—hooking it being the only way McZier thought he could get the half-court distance. He "gave the basket a glance over his shoulder and cut loose with a shot that zoomed through, to electrify the house," Dozer wrote.

But the shot was not quite as blind as it looked. "Interesting enough," McZier told me, "I used to shoot that shot playing horse, screwing around. I used to bet guys that I could make four out of five, or two out of three. Coach Ireland used to get on me for that. And I can understand why. You're never gonna take a shot like that, so why are you out there practicing it?"

CHAPTER 2: MISSISSIPPI
We were led to believe there were no Negroes.

In the summer of 1955, a sharp-dressing, smooth-talking young oil salesman from Baldwyn, Mississippi, somehow got himself hired as head basketball coach at Mississippi State College, his alma mater. Located in a town called Starkville amid cotton and cow farms in the northeast part of the state, Mississippi State was a land-grant school that had long been considered the poor country cousin of the University of Mississippi at Oxford—"Ole Miss." Basketball was not a big deal at Mississippi State; it was something that happened before baseball season started. Even the outgoing coach, Paul Gregory, seemed to share the institutional preference: dismissed after a horrible 6–17 season, he went on to achieve great success as State's baseball coach, winning four Southeastern Conference (SEC) championships in a celebrated 18-year career.

The new basketball coach was James H. McCarthy, age 31. Everyone called him Babe. He was hired as Mississippi State's first full-time basketball coach, but if that suggested a new commitment on the part of the college, his resume suggested otherwise. McCarthy, who stood about 5-6, had never coached or even played basketball at the college level, though one source said he played for a fraternity team while a student at Mississippi State. He did have some experience, though: he had coached his hometown high school team for three years, had taken them to the state championship, and after serving as a transport pilot in World War II he had coached a team in the Air Force. When he got the job at Mississippi State he had been out of coaching for a few years, though he had remained active as a referee in the SEC. Presumably he came cheap and won the job by force of personality, which by all accounts was his strongest suit. "He never met a stranger," one of his players told me. "He could have been governor of Mississippi," said another. "He could sell a refrigerator to an Eskimo," said a third. "When he walked into a room you'd say to yourself, 'The man has arrived. I don't know who he is, but there he is.'" They called him Little Napoleon. Several of his players remembered his voice: it was authoritative. Distinctive. You could pick it out of a crowd. Years later sportswriters would call him Magnolia Mouth.

He was not shy. As the rookie coach of a woebegone basketball program, installed in the job about two months before the start of the 1955 school year, he set out to recruit one of the most highly prized players in the Southeast, a 6-7 center from Middleton, Tennessee, named Bailey Howell, who years later landed in the Basketball Hall of Fame. Howell wanted to play in the SEC, and he had his pick of scholarship offers including one from Kentucky, one of the most storied basketball programs in the country. But he passed on Kentucky, and on Tennessee and Ole Miss, in favor of a team that had just finished dead last in the conference.

"Coach McCarthy was sort of ahead of his time in recruiting," Howell told me. "He visited me and my parents probably more than all the other coaches put together. He sent people by—for example Don Blasingame, who was a second baseman for the St. Louis Cardinals who had played for him in the service. He sent him by to say hello and to encourage me to consider playing for Babe. He was a great personality and he just sold himself, really, to me and my family."

In McCarthy's first year as coach, while Howell played on the freshman team, the Mississippi State varsity climbed to a 12–12 record and tied for sixth place in the SEC. When Howell joined the varsity as a sophomore in 1956, he led the NCAA with a 56.8 shooting percentage. The team's record improved to 17–8 and they tied for third place in the conference.

But if that 1956–57 season pointed to a bright future for Mississippi State basketball, it also revealed a tragic flaw. At the end of December, McCarthy and his team traveled north for a holiday tournament hosted by the University of Evansville in Indiana. They beat their first-round opponent, the University of Denver, in a close game on Friday night. On Saturday, McCarthy received a call from his athletic director, Dudy Noble. Immediately after that call—a few hours before they were to take the floor for the tournament final—the team packed up and went home to Starkville. Noble, it seems, had seen in newspaper accounts that the Denver team included two black players. Worse, Mississippi State's next opponent in the tournament, Evansville, would have a black player too.

"It's always been our policy that our teams would not compete against Negroes," Noble explained. At least it always had been since 1955, when the football team from Jones County Junior College in Mississippi played an integrated team from Compton, California, at the Junior Rose Bowl in Pasadena. In response to that mishap, Mississippi legislators threatened to withhold funding from state-supported schools that strayed from the Mississippi "way of life." Compliant college administrators began observing an "unwritten rule" against participating in athletic tournaments if there was any danger that Mississippi boys would have to play against a Negro opponent.

In the wake of the Evansville retreat, the president of Mississippi State, Ben Hilbun, at first told the press he'd had nothing to do with it, then admitted that he had ordered it. An AP story quoted him saying, "We were led to believe there were no Negroes....Our team wouldn't have gone up there if I had known there were Negro players in the tournament. I don't think our coach would ever have taken the team up there if he had known it, either."

The AP story went on, painting a picture: "Coach McCarthy firmly refused to comment on the action, and apparently instructed his players to do the same....McCarthy and his players packed up

hurriedly and left their hotel by bus for home. They were out of
Evansville within an hour."

Vance Hartke, who would soon be elected to the first of three
terms as a U.S. senator from Indiana, was mayor of Evansville at the
time. He said, "Basketball is a prime example of judging a man by
his ability—not by the color of his skin. Some day, perhaps, we all
will come before one Great Judge. I hope our Southern friends then
learn what justice really is."

This provoked a letter from a woman in Memphis, who shared
her thoughts with a carbon copy to Mississippi State president Ben
Hilbun. "Sir," she wrote to Hartke:

> Your remarks in regard to the action taken by the Mississippi
> State basketball team show that you know about as much
> about a nigger as a pig does about Sunday school.

A couple days later, the *Daily News* of Jackson, Mississippi, the
state capital, stepped forward to offer its perspective, showing an
attitude, and a level of acuity, that would become familiar in the
years to come:

> Managers and coaches of football, baseball, basketball, and
> other athletic teams in Mississippi's state-supported colleges
> should understand, once and for all, that they must not take
> part in games anywhere, or under any circumstances, where
> the opposing team has Negro players composing a part of
> the personnel.
>
> Insofar as public sentiment in Mississippi on that subject is
> concerned, the rule is as irrepealable as the law of gravitation.

CHAPTER 3: CINCINNATI
The Best Basketball Player in the World

While the separatists in Mississippi held tight to their status quo, the future they feared arrived about 500 miles north, in Cincinnati, Ohio—just across the Ohio River from Kentucky, about as close as you could get to the South without actually being there. In 1956 an unusual number of people began showing up for freshman basketball games at the University of Cincinnati. There was no doubt they were showing up for the freshman games, because many would leave before the varsity team took the floor. Their reason for coming was a shy young man from Indianapolis, the best basketball player that most of them had ever seen, or ever would. He was Oscar Robertson.

Robertson was not the first black college superstar, but he was probably the most appealing. By the time he arrived at Cincinnati, Wilt Chamberlain was at Kansas, Elgin Baylor was at Seattle University (a Jesuit school), and Bill Russell had led San Francisco (another Jesuit school) to two consecutive NCAA championships. But Chamberlain was 7-1 and Russell 6-9. They played close to the basket and what they did looked easy, given their freakish height, to those who were inclined to underestimate their talents. Baylor, a 6-5 forward, had a game that was easier to appreciate—he was a gifted passer and an acrobatic scorer—but he was less visible. He started his career at the College of Idaho, then sat out a year, and then played only two seasons way out in the Pacific Northwest before leaving school to turn pro.

Oscar Robertson, by contrast, arrived at Cincinnati a fully hyped phenom—a high school All American and winner of the honor they call "Mr. Basketball" in basketball-crazed Indiana. He could do everything—pass, dribble, shoot, rebound, post up. And he was a hero to blacks for having delivered the revenge of Crispus Attucks on the state that had once been the northern stronghold of the Ku Klux Klan.

Crispus Attucks High School was opened in 1927 expressly to remove and segregate black students from other Indianapolis high schools. It was named after a black Revolutionary War hero, one of the victims of the Boston Massacre of 1770. (The school board wanted to name it after a white slaveholder, Thomas Jefferson, but the blacks who were to be sequestered there objected and petitioned for the change.) Although the school was a center of racial pride in Indianapolis—it was staffed almost entirely by blacks, including PhDs who couldn't get teaching jobs in the white schools—it was also a symbol of oppression. After Crispus Attucks was opened, the cities of Gary and Evansville followed the Indianapolis example and established their own all-black schools. The discrimination became particularly poignant when high schools lined up for the annual state basketball tournament, which was (and remains) a very big event in Indiana. The schools in smaller communities were integrated—there weren't enough blacks to justify a separate school—and their teams were allowed to play in the tournament. But the all-black urban schools were excluded. Arthur Trester, the head of the Indiana High School Athletic Association, explained when Crispus Attucks opened that it wasn't eligible for the IHSAA or its tournament because it wasn't really a "public" school—it enrolled only blacks! This logic prevailed for 14 years. Black (and Catholic) schools were finally admitted to the association in 1942.

By the 1953–54 season, Oscar Robertson's first on the Crispus Attucks varsity, the state tournament was more than 40 years old and had never been won by a team from Indianapolis. Attucks reached the sectional championship that year before being defeated by the team that eventually won the tournament, tiny Milan High School, whose season inspired the film *Hoosiers*. In 1955, Robertson's junior year, Crispus Attucks won the tournament, to the delight of blacks in Indiana and beyond, and in 1955–56 they went undefeated and won again. Indianapolis sportswriter Bob Collins called Robertson "the best high school player in the world," and college coaches seemed to agree. In his autobiography, Robertson (or his ghostwriter, Charles Bock) wrote that he was contacted by 75 colleges. "Calls came to my home and school on a daily basis. Indiana, Purdue, Notre Dame, Illinois, Duquesne, Kansas, New York University, Duke, Connecticut, Marquette, UCLA, Arizona State, Kansas, Nebraska..."

Although Robertson was shy and quiet, by his own account, he was also proud, wary, and sensitive to racial insult. He wanted to go to school within a bus ride of Indianapolis. His first choice was Indiana University. Like a lot of kids who grew up playing basketball in Indiana, he wanted to be a Hoosier, even though he knew that the coach there, Branch McCracken, had a bad reputation among black players. "[A]lthough Indiana had five black players on the team, they did not play more than one or two at a time," Robertson wrote. "If they had all those guys on the bench, it followed that someone wasn't going to play." Nonetheless, Indiana's basketball tradition pulled strongly. "If that man had said, 'Oscar, we would like you to come to Indiana and play for us,' I would have taken a pen from my pocket and signed with him right there." But the coach seemed to be bitter about the loss of Wilt Chamberlain the year before. Chamberlain had committed to IU, or so McCracken thought, but landed instead at the University of Kansas. Chamberlain later claimed that Kansas had given him a Cadillac and all the spending money he needed, as much as $20,000 over his two-year varsity career.

When Robertson, the next year's highly touted black player, appeared at McCracken's door, the coach kept him waiting for half an hour and then opened the conversation saying, "I hope you're not the kind of kid who wants money to go to school."

Robertson wrote: "I didn't answer him and just walked out of his office, back to the car, seriously insulted....I came away thinking that I wouldn't play for Indiana University if it were the last place on earth."[3]

Another Big Ten school, Michigan, invited Robertson to visit. He got on an airplane for the first time in his life. When he landed in Detroit, there was no one to meet him at the airport. "I kept waiting, unsure of what to do or where to go," he wrote. "After half an hour, I called the coach. They'd forgotten I was coming. I got on the next plane for home."

He was received more adeptly in Cincinnati, courted not only by coach George Smith but also by a well-coordinated group of local businessmen and civic leaders. A booster arranged for his mother, an aspiring musician, to appear on the *50-50 Club*, a Cincinnati-based variety show that was seen in Indianapolis, and to make an audition tape at King Records, a successful independent label headquartered in Cincinnati. (James Brown, among many others, recorded for King.) Another booster, a prominent lawyer, chatted Robertson up at a Reds game and promised help and counsel in his college years and beyond. Robertson liked Cincinnati's unusual co-op program, which would allow him to earn money by alternating quarters of academic work with employment at Cincinnati Gas and Electric—all legal and aboveboard, with no threat to his eligibility as an athlete.[4] He didn't spend much time on campus—and would later regret being naive about just how white the student body was—but he committed to UC the day after he graduated from high school.

Almost immediately he began paying off on his extraordinary promise. In his first game as a freshman, against the Cincinnati varsity, he took 17 rebounds and scored 37 points. He finished his freshman season averaging 33. In his 11th game on the varsity, against Seton Hall at Madison Square Garden, he scored 56—more than the entire Seton Hall team, and more than any player, pro or college, had

3   It seems only fair to point out that under McCracken, Indiana was the second school in the Big Ten to have a black player, Bill Garrett, back in 1947.

4   The NCAA later objected and Robertson had to give up his co-op employment.

ever scored in the world's most famous basketball arena. Louis Effrat
of the *Times* called it "the greatest one-man show in Madison Square
Garden basketball history." And Robertson was just getting started.
Two polls named him college player of the year as a sophomore, over
both Chamberlain and Baylor, and four named him as a junior and
senior. (In 1998, the U.S. Basketball Writers Association named its
player of the year trophy after him.) He led the nation in scoring
through his three years of varsity play, finishing with an average of
33.8 points per game. From there, of course, he went on to a long and
legendary NBA career with the Cincinnati Royals and the Milwaukee Bucks. With the Bucks, and a young center named Lew Alcindor
(who would later change his name to Kareem Abdul-Jabbar), he won
an NBA championship in 1971. In 2000, the National Association of
Basketball Coaches named him Player of the Century.

Only one thing is missing from Robertson's long list of accomplishments: he was not able to lead his college team to a national
championship. Cincinnati made the final four[5] in his junior and
senior years, but both times they were turned back in the semis by
the University of California, a defense-minded team coached by Pete
Newell, who was also bound for the Basketball Hall of Fame. Cal
held Robertson to fewer than 20 points in both games. They won
the championship in 1959 and lost in the final to Ohio State in 1960.

When Robertson graduated, it must have seemed to many that
Cincinnati's chance to win a national championship had slipped
away. George Smith chose this moment to end his coaching career;
he moved up to become Cincinnati's athletic director and passed
the team on to his assistant, Ed Jucker. But if Robertson had failed
to bring Cincinnati a title, he had at least pointed the way. He had
proved, for one thing, that even a conservative and almost-southern
city like Cincinnati could learn to love a black basketball player. After
Robertson opened the door, George Smith began recruiting blacks in
greater numbers—and signing them. They wanted to play where the

---

5   The term "final four" was not yet common, but I'm going to use it anyway.

Big O had played. By the middle of the 1960–61 season, Cincinnati would be starting three black players.

Robertson also taught the white coaches at Cincinnati how to deal with black players once they arrived. In his sophomore year, on a road trip to Houston, he was rousted from his bed at the Shamrock Hilton and moved to a dorm room at all-black Texas Southern University while the rest of his team stayed put. Although he had been playing varsity for only about two weeks, he was already valuable enough to make his own rules. According to his autobiography, he told Smith in no uncertain terms that if it ever happened again, he would walk.

Finally, Robertson taught a valuable lesson to Ed Jucker, who had accepted the thankless job of coaching Cincinnati in the future. Two years in a row Jucker had watched from the bench as the Bearcats earned a place in the final four, and both times they were thwarted by a disciplined team that stressed defense. If a running, high-scoring offense wasn't enough to win the championship with the best basketball player in the world, it certainly wasn't going to win without him. Jucker knew he would have to find another way.

CHAPTER 4: CHICAGO
Out-of-Town Talent

It's not clear when, how, or even if George Ireland consciously decided to recruit black ballplayers from out of town, but it's a fair bet that Art White had something to do with it. White was the 1947–1949 Loyola player who had come from St. Elizabeth High School in Chicago. After college he returned there to teach and coach, and on the side he refereed freshman games for Ireland at Loyola. He would later become the first black ref in the Big Ten.

St. Elizabeth was a magnet for talented black players, the only black high school in Chicago's competitive Catholic League, which vied with the Public League each year in a high-profile city championship game played at the Chicago Stadium. In 1956 and '57 the team was led by Art Hicks, who is remembered as one of Chicago's best ever. In both those years St. Elizabeth won the all-city championship, and in 1957 they won the all-black National High School Basketball Tournament, sometimes called the National Negro Tournament, played in Nashville.

Part of the program at St. Elizabeth was a barnstorming trip during Christmas break. White and his fellow coach Charlie Gant would pile their kids into cars and drive them through Tennessee, Mississippi, Arkansas, and other points south, matching them against other all-black teams and along the way giving them an education in southern race relations. On one of those trips, St. Elizabeth played a high school from Algiers, Louisiana—the other side of the river from New Orleans. In that game White noticed a 6-5 center named Clarence Red. Soon after, George Ireland was in Algiers knocking at the Red family's door.

Red was a studious, sheltered kid. He already knew he wanted to be a dentist. His father was a hod carrier and an official in the union; his mother worked at a dry cleaner. They took education seriously and made sure Clarence did too. He ranked high in his senior class (the *Defender* erroneously reported that he was valedictorian), but his college options were limited. He had scholarship offers from Grambling, Southern, and other all-black schools, but the only northern schools that showed interest were two Jesuit colleges, Loyola and the University of San Francisco. Most black kids would probably have jumped at the USF offer. Coach Phil Woolpert and the Dons, as his team was called, had just won two consecutive national championships with three black starters, Bill Russell, K.C. Jones, and Hal Perry.[6] But Red visited the USF campus and didn't think it was the place for him. "The players"— by this time, Russell, Jones, and Perry had moved on—"they were a little different. I guess I would call them fast? Party guys. And I was just a high school graduate, I wasn't looking for a fast life." He liked Loyola better. And he really liked George Ireland.

"George Ireland was quite a unique person. He came to New Orleans and came right into our home and sat at the kitchen table with my mom and dad and me and my little sister. He came in like just a friend of the family. He was very much at ease sitting down and chatting with my parents and me. Different from other white coaches. He was just like any of the black coaches that came to my home. So I didn't view him as this white coach—I viewed him as hey, he's right at home with us.

"First of all he asked what I wanted to do. What do you want to be? What do you want to major in? I told him I wanted to become a dentist, and he said you know we have a dental school, and he started talking not only about my playing basketball but going to Loyola

---

6   Jones played the regular season in USF's second championship year, 1955–56, but not in the NCAA tournament. The California Basketball Association granted him a fifth year of eligibility because he had missed all but one game of the 1953–54 season due to appendicitis. But the NCAA wouldn't let him play in the tournament. His spot was filled by another black player, Gene Brown.

dental school. By the time he was done with what Loyola could offer, and what he could offer as a coach, my mom turned to my dad and said I think he should go to Loyola. And that's how it happened."

Young Clarence had some adjusting to do. He had never played against white athletes, and he was a 6-5 black man on a nearly all-white campus. "I always felt that because of the way I stood out, I had to be very careful how I acted." But even if he'd been inclined to get into trouble, it's not clear he would have known how. "Fortunately I had good parents and a good high school coach, and I thought I knew how to behave. I certainly didn't want to embarrass the school. George Ireland had given me this opportunity, I certainly didn't want to embarrass him."

Red hit the floor running and never slowed down. In his first game for the varsity, he scored 26 points against Carleton College. (Like many coaches, Ireland liked to start each season with a few "warmup" opponents.) A week later, against Western Ontario, he tied a school record with 15 field goals; he scored 34 points that night and took 29 rebounds. He finished the season leading the team with 20.3 points per game, and Ireland's world started to look a little better. At the start of the 1959–60 schedule, he told the *Tribune's* Richard Dozer that he was hoping for his best season ever.

He didn't get it, but he did succeed in making some history by taking Red home to play Loyola of New Orleans in February of 1960. Where Mississippi had an unwritten rule against integrated sporting events, Louisiana had it in writing—a state law enacted in 1956, after the University of Pittsburgh caused a stir by bringing a black football player to the Sugar Bowl against Georgia Tech.[7] That law had been successfully challenged in 1958, but no integrated sporting event took place in Louisiana until the two Jesuit schools contrived this battle of

---

7   The player was Bobby Grier. The incident, coming in the wake of *Brown v. Board of Education* in 1954, set off a flurry of legislative activity in the Deep South. Next door in Georgia, state senator Leon Butts, whose words appear in the epigraph, introduced a ban against integrated athletics in 1957. Butts's bill failed to pass, thanks in part to opposition from minor league baseball owners, but the state board of regents had already enacted a sports segregation policy of its own. In the Sugar Bowl game, Grier was called for pass interference in the first quarter, in what the New Orleans *Times-Picayune* called a controversial play. The penalty gave the ball to Georgia Tech on Pitt's one-yard line. Tech scored on a quarterback sneak and won the game 7-0.

the Loyolas. Clarence Red thought that Ireland (whose brother was a professor in the Loyola New Orleans pharmacy school) arranged the game at least partly as a favor to him. "I think George Ireland knew that I couldn't have attended Loyola of New Orleans and played basketball like I played in Chicago. I feel that he was trying to do something for me, to allow me to play in front of my hometown." The *Defender* reported "an estimated 2,500 braved a heavy thunderstorm to attend the contest, including 500 Negroes who watched from segregated stands. The crowd was about 1,000 more than the normal attendance at Loyola games."

Red was the attraction and he almost carried the day. After the Ramblers trailed by as many as 10 points, he sank two key baskets to tie the game with less than three minutes and again with 16 seconds left on the clock. But Loyola of New Orleans won on a layup at the buzzer.

The only jeering, the *Defender* reported, came from both sides of the stands when Red objected to a goaltending call. "The Rambler ace angrily slammed the ball high into the Loyola fieldhouse rafters." Red led the Ramblers with 17 points, but "handed the winners 10 automatic points with his five goaltending fouls."

Despite Ireland's high hopes, the Ramblers finished that 1959–60 season with a disheartening 10–12 record. Loyola had one of its best players ever and still seemed unable to get out of its .500 funk.

———————————

If the students held Ireland responsible, his boss was inclined to lay the blame elsewhere. He was Father Cletus Hartmann, chairman of Loyola's athletic board, the committee that steered hiring, firing, and policy for the school's sports programs. Father Hartmann thought that Loyola's basketball woes arose from excessive devotion to academic standards. After the lackluster (10–14) season of 1955–56, he wrote to Father James Maguire, the president of the university, seeking an audience with the board of trustees. "In my estimation," he said, "the plight was never more desperate." He continued:

> The Basketball Coach has knocked himself out trying to induce good prospects to come to Loyola....The coaches of the Chicago Catholic League will not recommend Loyola to any of their athletes because of the reputation for difficulty of the entrance exams.[8] The word has gotten around that it is very hard to enter Loyola and still harder to stay there...

> Do we want big-scale basketball or don't we?...Why are Marquette, Detroit, Xavier, Creighton, Holy Cross, Fordham, San Francisco, and some of our [Jesuits'] other schools permitted to recruit the way they do, and have the athletes accepted at those schools? I hear this time and again, and I know boys that have been rejected by Loyola have been accepted at another Jesuit University.

Athletic committee records contain no indication that Hartmann got his chance to address the trustees on this issue. He took a different tack after the 1957 season (14–10), asking Ireland to provide written proposals for improving the recruiting picture. Ireland asked for "permission to admit on probation some very good prospects who might otherwise be refused admission." He also requested a tutorial system to help athletes with their classes, full scholarships for up to 20 players at a time (including books and the NCAA standard of $15 a month for carfare and laundry), and a recruiting budget that the board pegged at $200 to $300 for the coach and an additional $500 for "outside assistance." Hartmann's committee voted to present these requests to the president and to give Ireland a new three-year contract.

In 1958, even as Art McZier was leading the Ramblers to a 16–8 season, Hartmann focused his attention on the admissions office. In a letter to Father J.J. O'Callaghan, executive vice president of the

---

8   The SAT was far from universal and the ACT wouldn't come along until 1959. Loyola and other colleges administered their own entrance exams.

university, he recounted some friction between himself and the admissions director, Mary Manzke, and complained that Loyola was "the only Jesuit University that does not have a Jesuit in charge of admissions." He asked O'Callaghan to provide Miss Manzke with written permission to admit a few athletes who wouldn't get in otherwise. O'Callaghan and Maguire insisted that the athletic department could achieve its goals under current university policy, which allowed deans discretion to admit students on probation. O'Callaghan wrote: "If you can convince a Dean that...a student merits a chance on a probationary status, you are working within the regulations of the University, and no one can gainsay this."

At Maguire's request, Miss Manzke produced a study showing that between 1953 and 1958, 17 basketball players had been admitted as exceptions to the regular norms, and 13 of them had either flunked out or were still on academic probation.

Hartmann replied to this slap with another letter, a passionate defense of his student athletes:

> None of them have an easy time at Loyola, and none of them get the breaks they get at other colleges, including Jesuit colleges. There are no snap courses, there is no physical education curriculum, there is no feeling among the faculty that the athletes deserve a break...

> Why do we expect an athlete to take a full schedule of courses in the same curricula as other students, ask him to add the hours of practice, the consequent injuries and aches and fatigue, the absence from class representing the university in competition with other schools, and expect him to do as well as other students who find it difficult to pass the courses unburdened with outside activities?

Hartmann said he knew many athletes who were "scholars Loyola can be proud of. I know the backgrounds that statistics cannot show.

I have been told on occasion that Loyola is not interested in back-grounds, circumstances, etc., but in percentiles, gross scores, senior high-school class averages, etc. This is a far cry from Jesuit education as I understand it...."

> I merely hope that you don't get the idea that we are cut-ting corners in athletics, and that we are admitting bums to Loyola. There are some circumstances known to the coach and myself which justify my asking for the admission of this or that athlete. If the university prefers to operate on statis-tics alone and not on some other values, then I suppose we shall have to conform. However, until such utopian time that good athletes are also good scholars I feel that we shall have to ask for special consideration.

If Hartmann thought he could get special consideration spelled out in a policy or memo, he was probably dreaming. But maybe he was just proposing an unrealistic extreme to soften the opposition. He may have been doing something similar when he suggested that the athletic committee consider dropping basketball and substituting football, which Loyola had abandoned in 1930. Or maybe that was just a joke. In any event, Loyola did admit a basketball player on probation the following fall, a New York kid with powerful lungs and an unusual left-handed push shot. He had finished high school a year before but had not been able to find a college that wanted him. He was the kind of kid Father Hartmann wanted to take a chance on. One day he would make Loyola proud. He was Jerry Harkness.

CHAPTER 5:
NEW YORK–CHICAGO
Hungry Young Men

In 1959 New York was the world capital of basketball and Harlem was its most important breeding ground, a place where professional and college players came together with the street kids whose energy and hunger fed the game and pushed it forward.

Basketball, it is commonly observed, requires less equipment and real estate per player than any of our other favorite ball games. But that's not the only reason it's "the city game," as Pete Axthelm titled his influential 1970 book. Whether it's five players against five or one on one, basketball is a game in which an individual can shine. More than most other team sports, it provides a way to get what's hardest to come by in the inner city: identity, attention, respect, self-confidence. Status. Invented in 1891 in Springfield, Massachusetts, the game quickly took root in the fertile asphalt of New York City. In the early part of the 20th century basketball was dominated by Jewish kids like Nat Holman from the Lower East Side. He started his professional career at age 14, playing with the barnstorming Roosevelt Big Five for $6 a game, and went on to coach at City College of New York for 37 seasons starting in 1920. They called him Mr. Basketball. In the 40s the game was embraced by Irish kids in Rockaway, Queens, where Dick and Al McGuire came up. Dick was a ball-handling wizard who starred for St. John's and the New

York Knicks. His younger brother Al also played for the Knicks but was better known as a coach—he led Marquette to an NCAA championship in 1977—and later as a broadcaster. They are the only brothers in the Basketball Hall of Fame.

After World War II, with "money available for cars and stereos and surfboards," Axthelm wrote, "the hunger vanished from many white playgrounds, and so did the top-caliber basketball. But the blacks of Harlem and Bedford-Stuyvesant more than filled the void."

In Harlem the scene was developed by and eventually named for Holcombe Rucker, a city playground director who in 1946 started a summer basketball tournament as a means of improving the prospects of the neighborhood's young people. Rucker was a teacher at heart; after his tournament was well established, he received an education degree from City College and taught English at Frederick Douglass Junior High School in Harlem. His motto was "Each one, teach one." In *Asphalt Gods: An Oral History of the Rucker Tournament*, Vincent Mallozzi writes that Rucker spent 14 or 15 hours a day in the park, "a weathered green bench serving as his office chair, an old streetlamp his night-light," receiving scores of boys and girls, basketball players and not, guiding them through their complicated lives. According to one source he personally taught reading, helped with homework, and scrutinized report cards.

Rucker's tournament quickly grew to three divisions and began to attract top players, amateur and professional, from across the city and beyond. Watching the games was a popular weekend pastime in Harlem. Mallozzi, who grew up in the neighborhood, wrote:

> The scene was carnival-like, with pushcart vendors hawking beer and ice cream, old ladies selling fried chicken at 25 cents a piece, and fans in the corners of the park huddled over small flames cooking mickeys (sweet potatoes) in pans from their own kitchens. Little children stood on milk crates to get a better look at the action while their parents worked out their vocal cords along the sidelines...

White players were welcomed and even respected for seeking out the competition—if they could play. One of them was Donnie Walsh, a skinny kid from Riverdale, Bronx, who later played at the University of North Carolina and went on to a fabled career as an NBA coach and executive. He competed in the Rucker tournament while a student at Fordham Prep and told Mallozzi he'd never played in front of so many people. "There must have been over one thousand people in that little fenced-in schoolyard....There really is no way to capture the feeling of what it was like playing up there, with all those great players, and it didn't matter if you were black or white, because if you showed the crowd you were a player, they respected you for it." By the time he talked to Mallozzi, Walsh had been to the NBA finals as president of the Indiana Pacers. But he said he had "never, ever had such a great feeling about being a part of the game."

It was the mixture of pros and talented amateurs that gave the Rucker tournament its special charge. Wilt Chamberlain played there. And Lew Alcindor, Bill Bradley, Julius Erving, Willis Reed, Earl Monroe...the list goes on. Fifty years ago, the NBA was disorganized and slightly disreputable compared to the slick entertainment conglomerate we know today. As late as 1960, if there was a college game scheduled at Madison Square Garden, the Knicks had to move downtown to play in the 69th Regiment Armory on Lexington Avenue near 26th Street. Pro players were not too rich or injury-averse to play on city asphalt, and not too proud to compete against playground heroes whose names were known only to the hardcore. Some of these pros were returning to the parks where they had grown up. Some of them had known Holcombe Rucker as kids. They nourished the neighborhood. A visiting pro paid respect. A returning pro was even better—a reminder that Harlem kids could make it. And if a pro was bested by a neighborhood player who hadn't yet made it, or might never make it—that was the stuff of basketball dreams.

Holcombe Rucker, a chain smoker, died of cancer in 1965 at age 38. In 1969, the park at 155th Street and Eighth Avenue, the last of several sites where his tournament was held, was named Rucker Park, and through the years "the Rucker" has become synonymous with Harlem playground basketball and the showy, improvisational style of play it engendered. This was not the systematic, geometric game taught in schools by coaches who emphasized discipline, teamwork, and unselfishness. It was the exuberant, improvised game of unrestrained young men who had something to prove, who wanted literally to rise up over their opponents and out of their circumstances.[9]

———————————

Rucker and his tournament are only the best remembered symbols of a basketball passion that pulsed throughout Harlem and across the five boroughs. Every church, playground, and community center had its team, and there were coaches and mentors and leagues and tournaments everywhere. As the biggest tournaments gained in popularity and prestige, they attracted a new kind of participant to the scene— the all-star coach or sponsor, who handpicked teams to compete in big tournaments like the Rucker and the Ray Felix tournament in Queens. The players were the cream of the New York crop; the sponsors were freelancers representing only themselves. "Outside ball," they called it—meaning not that it was played outdoors, although it usually was, but that it was beyond the reach of institutions like high schools and colleges.

In 1959 this scene was dominated by three white men. The first of them was Mike Tynberg,[10] who put together the Gems, a legendary team that at one time included Roger Brown and Connie Hawkins, two of the most celebrated of all New York playground players. Then came Howard Garfinkel, who was friendly with Tynberg, followed his example, and eventually became his rival. Garfinkel assembled a team that he called the Nationals, after the Syracuse Nationals, his

9   The name and organization of the tournament began changing as early as 1966. In the 80s, it was succeeded by the Entertainers Basketball Classic, which has brought commercial sponsors, rap musicians, and cable TV to Rucker Park. Big-name pros such as Kobe Bryant and Kevin Durant still come occasionally to participate in the pro-am playground romance.
10   Some sources spell it Tyneberg; see Notes and Sources.

favorite team in the NBA. (They eventually moved to Philadelphia and became the 76ers.) At one point Garfinkel's Nationals included Tom "Satch" Sanders, who later played 13 seasons with the Boston Celtics; Tony Jackson, a star for St. John's University, "one of the greatest shooters in the history of basketball," according to Garfinkel; and Al Seiden, who also played for St. John's, the "Cousy of his day," Garfinkel claimed, and the best who ever played for him. (Brown, Jackson, and Hawkins were casualties of the point-shaving scandal of 1961, on which more later).

Garfinkel recalled the scene some 50 years later in his "office"— the Carnegie Deli on Seventh Avenue. "We went 38–1 over two summers in the Grover Cleveland summer league in Queens" he told me. "I contend, and people agree, that it was the greatest outside team ever put together." Garfinkel, or Garf, as he's sometimes called, made basketball his whole life. After amassing a record of 511–151 as a coach-sponsor—he kept count—he quit the outside game to establish a scouting service for college coaches. He drove to gyms all over New York and New Jersey to sniff out talented prospects, issuing his reports first in a magazine and later a targeted newsletter for coaches called *High School Basketball Illustrated*. Later he cofounded the famous Five-Star basketball camps, where high school players like Michael Jordan, Alonzo Mourning, and LeBron James developed their games and showcased their skills for college recruiters.

Garfinkel told me that after he and Tynberg were at it for a while, a third guy came along, an insurance man named Walter November. He named his team the Reliables, after his company. "He was a tough opponent. We had our differences."

The outside scene was loose and informal. The rosters might change from one tournament to the next, and players would move from one sponsor to another. In return for their services, they would get uniform tops, maybe socks or sneakers, a ride to an exotic neighborhood, hamburgers or pizza after the game. One player told me that he and his teammmates were paid—the very best got up to $50 for a game, he said—but Garfinkel denied paying anyone and most of the players

I talked to insisted that when money changed hands it was carfare, or lunch money, or a gift or a loan to help a family strapped for cash.

What was in it for the sponsors? Garfinkel and most of the players I spoke with agreed it was a combination of things, including ego, competition, and "helping kids," in Garfinkel's words. "Because they're getting exposure. And you're sending some to college." In effect, Garfinkel said, the outside teams were the benign precursor of the AAU teams that play such a prominent role in recruiting today. Because they gathered the best talent from a wide area, their coaches sometimes had closer relationships with college recruiters than high school coaches had. Tynberg scouted for Frank McGuire[11] at North Carolina and Al McGuire at Marquette. Garfinkel was tied to Everett Case at North Carolina State. When Walter November had a good prospect, he told George Ireland at Loyola Chicago.

———————

Jerry Harkness played his first organized basketball under Holcombe Rucker. Later he played for Howard Garfinkel awhile—as a bench player on the greatest outside team ever put together—but he ended up with Garfinkel's "tough opponent," Walter November. "Garfinkel cared mostly about winning games and tournaments," Harkness recalled. "November cared about me. Not that Garfinkel didn't, but November would come to the projects just to talk. We'd sit on the bench and talk about life and things like that, about playing and going to college."

Harkness was a shy, sensitive kid. "I grew up in Harlem, on welfare," he told me, intending those words to explain a lot. The guys in the neighborhood called him Lonely Face.

His mother, Lucille, was 16 or 17 when she gave birth to him. A couple years later came his sister Marlene. Their father, Sonny, had a decent job as a window washer at the UN, but Sonny's first loyalty

11   Frank McGuire, the son of a New York cop, was not related to Al and Dick McGuire, the sons of a New York barkeeper. However, Frank did coach Dick and Al when they played for St. John's.

was to his brothers and sisters; they had been abandoned as kids. Harkness told me his father "stepped up" later in life, but he wasn't around much when Jerry and Marlene were young. "My sister and I would go downtown before he'd get off and he'd give us a little pocket money, but that's basically what we saw of him. My mom had to take it pretty much by herself. She didn't have any money. And she couldn't quite get a job. She was insecure about her skills, about herself. We didn't eat a lot of nights." Sometimes when they did eat, dinner was bread and Karo syrup.

Though Harlem could be rough, it was not an unrelieved slum. The "ghetto" meant segregation and discrimination, but it also meant a certain amount of black dignity and self-reliance. The son of a welfare mother knew plenty of people who went to work every day. The schools weren't so bad. The neighborhood was home to doctors and lawyers and teachers and famous musicians and athletes. They had nowhere else to go.

Jerry was what they called a clean-cut kid. He went to class. He wrote poetry. He wasn't a gifted or a particularly focused student, but he was lucky to land at DeWitt Clinton High School, a storied all-boys public school in the North Bronx. It was a subway ride from Harlem but a world away.

When I first met Harkness he had just come back from a 50-year reunion at Clinton, and he was dazzled by the people his schoolmates turned out to be: fashion designer Ralph Lauren; comedian Robert Klein; Ed Lewis, one of the cofounders of *Essence* magazine, who came to the reunion in a chauffeured limo; a surgeon who'd lived in Paris; a hugely successful dentist; a couple of guys who wrote for the movies. "It was predominantly a Jewish school," Harkness told me. "They were trying to integrate. It was a good experience with another race. You could see a different environment, a different makeup of kids. A lot of us black kids wanted to look cool, clean cut and nice and neat, and studies weren't a high priority. Right away I realized that the Clinton kids were really focused. They wanted to do something with their lives. They didn't dress nice and didn't care, but when I saw those kids and how far they seemed to be ahead of me, they moved me up. Started me thinking, hey, I ought to be doing better."

He didn't play basketball for Clinton until his senior year. Instead he focused on track and cross country, at which he excelled. He won Bronx public school championships in the 880-yard run and in cross country (2.5 miles), but characteristically he told me more about a race that got away, a cross-country race in which another runner outfoxed him and cut him off.

Harkness was behind him but coming on. "He knew I had a kick, and I'm coming out with about a quarter of a mile to go. I don't have much left, but I got enough to get him, and I feel it. So I'm coming down the straightaway and he sees me coming and just comes over in front of me." On a cross-country course, spectators sometimes line the finish; Harkness wanted to go around but couldn't find room. "He got me. I broke stride and finished right behind him." The winner of the race was 30 seconds ahead; this was a battle for second place. But Harkness had not forgotten it 50 years later. "I can still feel it, I see myself. Those things stay with you. All my life they just stay."

At about the same time he entered Clinton as a freshman, Harkness's mother moved the family north to the Patterson public housing project in the Bronx. Jerry hooked up with the Clowns, a basketball team from the project that played around the city in summer leagues. They did well. He came to believe that he might have been the reason, but at the time it didn't occur to him—he was slow to recognize his talents. He didn't even try out for Clinton's varsity team. "I said oh gosh, I can't make those teams, those guys up there are so much better. And I was real good with the community teams—really good—I just didn't have enough confidence. We were already struggling, with the poverty. I didn't want any more letdowns in my life."

In his junior year he did play on an intramural basketball team at Clinton, and in the intramural championship, which his team won, he scored 24 of the team's 28 points. That got the attention of Clinton's basketball coach, Hank Jacobson. Then, that summer, he had the fateful encounter at the Harlem Y with Jackie Robinson (who had played basketball and football at UCLA in addition to baseball). "I'm shooting around, I'm hitting jump shots, and he says 'You're not that bad. You know, you could get a scholarship.' Nobody ever mentioned that in my life. I never thought of college or a scholarship. I hardly hear what he's saying. I'm looking at the guy—it's Jackie Robinson! And I said well, if he thinks I'm pretty good, I'm gonna try out."

That year, Harkness's first and last as a high school player, Clinton won the citywide Public Schools Athletic League title in what the *New York Times* called a "smashing upset" over heavily favored Boys High of Brooklyn. The game was played at Madison Square Garden. Harkness was the team's leading scorer. But despite the exposure he received, the scholarship that Jackie Robinson held out to him did not come easy. Though black superstars were well-recruited in the late 50s, players who were merely excellent found their options limited. Coaches were reluctant to have too many black faces in their team pictures.

Harkness remembered that George Ireland saw one of his high school games, but he didn't play very well and nothing came of it. Maybe Ireland was there to look at someone else. That summer, playing for November, Harkness had a great game against Connie Hawkins and the Gems; NYU coach Lou Rossini was there and approached him, even got him a small summer job, but Harkness couldn't pass the NYU entrance exam. Bowling Green offered a half-scholarship, though Harkness did not think anyone from the school ever saw him play. In any case, he had no chance of coming up with the other half of the tuition. His only real option was Texas Southern, the all-black school in Houston; they sent him a yearbook and offered a full scholarship. He didn't remember meeting anyone from the school, but he was ready to go. Then he received a letter saying that his dorm had burned down and the university had to rescind its offer.

When the 1958–59 school year started—the beginning of what should have been his freshman year of college—Harkness had nothing. He stayed home, worked odd jobs, and continued to play outside ball. "I was so depressed, because I don't have any school to go to. And we didn't have any money. We're struggling in the projects.

"At that time the bookies come and ask me, Hey, you want to make some money?"

———————

The bookies had nearly sunk New York basketball once already. In 1950, the city game was riding high. Both the NIT and the NCAA tournament were played in Madison Square Garden, and Nat Holman's CCNY team won them both—the only team ever to do so. But in 1951 the swagger turned to shame. Three members of that championship team were arrested in a point-shaving scandal that eventually involved more than 30 players from seven schools, including Manhattan College, NYU, and Long Island University. The fixer was Salvatore Sollazzo, a New York gambler. Though the scandal reached as far as the University of Kentucky, it was chiefly a blot on New York City basketball. The managers of Madison Square Garden considered dropping the game altogether. They banned CCNY, cutting off an important source of revenue for all the school's athletic teams. Nat Holman was besmirched, though eventually cleared of wrongdoing. The CCNY basketball program never recovered.

But the gamblers barely missed a beat. In March of 1961, a second scandal erupted when two New York gamblers were arrested for fixing games with players at Seton Hall University and the University of Connecticut. Ultimately 47 players from 27 schools were implicated and the "master fixer" was identified as Jack Molinas, a lawyer and onetime All American player at Columbia University. All the players accused in the scandal cooperated with the investigation and avoided prosecution, but not all of them avoided punishment. Art Hicks, who went to Seton Hall after starring for St. Elizabeth in Chicago, was one of the players who admitted accepting bribes. He was kicked out of school and his promising career was finished. Tony Jackson of St. John's—the player Howard Garfinkel called "one of the greatest shooters in the history of basketball"—rejected a bribe attempt but failed to report it. He was banned for life from the NBA; his pro career was limited to the short-lived American Basketball League and later the ABA.

The most famous casualty was Connie Hawkins, who was a naive freshman at the University of Iowa when the scandal broke. He couldn't have shaved a point because he hadn't played in a varsity game. But he had accepted a $200 loan from Molinas, and had been seen riding around in his car. Years later he was quoted saying of Molinas in the *New York Times*: "I just thought Jack was a nice guy. He'd buy us food, drive us home from the beach, lend us his car." Hawkins was punished severely for failing to see the difference between Molinas and a coach-sponsor like Mike Tynberg or Walter November. Though he was never charged or arrested, and both he and Molinas protested his innocence, Hawkins too was expelled from school and banned from the NBA. He played for the Pittsburgh Rens of the American Basketball League, then for the Globetrotters, then for the Pittsburgh Pipers in the ABA's first season, 1967–68. He sued the NBA and was finally assigned to the Phoenix Suns in 1969. Though his best years were behind him by then, he was named to four NBA all-star teams and to the Basketball Hall of Fame.

Molinas served four years at Attica state prison in New York. After his parole he moved to Los Angeles, where he was arrested for shipping pornographic films over state lines. In August 1975, about a week before his trial date was to be set and less than a year after the fatal beating of a business partner on whom Molinas held a half-million-dollar insurance policy, he was killed by a bullet to the head while standing in the backyard of his home in Hollywood Hills.

When the fixers approached Jerry Harkness in 1959, they wanted him to be their messenger—to talk to a couple of players who had graduated ahead of him at Clinton and were scheduled to play soon at Madison Square Garden. He didn't know the players well, but the fixers didn't know that. He remembered them asking "'Could you talk to them? Why don't you get 'em to cut back, just hold off a little bit. Win the game, go win the game, but don't win by as many points.' They said, 'If you do that, there's a couple grand for you.' A couple grand??!! 'If it works out, yes.' I said oh my gosh. I said, this is not right. But I could use a couple grand. I don't have any money, my mom's on welfare, NYU just said no. I went down to Madison Square Garden, I saw the guys, but I couldn't approach them. My makeup, my personality, I just couldn't. Because how am I gonna ask guys—I don't know how to do this! And I left the Garden and went home."

Years later, Harkness said, one of the players he was asked to approach became an FBI agent, which led Harkness to believe that if he had made the attempt that day at the Garden, the future fed would have turned him in. "I came that close to being a part of it," Harkness said. "I would have been gone. I wanted to do it, I just didn't know how. I was embarrassed, you know? I needed the money, we got nothing going on. But thank heaven someone was looking after me."

That summer Harkness played well for Walter November's Reliables. November contacted George Ireland and urged him to have another look. Ireland had just finished an 11–13 season. Perhaps he had new reason to believe that he could get a promising player admitted to Loyola on a probationary basis. In any event he offered a scholarship and Harkness eagerly accepted. "He was very good. He came in and he told my mom that I would get an education, and that he would see to it, if I worked hard, that I would graduate. And he said basketball would be secondary—all that stuff that mothers like. The emphasis was on her more than me. Mom was really excited about him. And subconsciously, I liked that a lot. I wanted somebody to treat her good, because I hadn't seen that."

CHAPTER 6: MISSISSIPPI
A Big-Time Major Mistake

At Mississippi State, now officially Mississippi State University, the Bailey Howell era was in full swing. In 1957–58, his junior year, Howell averaged 27.8 points per game, fourth in the nation behind Oscar Robertson, Elgin Baylor, and Wilt Chamberlain. His average of 16.2 rebounds was ninth in the nation. Mississippi State won 20 games for the first time ever, losing only 5, and finished the season ranked 15th nationally in the AP poll.

The following year was even better. Howell again finished fourth in scoring, with 27.5 per game, and broke the SEC career scoring record previously held by Bob Pettit of LSU. He was second in the nation in rebounds, with 15.2 per game, and a consensus first team All American. Mississippi State won their first nine games, all against nonconference opposition. They were trounced by Auburn in their first conference game, then ran off 15 straight wins, including a 66–58 victory over number-one-ranked Kentucky, the defending national champions and supreme rulers of the SEC. MSU finished the season at 24–1. The AP poll ranked them third in the country, behind Kansas State and (still) Kentucky, but the Bulldogs were SEC champs for the first time in the school's history.

As they closed in on that conference title, which would mean an automatic invitation to play in the NCAA national tournament, an article in *Sports Illustrated* raised the specter of Mississippi's unwritten rule on integrated play. By being careful and selective, a Mississippi school might get through a holiday tournament without facing an integrated team. But when it came to the NCAA tournament, with more than 20 teams competing in a five-step draw, there was only one way to safeguard the Mississippi way of life: stay home. Which is what most observers assumed Mississippi State would do. But "a strong statewide rumor has it that, if his team is refused permission to play in the tournament, Babe McCarthy will resign," *Sports Illustrated* reported. "And on the campus at Starkville students are saying, 'If they don't let us play, we'll march on the Capitol.'"

There was no march and no resignation. The prospect of a tournament appearance died a quick and quiet death. Mississippi State clinched the SEC championship in their last game of the season, winning a ball-holding contest at Ole Miss by the stupefying score of 23–16. The day before the game, McCarthy signed a new long-term contract. Immediately after, university president Ben Hilbun announced that Mississippi State would reject the NCAA's invitation. Kentucky, of all schools, would go to the tournament in its place. The *Clarion-Ledger* of Jackson, Mississippi, announced it all in a single story: State beats Ole Miss, wins conference, rejects tournament bid.

Though they could not play for the national title, the paper reported that "the Maroons[12] were well satisfied with their first Southeastern championship in history," and that McCarthy had no problem with Hilbun's decision, quipping, "We'll stay home and tell everybody we're the best."

But Bailey Howell had a problem. He was not satisfied. "We all wanted to go," he recalled years later. "It was a real bitter disappointment." Howell was fairly certain that his own basketball career would go on, and it certainly did: he was the second player selected in the 1959 NBA draft (by the Detroit Pistons), and he starred in the league for 12 years, including six all-star games and two championships with

---

12   Sportswriters used the nicknames Bulldogs and Maroons interchangeably. Maroon and white were the MSU colors. No reference to runaway slaves appears to have been intended.

the Boston Celtics. But he felt bad for some of his senior teammates, who played the last basketball of their lives that night against Ole Miss. They should have been allowed to play for the big prize, to test themselves against the best teams in the country. In a 2002 documentary film, Howell speaks gravely and sadly: "I think in America...we need to be able to go just as far as our talent and our commitment will take us in whatever it is, no matter whether it's science or literature or athletics or what. I think we need to provide our young people with the opportunities to just see how far they can really go, what they can accomplish, how good they can get at whatever thing it is that they enjoy. And we were denied that. So that was a big-time major mistake, I think, on the part of the politicians of Mississippi."

In the film, Howell wears the maroon and white stripes of Mississippi State. After his pro career, he returned to Starkville and became active in university public relations and fundraising. When we spoke about the 1959 season he was careful to say that he found no fault with the university or its officials. In his mind the politicians were responsible.

Ultimately they were. But what Howell didn't say, and perhaps didn't remember, is that the politicians didn't have to act in 1959. The president of the university acted for them, and the basketball coach went along, with a new contract in his breast pocket. Of course none of the players complained. McCarthy told them not to talk about it, Howell said. And "back then you kind of did what you were told to do."

CHAPTER 7: CHICAGO
Stranger in the Heartland

———

Jerry Harkness landed in Chicago in the fall of 1959. A few months later, he was packing his bags to go home.

Art McZier met him at the airport, drove him to campus, and showed him around. It was not exactly what Jerry had in mind. In the pictures Ireland had showed him, the campus looked bigger and the dorm room had a TV. And though he was used to being among the minority at DeWitt Clinton, he wasn't used to the minority being quite so minor. At Clinton there were enough blacks to make a tribe. At Loyola he'd be lucky to find a posse.

But he wasn't complaining. The dorm was just a couple years old. It was a lot nicer than the Patterson projects. "It was like, dang, where's my TV? But it was so much better than what I was used to. Everything was clean, neat. And then you had the lake. I wasn't used to lakes. We had the Hudson River but this was beautiful. The scenery, and the grass. This was *nice*." After practice he didn't have to get on the subway, he just walked back to the dorm. He could sit downstairs in the lounge and watch the world go by on Sheridan Road. He could go upstairs and stretch out in his room. No need to wonder how or if he would eat. Step into the dining hall. Dinner is served. "Oh, I liked it."

There weren't many girls to meet, but they were easy enough to pick out. Standing on a line during freshman orientation, he spied a black girl and introduced himself. She was Judy Carroll, a freshman from the South Side. The next night or the night after, Jerry and Judy met up at the beanie hop with her high school friend Marie Leaner, who was attending Loyola's downtown campus, and a basketball player named Herman Hagan, a Chicago native who soon became Jerry's running buddy. The beanie hop was a mixer; the girls would throw their freshman beanies into a box and a guy would pick one out and they'd dance. Unless, of course, you were one of the four blacks in the gym. No need for beanies in that case.

Judy and Jerry got along. She was a woman who knew her way around the sports world. Her father was Ernie Carroll, the chef at the Bards Room at Comiskey Park, the home of the Chicago White Sox and the NFL's Chicago Cardinals. The Bards Room was where sportswriters, players, coaches, and assorted VIPs gathered after the games to eat, drink, and tell tales. According to the legend, Ernie had been hired as a teenager by Charles Comiskey himself, whose nickel-clenching ownership of the White Sox supposedly drove his players to the Black Sox Scandal of 1919. Ernie started boiling hot dogs for the Old Roman (as Comiskey was known) and in time became a well-known figure at the park and around town. White Sox broadcaster Bob Elson would rave about his chili on the radio, and for a dime Ernie would send you a mimeographed copy of the recipe. At Christmas he would make eggnog and take it around to his friends and acquaintances, and he had all kinds. You'd go over to his house and Ernie Banks or Minnie Minoso would be sitting in the living room. You'd dine at a restaurant with him and they'd bring out dessert on the house. You'd go somewhere in his car and the cops would say, "Park right here, Ernie." He never had to walk far. Mayor Daley knew his name. Abe Saperstein, the owner of the Globetrotters, was his friend, and so was Andy Frain, whose company provided the ushers for all the big events: baseball and football games on either side of town, basketball games at the International Amphitheatre, hockey at the Chicago Stadium, concerts, the Ice Capades, the Ringling Brothers and Barnum & Bailey Circus. If you were Ernie's kid, or her date, or one of his teammates, you could go anywhere.

If the Loyola dorm was a luxe lakeside apartment beyond Harkness's dreams, the Carrolls were the warm, engaged family he'd never known. There were four kids, three girls and a boy. Their mom, Adele, worked for the IRS. They took two newspapers and talked about politics. Education was important to them, and on the South Side of Chicago that meant Catholic schools. Adele had attended St. Elizabeth and Judy followed in her footsteps. Judy and her older sister participated in the Catholic Interracial Council, which often met at St. Ignatius High, the Jesuit high school left behind when St. Ignatius College moved to the far north side of the city and became Loyola University. The Jesuits impressed her; when the time came, she went north too. And soon came home to the South Side with the star of the freshman basketball team, who fit right in.

On the basketball court, Harkness was tearing it up, having an "awesome" freshman year. Though he had come off the playgrounds of New York, he was not the kind of player you would notice in a warmup or shootaround. He was listed at 6-3, but in the way of basketball rosters everywhere that was a bit of a stretch. He didn't have a great shot or flashy moves. He wasn't a big leaper. He couldn't dunk. But he had speed, remarkably quick hands and feet, and uncanny physical instincts—an ability to anticipate where the ball was going, a mastery of the ever-changing geometry of bodies in motion. In short, he had a step. He could go right by you and leave you wondering how. He could cut off your pass before you knew you wanted to make it. He was aggressive and he moved well toward the basket. And he was left-handed. He went ways you weren't used to. His unorthodox one-handed jump shot, more of a push than a shot, came at you from angles you'd never seen before. Often he took his right hand off the ball and used that arm to hold his defender away.

Most important, perhaps, he had the stamina of a cross-country runner. With five minutes left in the game, when everybody else was dragging, Jerry Harkness was still going full-tilt.

He was about as quiet as a star could be. "I was not a talented basketball player," he said. "Not an athlete. I was just a guy who got a ton out of my small amount of talent. I'd get four or five layups, four or five free throws, and a couple of small jump shots, there's my 20." His New York buddy Freddie Crawford, who later played for the Knicks and the Lakers, said you might not know that Jerry had beat you until you looked at a score sheet. "He got 20 points?! How? Who saw this? Who is that guy?" His ability was the kind you might miss if you saw him play in a single game, but over a week or a month or a season you'd see it. "Jerry's steady, boom," Crawford said. "You know what you're going to get."

He had never felt like the star before, but here he was on a major college campus, leading a team that was smoking the opposition freshmen and holding its own in scrimmages against Clarence Red and the Loyola varsity. Still, he was a black kid from the New York projects on a white Midwestern Catholic campus. It wasn't easy. For one thing, his first semester grades were terrible—four Ds and two Cs, as he remembered. Ireland had him rooming with Clarence Red, hoping some of Red's studiousness would rub off on him, and Red tried to keep him focused. No long speeches, just a comment here and there. Aren't you going to study tonight? Didn't you tell me you have a test tomorrow? But Harkness didn't know much about studying and he didn't have much discipline. He wasn't a wild party guy, but he thought weekends were for fun, not work. At home in New York, living in a single woman's home, he'd come and gone as he pleased.

He was acquiring some attitude, too. The self-confidence he was finding as a player sometimes tipped over into hubris. Looking back on it as an adult, he said, "I was not really the type of person I would be proud of now. I was big-headed." Though he came to believe that Ireland treated him very well, he didn't see it that way at the time. Like many if not most coaches then, Ireland believed that a good coach was a tough coach. He told his players he didn't want to be their friend, that his family were all the friends he needed. The players called him "the man" and he liked it. He had a temper. On at least a couple of occasions he showed his displeasure with a smack or a punch.

One night Harkness stayed too late at the Carrolls' house and got back to campus after curfew. He was invited to leave the dorm. He and Ireland had heated words. "I wasn't used to people getting on me like that. My mom never would get on me like that. So I'm away from home and here this guy is jumping on me, and I'm highly sensitive anyway as a person, always was that way. So I'm ready to go. Shucks. I went and packed my bags."

Ireland sent the team trainer to the dorm to settle Harkness down. "Don't be silly now, don't pack your bags, let's deal with this thing and we'll get you through it." Ireland arranged for Harkness to stay in Evanston with another player's family until he could get back into the dorm. Later Harkness would say that the experience was good for him—taught him some discipline and humility. He had to get up early and take a bus to campus every day.

He wondered later if he really would have gone home. "Deep down," Harkness recalled, "I thought somebody would come and say, 'Hey, let's work this out.'" Sounding a theme that would become familiar among Ireland's players, he added, "I thought he wouldn't allow me to leave. Because I was averaging like 22 or 23, and I was playing very well."

Harkness led his freshman team to an 8–1 record and finished the year with a 23 point average. In his second semester he managed to improve his four Ds and two Cs to four Cs and two Ds. When he returned to campus for his sophomore year, George Ireland took him aside and said, "I've got a surprise for you."

CHAPTER 8: CINCINNATI
Life Without Oscar

"As newly appointed head coach of the University of Cincinnati basketball team, I viewed the 1960 Commencement Exercises with a variety of emotions, none of them joyous."

So said Ed Jucker (or more likely his ghostwriter, Robert Portune) at the beginning of *Cincinnati Power Basketball*, a book published in 1962 to capitalize on Jucker's new fame.

On that graduation day in 1960, the university said good-bye not only to Oscar Robertson but also to his teammates Ralph Davis and Larry Willey. "Just in case I had forgotten," Jucker's book went on, "the local newspapers reminded me that (a) I had lost 55 of our 87 point per game average, (b) I had lost an average of 21 rebounds per game, (c) tickets were sold out for the 1960–61 home season, and (d) there was a long line of fearsome opponents waiting to get revenge for defeats suffered over the three years just past."

Was Jucker daunted? If he was, he didn't admit it. "In answer to a question, I said, 'There is not going to be any drop in the quality of University of Cincinnati basketball; this year's team will rank among the nation's leaders.'"

Jucker was a thoroughbred Bearcat, captain of the school's 1940 team and also a letterman in golf and baseball. According to *Cincinnati Post* sportswriter Wally Forste, he had been dreaming about becoming Cincinnati's basketball coach ever since. He started his coaching career at Batavia High School in Ohio, coached and played basketball at the Norfolk naval base during the war, and moved up to the college level at the U.S. Merchant Marine Academy and later at Rensselaer Polytechnic Institute in Troy, New York—where he met his wife Joanne, a basketball star at Russell Sage women's college. He returned to Cincinnati as a baseball and basketball assistant in 1953.

He probably wasn't the jaunty, confident card embodied in his ghostwriter's prose. *Sports Illustrated* writer Walter Bingham, who profiled him in 1963, portrayed him as a nervous wreck:

> Successful though he is, Jucker usually has the harried mien of a longtime loser. Basketball coaches are a notoriously nervous lot, but shortly before the start of every Cincinnati game Jucker looks like a man condemned to die. His skin turns several shades paler than normal, accenting his heavy beard and making him look old (he is 45). His eyes are strained, as if pleading for help, and beads of sweat line his forehead. He develops a cough, though his health is perfect. He keeps glancing at his wrist as if checking the time, but he wears no watch. "In the last few minutes before a game," says Tulsa's coach, Joe Swank, "Juck wouldn't even remember his name." Backslapping well-wishers stop by the bench to wish Jucker luck. "I nod yes and no," admits Jucker, "but I don't even know what people are saying to me."...
>
> A foul called against Cincinnati will bring Jucker leaping to his feet, arms stretched toward heaven, his face a picture of amazement. "He's very quick to come off the bench on a call," says a rival coach. "He certainly lets the officials know what's on his mind, even to the extent of buzzing the buzzer at the scorer's table." In a recent game against Houston, Jucker did just that, not once but twice. Later, when asked about it, he looked wide-eyed with disbelief. "I didn't do that, did I?"

"He disrobed very quickly," recalled Tom Thacker, who was a sophomore on Jucker's first Cincinnati team. He'd be wearing a jacket and tie at the start of the game, but within two minutes the jacket was gone. "Highly intense guy, highly intense. He couldn't sit still for nothing....You had to laugh at some of his antics; he'd go for the referees, people had to grab him back. He'd get wound up tight, he'd go off, and we'd say 'Juck, take it easy!'"

According to his players, Jucker's over-the-top excitability was mostly a gametime phenomenon. What they remembered more was an infectious, upbeat enthusiasm, an ability to motivate and win people over to his point of view.

He needed that ability when he took over the team, because he had decided to scrap the high-scoring, up-tempo offense that George Smith had played with the Big O. In its place Jucker intended to play the kind of game that had defeated Cincinnati twice in the NCAA tournament—tight defense coupled with a slow, strictly controlled pattern offense. Instead of Robertson's glorious athleticism and crowd-pleasing freelancing, Cincinnati would now play by a new book. As Jucker wrote in *Cincinnati Power Basketball:*

> Some players are better at the jump shot than others, some are better at hook shots, some are better at set shots. *But all men are better close to the basket....*We planned the new Cincinnati offense, therefore, to bring the maximum scoring opportunity for all five men within a tight semi-circle whose radius was the distance from the foul line to the basket.

It didn't work too well at first. After easy warmups against Indiana State and Western Michigan, and a 70-62 victory over Miami of Ohio in the Cincinnati Gardens, the Bearcats went east to play Seton Hall in a tripleheader at Madison Square Garden. Tom Thacker later came to believe that this was one of the games that Seton Hall players were accused of fixing when the second national basketball scandal broke open a few months later. The *Cincinnati Post* noticed that the odds moved just before the game, increasing the point spread from two to eight points in Cincinnati's favor. But instead of winning by eight points or more, Cincinnati lost by eight, 84–76. "We couldn't even win the game they were supposed to throw," Thacker recalled. "That's how bad we were."

A week later they went west to start their conference schedule against St. Louis University. Cincinnati played in the Missouri Valley Conference, which was major at the time: four of its teams would appear in the top 20 at some point that season. In those days only one team per conference went to the NCAA tournament, so every conference game was important.

St. Louis did not look like a problem. They hadn't beaten Cincinnati in four years, home or away. Jucker had prepared a zone defense just for them and worked on it all week. "We were completely ready for them," he said later. "We knew their every move."

Cincinnati turned the ball over 19 times. They scored only 40 points, their lowest total since 1949. St. Louis hit on seven of their first eight attempts, shooting over the zone from the outside. "Two guys named Joe did it," said Jucker later, referring to Glen Mankowski and Gordon Hartweger. "Two we weren't even worried about as far as long-range shooting was concerned." He had to abandon his zone defense midway through the first half. The final was 57–40.

Carl Bouldin, a senior cocaptain on the Cincinnati team, recalled that Jucker was shaken by the loss. A week later the Bearcats would face Bradley, the class of the MVC and the second-ranked team in the country. Bradley had won the NIT the year before and had most of that team back, including future NBA star Chet "the Jet" Walker. They played their home games in a fieldhouse that opponents called the "Snake Pit." Their fans were once described by DePaul coach Ray Meyer as "10,000 natives ready to riot." Bradley had won their last 40 games there and Cincinnati was not likely to break their streak. So the surprise loss to St. Louis was serious. Despite Jucker's confident prediction, there seemed to have been a drop in the quality of University of Cincinnati basketball. Bouldin recalled that the coach gathered the team in a hotel meeting room after the game. He got a little emotional. "He said, 'You guys gotta stick with me. I know this is gonna work, you just gotta believe it.' And he kind of broke down there."

A week later they went down in the Snake Pit by a 19-point margin, 72–53.

At this point the Bearcats looked exactly like a team that had just lost the best player in the world. Their season was little more than three weeks old and already they had lost more games than they had the previous year. They were 5–3 overall, 0–2 in the MVC. Bradley, 8–0, looked uncatchable. The home fans started booing. People would accost sophomore guard Larry Shingleton on his way to practice: "When you guys gonna start runnin' with the ball? Just run. Why don't you run with it?" *Cincinnati Enquirer* columnist Lou Smith asked Santa to bring Jucker something special for Christmas: another Oscar Robertson.

But after the Bradley game, Jucker later remembered, three of the players who had been Robertson's teammates came to him and silently patted him on the back. "They let me know, 'We respect you and we'll stick with the system,' and they did not say a word. It was in their eyes."

Their next game was against Dayton at the Cincinnati Gardens, where most of the Bearcats' regional rivalries were played. It was a home game for Cincinnati, but Dayton was favored; they were 6–1 on the year and had just trounced Seton Hall 66–45. They took an 11-point lead late in the first half, and then...something happened. In the opening minutes of the second half, the Bearcats made a "fire-engine bustout," in the words of the *Enquirer*'s Dick Forbes. They went on to win the game 71–61, and they won every game after that.

What happened? Jucker's book says merely that "the entire system of pattern offense and pressure defense blended into a distinct style." A rival coach told *Sports Illustrated*'s Walter Bingham that Jucker gave up on his zone defense and switched permanently to a pressing man-to-man. Looking back on it 50 years later, several of the participants said it had a lot to do with a couple of new players: Tom Thacker and Tony Yates.

Since the beginning of the season, Jucker had been shuffling his lineup around a core of three upperclassmen: center Paul Hogue, forward Bob Wiesenhahn, and guard Carl Bouldin. At the second forward he started junior Sandy Pomerantz, a highly touted high school player who had been waiting patiently on the bench for Oscar Robertson's class to graduate. But Tom Thacker was eating him up in practice and everyone could see it, including Pomerantz himself. He left after a few games and went home to St. Louis, where he starred in a smaller pond for Washington University.

At the other guard Jucker started the season with Tom Sizer, but by the Bradley game Sizer had been pushed aside by Yates, who was quickly emerging as the team's floor leader. Though Yates was a sophomore, he had spent four years in the military. He was married. His teammates called him Gramps. Before long he became the middleman between the coaches and players.

Certainly Jucker was looking for the right combination. And he was probably trying to give his upperclassmen a chance to prove themselves before benching them in favor of the sophomores. But he may also have felt the pressure of an informal racial quota. Hogue, Thacker, and Yates were all black. Sizer and Pomerantz were white, as was reserve forward Fred Dierking, the younger brother of former Cincinnati star Connie. In other words, Jucker started the season with one black starter and four white. When he replaced Pomerantz with Thacker, there were two black starters. When he tried replacing Sizer with Yates at guard, he also replaced Thacker with Dierking at forward—albeit briefly—so there were still two blacks. No one ever suggested to me that Jucker was prejudiced in any way—quite the contrary—but in 1960 even the most open-minded coaches had to wonder if it was possible to play too many blacks at a time. They had a joke that has been repeated often and in many variations: two at home, one on the road, three if you're way behind.[13]

---

13   This formula is sometimes expressed as "One at home, two on the road..." and some-times "Two at home, three on the road..." I prefer the version in which the home crowd is more accepting, not less. Here's another joke I heard in my travels: Bigoted fan: Why do you have three black players on the floor? Coach: That's all we have!

Jucker started Thacker, Yates, Hogue, Bouldin, and Wiesen-hahn—three blacks and two whites—in the loss to Bradley on December 23. He used the same lineup six days later against Dayton, and that's when the Bearcats became unbeatable.

———————

The crucial game of that season was played on January 31—the rematch with Bradley, in Cincinnati's Armory Fieldhouse. Bradley was now ranked number three by the AP. Another loss to them would virtually kill Cincinnati's hopes of going to the NCAA tournament.

The lead changed hands several times; with 3:40 left to play, Bradley led by three, 70–67. But then Wiesenhahn scored to bring the Bearcats within one point, and Thacker put them ahead for good with a 20-foot jumper. He had a big night, 22 points and 11 rebounds.

Jucker was jubilant after the game, and uncharacteristically singled Thacker out for praise. "That long shot that put us on top in the final minutes of the game—never saw such a pretty basket in my life," he said. A few days later he conceded that when Thacker launched the shot, he was far beyond the tight semicircle whose radius was the distance from the foul line to the basket. "It certainly defies any of my theories of basketball," Jucker told the press.

A week later the Bearcats climbed into the AP top ten, and as their streak went on they continued to climb. On March 4, the last day of the regular season, they were ranked third in the country, ahead of Bradley—but they did not yet have a place in the NCAA tournament. Their conference record was 10–2; Bradley's was 9–2, and that afternoon Bradley was to play St. Louis in the Snake Pit. If Bradley won, which seemed likely, they would tie for the conference title and Cincinnati would have to play them a third time, on a neutral court at Purdue, to determine which school would represent the MVC in the tournament.

Cincinnati was playing away that night against 11–12 Marshall in Huntington, West Virginia. Before their game, they watched on national TV as St. Louis, which had all but dashed their conference hopes early in the season, now clinched the Bearcats' MVC championship by upsetting Bradley 70–63.

With a rookie head coach and without Oscar Robertson, Cincinnati was in the tournament again. Wally Forste of the *Post* wrote, "[I]f Ed Jucker isn't named coach of the year, there is no justice."

CHAPTER 9:
NASHVILLE-CHICAGO
Fast Break Basketball

New York was not the only basketball hotbed that George Ireland cultivated. In the spring of 1960 he was in Nashville, sitting in a gym on the campus of Tennessee A&I State University[14] watching two all-black high school teams competing in the most prominent tournament that would have them. Later Ireland would be quoted saying that he was the only white man there, in a crowd of about 4,500, but if he said that it was an exaggeration. Ted Owens, who was then an assistant coach at the University of Kansas, was there with him, and according to Owens's recollection so were a couple white bus drivers.[15]

If New York was the capital of playground basketball in the late 50s, Nashville was the center of black scholastic basketball: Tennessee State not only had the best black college team in the country—probably the best college team, period—but also hosted the National High School Basketball Tournament, which crowned the nation's best black high school team. The still point at the center of all this activity was Tennessee State's coach, one of the most important figures in the integration of American sports, a reserved, dignified, upright man named John B. McLendon, the "father of black basketball."

---

14   Often and now officially called Tennessee State; the A&I was dropped in 1968.
15   Owens became head coach at Kansas in 1965 and kept the job 19 years. He compiled a record of 348–182 and took his team to the NCAA tournament seven times.

Basketball's history is short. McLendon, who was born in 1915 and died in 1999, was a protégé of the game's inventor, James A. Naismith. McLendon's father was descended from slaves and his mother was a Delaware Indian. He grew up in Kansas City and fell in love with basketball as a sixth-grader visiting the new junior high school he would soon attend. "The door to the gym swung open," wrote biographer Milton S. Katz, and McLendon saw "a polished basketball floor and a man sinking shots one after another. The man was P.L. Jacobs, the new school's physical training instructor. 'I was spellbound,' McClendon recalled. 'I ran home to tell my mother I was going to be a physical training teacher and a basketball coach.'"

When McLendon entered the school the following year, P.L. Jacobs became his first basketball coach and promptly dispensed this essential advice: go out for gymnastics. Though he tried, McLendon never did get to play much organized basketball. But that was all right with him. He liked being the student manager and sitting on the bench next to the coach.

He wanted to go to Springfield College in Massachusetts because that's where Naismith had invented basketball. His father couldn't afford to send him there, but after he enrolled at Kansas City Junior College his father discovered there was no need for him to go—Naismith had been 40 miles away, at the University of Kansas, since 1898.

As McLendon later told the story, his father took him to the campus at Lawrence and told him to seek Naismith out. "He said, 'Tell him that he's to be your adviser.' And I did just that, but Dr. Naismith asked me, 'Who told you this?' So I told him 'My father,' and he replied 'Fathers are always right.'"

KU was integrated, but barely: McLendon recalled that when he attended, there were about 60 blacks in a student body of 4,000. With Naismith as his mentor and supporter, McLendon became the school's first black physical education student. From the start, he was on a double mission: not only would he use basketball as a way to mold men of high character, he would also try to surmount racial barriers wherever he found them. Though the Kansas basketball team would not accept blacks (because other schools would refuse to play integrated games), he tried out for the team anyway. With Naismith helping and cheering him on, he forced the integration of the KU swimming pool, which was drained after the first time McLendon swam there. He and his girlfriend integrated the annual spring dance, and McLendon successfully circumvented a university policy that prevented black students from teaching whites.

McLendon graduated from Kansas in 1936 and with Naismith's help got a scholarship to study for a master's degree at the University of Iowa. He and William Burghardt, the only other black in the master's program, had to live off campus in an all-black boardinghouse. As a research project McLendon studied physiological characteristics across racial lines. (He found no measurable differences between blacks and whites.)

By 1937 he had received his degree and followed his friend Burghardt to North Carolina College for Negroes (now called North Carolina Central) in Durham. There he became head basketball coach in 1940 and immediately installed a fast-break offense that he later described in a book titled *Fast Break Basketball: Fundamentals and Fine Points.*

"Contrary to its reputation," McLendon wrote, "the fast break is not an 'aimless,' 'helter-skelter,' 'run and shoot,' 'fire-horse' game except in the appearance of its rapid, often demoralizing action. It is a planned attack with multiple applications..."

Most coaches taught their teams to set up at half court and try to create easy shots by passing and moving in preset patterns. They used the fast break, but they preferred to do so when given the opportunity by a steal or an opposing player's mistake. Their inclination, in McLendon's words, was to play a "set offense first and fast break when you can." McLendon taught his teams not to wait for opportunities but to create them: "fast break first and set offense when you have to"—a strategy that came to him directly from basketball's inventor. Naismith had taught him that the "ultimate game" was running and pressing: that offense begins not at half court, but wherever your team takes possession of the ball; that defense begins wherever the other team takes the ball; and that offense and defense are intimately intertwined. Steals and interceptions are not only defensive, they are crucial first steps in an offensive attack. A defensive rebound is the beginning of an offensive play. "Get the ball! Get it out! Get going!" he wrote. [16]

He proved his case on court. In his first year as coach of North Carolina College, the Associated Negro Press voted his team "Negro National Champions." Over 12 seasons there he amassed a record of 239–68, a .779 winning percentage. Playing in the CIAA, the Colored Intercollegiate Athletic Association (now called the Central Intercollegiate Athletic Association), his teams won their conference championship eight times. They became so popular with fans that in the fall of 1952 the college opened a new million-dollar gym to handle the crowds.

By that time, however, McLendon was gone. The North Carolina legislature had disallowed the use of state money for college athletics, and at the end of the 1951–52 school year the college's president canceled the scholarships of McLendon's players. He left in a huff for another CIAA school, Hampton Institute in Virginia.

During his years in the CIAA, McLendon actively promoted the integration of both professional and college basketball. The first two black players to sign NBA contracts, in 1950, were Harold Hunter, who had played for McLendon at North Carolina College, and Earl Lloyd of West Virginia State, a conference rival. The Washington Capitols contacted both players through McLendon and he drove them to their tryout, stopping on the way in a cul-de-sac to give Lloyd a few pointers on defensive switching.

In 1948 McLendon formed a committee that requested the inclusion of "colored colleges" in the NCAA and its tournament. The NCAA was slow to respond (it did not allow black schools into Division I until 1970), prompting McLendon to crack, in what seems to have been a rare eruption of sarcasm, that the abbreviation NCAA

---

16   Myles Dorch, who grew up in the Bronx and played for St. Anselm's College in the early 60s, told me: "The New York style of basketball was take it off, kick it out, and run."

"may mean *National Collegiate Athletic Association* to some people, but to us it means *No Colored Athletes Allowed.*" The other national athletic organization, the National Association of Intercollegiate Athletics (NAIA), was more amenable. The NAIA, descended from the National Association of Intercollegiate Basketball (NAIB), grew out of a Kansas City tournament established in 1937 by Naismith, among others, to decide a national basketball champion for small colleges. In 1952, in response to pressure from the machinery that McLendon had set in motion, the organization voted to establish a "district at large" for black colleges: they could compete with each other as though they constituted a separate region of the country (which they did in all but geography) and the winner of their tournament would then go on to compete as one of 32 teams in the Kansas City tournament. That may look like a crumb by modern standards, but it was eagerly accepted by black colleges, which quickly joined the organization.

The first play-in tournament for black teams, in 1953, was won by Tennessee A&I, which thus became the first black school to compete for a national championship. (In the Kansas City tournament they advanced two rounds before being eliminated by East Texas State College.) Tennessee A&I was embarked on an ambitious program to raise its athletic profile. In 1945 it had revived the National High School Basketball Tournament, which gave the college an advantage in recruiting the best young prospects. In 1952, when the NAIA established the district at large and the play-in tournament for black college teams, Tennessee A&I quickly offered to host it. Academic programs were also expanding, following an increase in state support begun in 1941.

Tennessee A&I wanted McLendon to become part of their effort. They contacted him while he was at Hampton Institute and said, as he told interviewer Alan Govenar, "If integrating basketball is going to be the mission of your life, you better come on out here. We have the athletes; we have the government behind us. Here you can manage this on a national level, and this is the place for you to be." Biographer Milton Katz quotes him as having said simply, "I was brought to Tennessee State to continue the process of integration."

He didn't mean the process of integrating basketball, he meant the process of integration. He believed basketball was a means to that end. In the book *Learning to Win: Sports, Education, and Social Change in Twentieth-Century North Carolina*, historian Pamela Grundy quotes him saying:

> If you can get the sports thing going, that's the best way to go. Because everybody pulls for their team. They don't pull for part of their team....You can't divide up your loyalty. And then you begin to think—you might start admiring [a player]. And then you want your son to play like he does.... Pretty soon, race is not the most important thing.

One of McLendon's first acts as coach at Tennesse A&I was to break the accommodations barrier in Kansas City. In addition to its national championship tournament, the NAIA hosted a smaller tournament over the Christmas holidays. Tennessee A&I was invited, but McLendon had a condition. He told Alan Govenar:

> I said I wasn't coming unless they let us stay in the same hotels and eat in the same restaurants as the white teams....I never did take this up with the administration, because I knew one thing: If they said no, that would have been an impasse. If they said yes, then they would have gotten in trouble with the state authorities. So it was better for me to do it and get fired or get chastised or reprimanded or something than for the president to get involved because he could always say, "Well, I didn't know anything about it. I didn't have any idea he'd do something like that..."

> The late Al Duer, who was executive secretary of the NAIA at the time, was the one that called me and told me my team was supposed to take part in the tournament. And I told him yes, I knew it, but I wasn't planning on coming.

> He said, "What's the problem?"

I told him.

So he said, "How long will you be by the phone?"

And I told him, "All day, if necessary."

He said, "I'll call you back in 20 minutes."

In 20 minutes, he canvassed the Chamber of Commerce, Junior Chamber of Commerce, and his committee, who had apparently been studying this anyway, and called me back and said we could stay at the Hotel Kansas Citian, and we could eat at any of the restaurants that the other teams do. And that's how Kansas City was integrated. That was 1954. Up until that time, even Lena Horne couldn't stay in downtown Kansas City.

McLendon's team, unseeded as the Christmas tournament began, won it handily. They went 29–4 that year and scored more than 100 points seven times.

By 1957 he had his program running full tilt: he had installed his fast-break system, implemented the rigorous conditioning program needed to run it, and gathered his recruits, helped by an extensive network of contacts at black high schools, including coaches who had assisted or played for him in the CIAA. In 1957 Tennessee A&I won their way into the NAIA tournament and then won the championship—the first black team to win a national title. They won it again in 1958, and again in 1959. Given the cockeyed distribution of basketball talent caused by the racial attitudes of the time, they were likely the best college basketball team in the country. Chuck Taylor—the player the shoes were named for, who was something of a basketball ambassador—said as much after the 1958 NCAA final, in which Adolph Rupp's Kentucky team beat Elgin Baylor and Seattle. According to McLendon, who told the story to Milton Katz, Taylor remarked to some friends that Tennessee A&I could beat both finalists on the same afternoon.

These victories, in integrated national tournaments played in his hometown of Kansas City, must have been especially gratifying for McLendon. He had always bridled at the effect that racial exclusion had on the psyches and self-image of his young players. He told historian Pamela Grundy:

> Because of the exclusion of blacks in sports, if you were practicing the games that other people were playing, you really had no way to decide whether you were really playing well. Because [the white teams] were the ones you read about in the newspapers. You read about some of our teams once a week in the weeklies....It's almost like you're in another world and you don't know whether you're really doing what you're supposed to do or not.

For this reason McLendon actively sought games against white teams, even in the 40s when they were almost impossible to come by. In 1942 his arranged for North Carolina College to play against Brooklyn College.

> When we played that game, and our guys won the game, they felt like, "Well, we're really playing basketball. Coach is a real coach here. He's not just coaching a game that only we play, but he's coaching a game that they play, and all these pictures we see on Sunday—we're better than they are."

McLendon is perhaps best remembered today for the "Secret Game," in which his North Carolina College Eagles played an all-white team from the Duke medical school. Although this game was played in 1944, McLendon did not talk about it until 1996, when he was 80 years old. He spilled the tale to historian Scott Ellsworth, who was interviewing him for the *New York Times* on the 50th anniversary of the first CIAA tournament. Ellsworth published it in the *New York Times Magazine* and it has been recounted and elaborated on several times since.

In 1944 race relations were tense in Durham. As a professional courtesy, McLendon was invited to come across town to watch Duke varsity basketball games, but only if he agreed to sit on the end of the bench in a waiter's coat. (He didn't.) A white bus driver, annoyed by a black G.I. who did not move with enough alacrity to the back of his bus, shot and killed the man and was then freed by a jury of his peers after 20 minutes' deliberation. The Ku Klux Klan was active and segregation was strictly enforced by the Durham police. When YMCA members from Duke and North Carolina College got together occasionally, some of them felt the need to ride to the meeting on the floorboards of their car.

At one such meeting, George Parks, one of McLendon's players at North Carolina College, heard someone boast that the intramural team from Duke's medical school, which was packed with former college players in wartime training, was the best basketball team in the state—better even than the Duke varsity, which had just won the Southern Conference championship. Parks challenged this assertion, and soon the students were talking about a game to settle the issue.[17]

McLendon seized the opportunity for a black-white game and arranged a contest in the North Carolina College gym. (His players would not have been able to get onto the Duke campus without causing unfortunate commotion.) The game, complete with a ref and a time clock, was scheduled for 11:00 on a Sunday morning— when most Durham residents would be in church. No spectators were allowed. No one was to be told. Still, Ellsworth wrote, it was "an endeavor fraught with peril." The Duke players rode to the gym with quilts over their car windows so they wouldn't be seen driving through the black part of town. They walked into the gym through the women's dressing room, their jackets up over their heads. Once they were inside, the gym was locked. The windows were six feet

---

17   This is the most common explanation of how the game came about. McLendon's biographer Milton Katz also offers an alternative possibility: "[T]he boys from Duke were feeling so good about their team that they commissioned an article in the local paper declaring themselves state champions....McLendon once recalled that his student trainer...read the newspaper article and called Duke's unofficial coach, Jack Burgess, to issue the challenge."

high, which seemed safe enough, but a few students got wind that something was up and were able to peer in by climbing up or standing on boxes.

The game started sloppy. A taboo was being violated and the players were nervous. Edward Boyd, the manager of the North Carolina College team, told Ellsworth, "For the first five minutes, you felt like you were the biggest sinner in the world. But then we found out the black wouldn't rub off, and the white wouldn't rub off." Once the sweat started pouring it was just basketball. The teams settled down and found their rhythms and McLendon's team started to run away. "We represented every black soul in Durham, whether they knew it or not," Boyd said, "and when we got a lead, we wanted a bigger one."

"By the second half," McLendon recalled, "we were scoring on nearly every possession....The Duke team was stunned." McLendon's invisible black boys slaughtered the alleged best team in North Carolina. The final score was 88–44.

Then half the players switched sides and they played mixed teams. Then they repaired to the North Carolina players' dorm for refreshments and a bull session.

McLendon later said that he considered the Duke players "very special people....They were very special to even take the chance, because they would have been penalized worse than we were. They would have been socially ostracized and everything else."

The leader of the Duke players was Jack Burgess, who had played his college ball way out west at the University of Montana. He found Durham's racial attitudes a little strange. Ellsworth wrote that he had once been chased off a city bus at knifepoint for expressing an opinion on the complicated seating customs. A few days after the Secret Game, he wrote a letter to his parents back in Montana, which Ellsworth quoted at the end of his *Times Magazine* story:

"Oh, I wonder if I told you that we played basketball against a Negro college team. Well, we did and we sure had fun and I especially had a good time, for most of the fellows playing with me were Southerners....And when the evening was over, most of them had changed their views quite a lot."

———————

The National High School Basketball Tournament was the last in a line of all-black tournaments begun in 1929 at Hampton Institute. McLendon directed one of these tournaments while he was at North Carolina College. Another prominent tournament was held at Tuskegee Institute from 1935 to '42. The Nashville tournament, hosted by Tennessee A&I starting in 1945, flourished in the postwar years but its importance dwindled as integration progressed: black high schools were slowly being accepted into the state athletic associations from which they previously had been barred. By 1960 the tournament had shrunk to nine teams, but for the rare white coaches who knew the secret it was still a large gathering of unwanted black basketball talent. Ted Owens, the Kansas assistant coach who scouted the tournament with George Ireland, was probably there through connections with Kansas alum McLendon. Ireland had no doubt been tipped by Loyola alumnus Art White, whose St. Elizabeth team, a perennial participant, won the tournament in 1957.

Ireland had been in Nashville the year before, trying to recruit a player named Ronnie Lawson, from Nashville's all-black Pearl High School. Lawson starred in the 1959 tournament and Pearl won it. He wound up going to UCLA (and was forced out of school for failing to report a bribe attempt in 1961). According to a story told by Ireland, Pearl's coach, William Gupton, told Ireland he shouldn't be discouraged about losing Lawson to UCLA; come back next year, he said, there are more where he came from.

In the 1960 tournament, which Pearl won again (for their third consecutive championship), Ireland saw two seniors: Victor Rouse, a 6-6 forward, and Leslie Hunter, a 6-4 center. I was not able to interview Rouse for this book; he died in 1999. According to Hunter, the two were friends—and rivals—and they wanted to go to college together.

Hunter grew up in West Nashville, in what he described as a completely black pocket of the city about four blocks by five. Tennessee A&I was just over the hill, and Fisk University, another all-black school, just a mile and a half west of that. Hunter's grandfather had been a carpenter and the family owned several houses in the area. His grandmother was a neighborhood leader. Politicians would pay her a visit around election time. Senator Al Gore (the elder) spoke once from their front porch. Hunter's father was a laborer at a chemical plant (and, Hunter said, so painfully shy that if people came over for dinner, he would eat upstairs). Neither of his parents graduated high school, but he and his two sisters all went to college.

"I went to a little grade school, Clifton School, it was right across the street from my house," Hunter remembered. "The crossing guard for that school was my mother. My grandmother worked in the cafeteria. You have to picture this, it was a three-room school. It had first and second grade in one room. Miss Foster was the teacher, she had taught everybody in West Nashville, everybody knew her, because she had been at that school a long, long time. And you were getting teachers who had doctorates and stuff, because they had gone to Fisk and Tennessee State. The third and fourth grade were taught by Miss Hudson, who had been there for years and years, and the fifth-grade teacher, who was in another room, was also the principal of the school. And she was the wife of the president of Tennessee State University. Mrs. Davis was her name, she was Dr. W.S. Davis's wife. She would take us over to Tennessee State, to all the plays that they had, we could get into all the sporting events, the basketball games, the football games. And I had an uncle who taught at Tennessee State also. So even though we had a little dinky school—our bathrooms were outside, we didn't have indoor plumbing. To this day my two sisters have never gone in those bathrooms. They went home if they had to go to the bathroom, they crossed the street. But the lunchroom was kind of separated and there was a long trailer, and we had great

lunches, the best food anywhere. So even though from outside looking in, you'd have thought, oh, those poor kids, that wasn't the case.
We actually grew up on Tennessee State's campus. We had access to
all the facilities, all the cultural stuff. We'd get loaded into cars and
go right across the hill."

Vic Rouse grew up in East St. Louis, Illinois, the wrong side of the
river from St. Louis, Missouri. His father was a prominent preacher.
It was a tough place for a teenaged male, so before his junior year of
high school his family sent him to Nashville to live with his grandmother. He came to Pearl High and took the starting center spot that
Hunter thought he was going to get. When they were seniors, Rouse
moved to forward and Hunter started at center.

McLendon and Tennessee State were then in the midst of their
three-year NAIA championship run. In the summer, McLendon's
players would work out in the Tennessee State gym, and promising
kids from the neighborhood were invited to join them. It was a combination youth center, conditioning camp, and basketball academy
where both Hunter and Rouse learned McLendon's rip-it-and-run
style of play—particularly the rebounding skills that got the fast
break started. "We would have two courts going," Hunter recalled,
"and McLendon would never turn the air on or have the doors open.
You played in the heat, three-on-three, full court. And you played
constantly because if you'd lose on this court you'd go play on the
losers' court. Just constantly going three on three. And that got you
in shape and that got you to where you could run. It worked a lot
of weight off me and gave me some pointers playing with the best
basketball players in the country."

When they finished high school, winning Pearl's third consecutive national high school title, Hunter and Rouse had nibbles from
college recruiters but few if any solid offers. Hunter recalled that he
had an expression of interest from UCLA, via Ronnie Lawson, but
they didn't seem to be interested in Rouse, perhaps because of a knee
injury he'd suffered. Hunter also had letters from Notre Dame—the
mother of a guy who went there lived across the street from Hunter's

grandmother—and from several black schools. He thought his high school coach wanted him to go to Fisk, but they offered only a partial scholarship and wanted him to live at home. Tennessee State didn't seem interested at all, despite Hunter and Rouse's summer play. McLendon's kids went to Pearl High, Hunter recalled, and he felt pretty friendly with the whole McLendon family. "But I never asked and they never offered," he said. "You know, when you're on top of the basketball world, sometimes recruiting isn't a priority because people will find you, they want to come there. And I just never showed the interest. Maybe Tennessee State was waiting for me to ask for a scholarship there. I may have felt inadequate as a player, because I hadn't fully developed yet. And after my senior year, they were still a damn good team. I mean I probably didn't feel that I could really compete with them."

Loyola, that was a different story. Hunter had never heard of Loyola, so he figured he could play there.

George Ireland was the only coach who came to Hunter's house. "When George Ireland came, my mother and father were at work, my grandmother was at home. He went straight for my grandmother. And she was impressed by him pretty much."

Hunter himself was not so sure. Where Ireland had won Clarence Red's trust by coming into his home, Hunter felt it was unusual. The only white people he knew owned the little grocery store down the street. "Me not knowing or not interacting with many whites at that time, I looked at it as being a little odd for him to be there recruiting at a black national tournament. My whole world was black schools. All my friends were going to Florida A&M, down to Tuskegee, Talladega, Fisk, Tennessee State, Morehouse, or Clark."

But Ireland was an "amiable guy. He charmed people by saying the right things. He sold my grandmother on the school. And I was kind of sold because he was going to take both me and Rouse. I didn't have much confidence in myself, but I knew that both of us together could probably form the nucleus of a good team. So a lot of my decision was predicated on whether Vic was going to go." At the time

Rouse was the taller and more polished player, and Hunter admitted that going somewhere together was probably more important to him than to Rouse. But he didn't think he was piggybacking. He thought Ireland wanted them both. "I wasn't privy to their conversation, but I do think that Ireland made it known he was offering both of us scholarships. Rouse and I talked and he was saying he was going to accept it, because Illinois, East St. Louis—going to school in Chicago would suit him pretty good. And I said fine, I've got relatives in Chicago. Let's do this."

So Rouse and Hunter chose Loyola, and George Ireland had the two players who would collaborate on the most important shot of his life.

CHAPTER 10: CHICAGO
Four Fab Freshmen

At the start of the 1960–61 school year, George Ireland promised Jerry Harkness a surprise. A few days later it arrived: the two-man package from Nashville. Harkness could not remember the exact circumstances of the meeting. Was it in the gym or the dorm? Probably the gym. Were they dressed in basketball or street clothes? Probably street clothes. Probably the taller guy hung back a little and the other one took the lead. He was probably dressed sharp and wearing a short-brim hat. Harkness did not remember what was said, but his teammate Ron Miller never forgot meeting the guy in the hat. He stuck out his hand and announced, "Vic Rouse, Pearl High."

Miller was still laughing about it 50 years later. "As if I'm supposed to know, one, who the hell Vic Rouse was, and two, Pearl High.

"I remember when Jerry called to tell me that Vic had passed away," Miller continued. "I spent about two months where I could not get that image out of my head. He's got his hat, and he walks in and he says 'Vic Rouse, Pearl High.' I remember telling my wife, oh, I got this image. You know, you're 17 years old, you're invincible; you can run through walls and you think you can do anything. Now he's dead. But I kept thinking, 'Vic Rouse, Pearl High.'"

Harkness was impressed just by the look of the two. He saw their height, he gauged their weight, he liked the way they moved. "They looked agile," he said. "I could tell they could play ball. I just knew when I saw them."

He knew better when he played them. Harkness was now on the varsity team with Clarence Red. They scrimmaged often against the freshmen, and "the freshmen cleaned our clocks every time," Red recalled. "They were quick and fast and they could jump," Harkness said. And Rouse could score from the outside, with a quirky shot that he released from behind his head, almost. It was nearly impossible to block that shot, and if you did Rouse would get mad and throw you an elbow. That's what impressed Harkness most at first: "They were physical. You didn't just go in and get an easy shot—these guys would knock you down. They would hold you and things like that. They're physical and hard and don't care about you, they'll run through you."

There was another physical player on that freshman team. He didn't look much like a basketball player. He was 5-10 and stocky. But he was quick and pugnacious and he had such a taste for contact that he used it as a way to get into his rhythm at the start of a game. "For me, to get hit or hit someone physically, it makes you feel better, it just loosens you up a little bit. It's just a regular game now." This was Jack Egan, from Chicago. The white guy.

————————

Egan was one of nine children in a thoroughly Irish Catholic family. His father was a fireman, then a motorcycle cop, then a detective. His mother was a homemaker. Between the oldest and youngest kids was a span of 21 years. They lived in a three-bedroom apartment on the Southwest Side of Chicago. The neighborhood was properly called Chicago Lawn, but many people called it Marquette Park, after the large city park it surrounds. All four grandparents lived nearby.

Here's a story Egan told about himself and his father and a sandlot baseball game:

"I had an older brother, and around the neighborhood there were more kids my brother's age, which was three years or four years older than I, who used to play sports. And I would be like a tagalong. I would go where my brother was going to play with them. And as a result of playing as much as I did, I became pretty proficient at most of the games that they played. Not as good as they were—I was in fourth grade and they were in seventh or eighth grade—but in my mind competitive. And there were some guys that age that I was better than.

"One time when my brother wasn't in the game, they chose up sides and if you were the odd man, you got chosen out, you had to wait—you didn't play. And so I was, I thought, the second-least-talented player out there, but there was one less than me, who was older than me, and of course he was chosen as opposed to me. And maybe he was chosen because my brother wasn't there, or maybe they disagreed that I was more talented, but when they tried to play their game, I went over to first base and sat on first base. So they couldn't play. Now these are all guys three or four years older than I, but I don't want them to play the game if I can't play. So now they have to run around me for first base.

"But one guy, the toughest guy, he kept on kicking me in the ribs as he ran by. And you know, the kicking was getting harder and harder because I wasn't moving. And pretty soon I went home crying to my father, and I tried to tell him that the big tough kid was kicking the shit out of me. He said well, what do you want me to do about it? I mean, my father understands you can't sit on first base. He's not going to go out there, because I'm probably wrong. He says well, if you're right, you go out there, and you get the biggest rocks you can get, and bust him in the head if he's kicking you. I said oh God, that made so much sense to me. And I went out and I got about six or seven bricks, something big. Something I can fire. And I fired. I was trying to hit him right in the head, OK? I chased him all the way home. I just felt so much better.

"I'm not sure what the lesson was, but one of the things I think was, it doesn't make any difference how big they are or how tough they are, you can't let 'em walk on you. I mean I thought I was justified, which of course I wasn't. But it was like getting the imprimatur. You have permission, go do it. So no matter what I did to that kid, if I would have fractured his skull with a brick, my father would never have yelled at me. Because he told me to do it."

What were the other guys doing all this time? Did they also kick him going around first base? Did they come to the aid of their big tough friend? No, they let the little kid do his thing. "They were saying he's being a jerk, he's Jim's brother, let the asshole go.

"And they also probably knew I was right about the other guy not playing. Because I would point out he shouldn't be playing, I'm better than he is."

Chicago was (and in many respects remains today) a city of immigrant tribes and territories, a place where ethnic consciousness runs high. Chicagoans always want to know where you come from— what neighborhood, what parish, what high school, what foreign land. The neighborhood Jack Egan grew up in was mostly Irish. There were also Italian kids, Germans, Polish...but no blacks. Blacks were not welcome.

In addition to their perceived character defects, blacks were a serious economic threat to Chicago's white working-class neighborhoods. These neighborhoods were being attacked by a rapacious real estate industry that had learned how to profit from racial change. In a practice that came to be known as blockbusting, an unscrupulous dealer would buy or broker a home on an all-white block and sell it to a black family. The new owners might or might not understand how hostile the neighbors would be, but in either case they had a strong economic incentive: as long as they were confined to the ghetto by discrimination, their housing options were limited to substandard buildings for which they paid inflated prices. They could get a better deal by venturing into a "nicer" neighborhood, even after paying the blockbuster a substantial markup.

Once a block was busted, the rest of the residents would predictably flee, encouraged when necessary by agents who would swoop in to help them sell their property "before it's too late." Even those who felt no animus toward blacks were convinced that the value of their homes would plummet. Whole blocks could change from white to black in a matter of months. A tide of blackness was moving west from the ghetto, straight toward neighborhoods like Marquette Park. Martin Luther King Jr. led a fair housing march in Marquette Park in 1966. He was hit in the head by a rock.

"It was a real issue for a black person, especially a young black person, to walk down the street," Egan recalled. "What's he up to? What's he doing here?" Would he be chased? "Many times. And worse. Never a weapon. I don't think the idea was to maim or kill or anything like that. But he wouldn't want to walk down that street. I'm talking about a busy street, 63rd Street, let alone a side street. They would never walk down a side street. Or *should* never walk down a side street."

Egan played his high school basketball at St. Rita, which was all white. St. Rita competed in the Chicago Catholic League with St. Elizabeth, the all-black basketball power attended by Judy Carroll, Jerry Harkness's girlfriend. When St. Rita traveled east to play St. Elizabeth, very few St. Rita fans made the trip. When St. Elizabeth played at St. Rita, the game had to be scheduled for a Sunday afternoon. The usual Friday night game would be too risky.

"Playing against St. Rita was not very nice," Judy Carroll remembered. "Because they were not very nice. A lot of times there was name calling, there were things being thrown at you. You knew you weren't welcome. I never was afraid that someone was going to come and beat me up or try to fight me; I just always knew that maybe somebody would throw something like a bottle—not an egg—or if you were walking through the doors, somebody would just want to shove you. That kind of thing—just to make you uncomfortable."

"It was such a bigoted time," Egan said. "Obviously the neighborhood was very, very prejudiced. See, most of the people who lived in this neighborhood had lived in another neighborhood before that. And it was a movement from east to west, and all these people are escaping. Oh my God, don't let a black move in there, you're gone, you're dead. That's how everybody felt. St. Elizabeth couldn't play at St. Rita at night. They could only play on Sunday afternoons. Because guys went up on top of Walgreens, on the corner of 63rd and Western, and threw garbage cans down on the people waiting for buses. I mean I didn't know anybody—none of my friends would do that. They might chase blacks, they might fight with blacks, but taking a garbage can and throwing it down on people waiting for a bus, that's too much. There's kids there and there's mothers—you know, you don't do that. Obviously it's a criminal act. But people wouldn't say oh, let's turn them in. That wasn't the thought."

It's not that everyone in Marquette Park was a rabid racist, but the rabid racists were tolerated with a shake of the head, if not the wink of an eye. If he'd been there at the time of the open-housing marches, Egan told me, he would not have been one of the angry mob raining rocks, bottles, firecrackers, and abuse down on Martin Luther King and his followers—but he wouldn't have been on King's side either.

———————————

Egan was recruited by colleges that would not have touched most of his black teammates: Duke, Houston, Illinois. In all he had letters or contacts from 15 or 20 schools, he once said. He liked the idea of the Big Ten; it was major basketball and good exposure for a Chicago kid. He thought he would play for Sharm Scheuerman at the University of Iowa. They had been watching him since his junior year of high school and he had visited the campus a couple times. He would have been a freshman there with Connie Hawkins. But his last trip to Iowa did not go the way he expected. "I worked out there, with their freshman team and other recruits. And after the scrimmage was over, I felt good because I thought I probably played about as well as I could play. We went to Sharm Scheuerman's house with the other recruits and he and the assistant coach would talk to each guy about their plans for him. I wasn't terribly concerned about what he was going to say to me, because a center from my high school team was also recruited by Iowa, and he came out of that meeting and indicated to me that he had gotten everything—room, board, books, tuition, 60 bucks a month—whatever it was. He had gotten the full scholarship. So when it was my turn to go in there—and I liked Sharm Scheuerman, he was a nice person—he told me some nice things, which made me suspect, and then he said we're prepared to offer you a one-year scholarship, which would be renewable every year. I guess I must have shown how shocked I was. I said are you kidding? I said do you think there are guards out here that are playing better than I played? I said I would never go here. There's places I can go with a four-year scholarship. I don't go there and renew it. Renew it! I said absolutely not, I won't do it."

Like many of Egan's stories, this one ends with a twist: "And so then Loyola winds up playing Iowa at the Stadium a couple years later. I get 20 points, and then I go over and talk to Sharm afterwards. Not rubbing it in completely, but just..."

And then there's a twist back. "We've talked since I graduated. He turned out to be a very nice guy."

Egan was recruited in the old style by DePaul's Ray Meyer. Meyer knew the coach at St. Ignatius High School, and that coach had a son Egan's age. The son called and said if Egan was interested in DePaul he should give Coach Meyer a call. He didn't.

On the other hand there was Guy Lewis at the University of Houston; he recruited in the new style. "He's the one who sent the letter, and he's the one who met you at the plane. He was impressive. I really liked that guy. He showed, I don't know, call it respect or whatever it was, but he recruited you, he wanted you. I didn't even work out at Houston. My first time ever on a jet plane was going down to Houston around March of my senior year. So I go down there and we're going into this restaurant and evidently I was fawning over this car, this brand new 1960 Pontiac Bonneville. At that time that was the big car. He says you like it? Yeah, of course I like it, how could you not like it? The next day, we're not going to work out, we're going waterskiing! We're going waterskiing with some freshmen and sophomores and all these girls, maybe about four or five carloads. They throw me the keys for a new Pontiac convertible! I said oh shit, this is wonderful. And then we had this wonderful day, night, I mean it was just a party. And so the next day, Sunday, I meet up with Guy Lewis, we're going out to breakfast and then he and I are going for a walk on this beautiful campus. And I mean I was sold on that place, OK? And all I said to him, the only thing I need is some sort of commitment for law school." Egan had known he wanted to be a lawyer since he was in grade school. He liked Perry Mason. "I said if I could get some sort of commitment for law school, I'm done. I'm here. But Guy Lewis, he said I can't do it. He said I'm not gonna tell you I can do what I can't do.

"At that time it was all white, Houston was. And it turned out to be the most bigoted place we ever played!"

Egan played in a high school all-star game at Loyola's Alumni Gym. His father's cousin was Robert Quinn, the city fire commissioner and a personal friend of George Ireland. Quinn called and told Egan that Ireland wanted to meet him. Egan thought Loyola was a step below the Big Ten, but it had its advantages. He figured he'd probably end up living and working in Chicago. Loyola had a law school, and they played a few big games in the Chicago Stadium every year. Egan calculated that it might be a good place to make a name for himself. Ireland could not promise him a law school scholarship either, but by the time Egan was ready for it Loyola University was only too happy to oblige.

———————————

When Judy Carroll learned that Jack Egan would be playing for Loyola, she got her guard up. She didn't know Egan personally, but she knew all she wanted to know about St. Rita. She shared her misgivings with Harkness and he leaped to his own conclusions. Harkness recalled, "Judy would tell me how it was when they played against St Rita's, and what those guys would do. So in my mind, Egan is aggressive, he's a leader. He's gotta be in front of this, he's gotta be a part of this. That's the kind of guy I knew he would be—I thought he would be. That's the way I'm thinking as a young, stupid kid. I was awfully wrong. I was awfully wrong."

Harkness was chilly. Egan picked up on it and retaliated in the Irish tough-guy way he learned from his father. "If I was going down the street on campus and I would see him, I would normally say hello to any of my teammates, OK? And if I got 'Oh how ya doin'"—mumbling and turning his head away—"sloughing off the hello, and if you did that three times to me, OK, then I'd say to myself, what am I doing, am I nuts, what am I saying hello to this asshole for? I'd say it's not as though his mind is wandering, this is consistent, this is intentional. And then I could make the conscious effort to never say anything to him. Walking into a room, he's the only one in the room, walking right by him—which is a lot different from walking past each other on the sidewalk. In fact I would enjoy it."

Egan and Harkness never really trusted each other during their days at Loyola. Later in life they became fast friends. They kept in touch as though they were frat brothers, and when Harkness and his wife came to Chicago for a Loyola reunion or golf outing, they would often stay at Egan's house in the suburbs. Both insisted that the bad feeling did not affect their ability to play together as teammates. On the court, they said, all that stuff went away.

The other guard on that freshman team was Ron Miller. Like Harkness, he was a black New Yorker who came to Loyola by way of Walter November. He would become an integral part of the team, but at first he didn't quite fit—and in some ways he never would.

Miller was born in rural Georgia in 1942, in the same room where his mother was born. Her parents were sharecroppers. She was 15 when Miller was born, his father 17. "They got married, but just because that was what they had to do. And then he went off to World War II, and they had never really lived together." Miller's mother had siblings in New York. When he was seven or eight, she went up there to find work, leaving young Ron with his grandparents. That was all very common then, he said. Everyone married young, the young men went off to war, all the kids lived with grandparents. He could barely remember a kid his age who didn't.

In New York his mother found a job with the phone company and a new man to marry. When she sent for Ron, he was about nine. They lived in the South Bronx, which was not then as rough an area as it would later become. "Winos, but nothing violent. We had gangs but not gun gangs. More like little packs. I think what helped me was the fact that I was in sports. Once gang members knew you were not a part of that, they treated you different. You didn't have to worry about having a problem with anyone."

He first attended Samuel Gompers High School, but that didn't work out. At Gompers, Miller recalled, all the black kids were channeled into the vocational classes. The school had Miller on track to become an electrician. "I probably would have been dead in a year, because I'm absolutely brutal on concepts like this wire goes here—I can change a lightbulb, that's about it. I hated what I was doing and they wouldn't let me do anything else." He played hooky for about a month before his mother found out. She had heard good things about Christopher Columbus High School in the North Bronx and got him in there by using a phony address. "It was 97 percent white and 90 percent Jewish," Miller recalled. "I had to take algebra, I had to take geometry, I had to take my half year of physics. Things that I struggled with. But I still had to take them. If I had stayed at Samuel Gompers, I would have never taken those courses."

More important, he would never have met Roy Rubin, the basketball coach, who spotted him in the gym and invited him to practice.[18]

---

18   Rubin later had a successful run as head coach at Long Island University and a not-so-successful run with the 1972–73 Philadelphia 76ers, the team with the worst season record in NBA history. He went 4–47 before being replaced in midseason by player-coach Kevin Loughery. Loughery went 5–26.

Miller's stepfather died when he was 16. Rubin gathered him in. "I would say that probably changed everything, getting involved with him. He absolutely dominated my life from that point. He made sure I took the right classes, he talked to the teachers, and everything was geared to being able to get into college. Up until that point in my life I'm thinking if I could get a job making a hundred dollars a week, I'd be set. What he did for me, he made me aware of other things, another world. He used to tell me, if you hang out with bums you'll be a bum. He used to drive me nuts with that." (Miller in turn drove his daughter nuts with it, and shortly before we spoke he had heard her repeat it to a class of teenagers. He was very pleased. "The tradition lives on!")

Miller played center for Rubin's Columbus team, which in his senior year went undefeated in its regular season. He was short for a center, only 6-2, but he could jump. He didn't play outside ball in New York City, but Rubin did send him up to the Catskills, where city ballplayers could get summer jobs at the Jewish resorts. Supposedly they were paid to do kitchen work and the like, but their real purpose was to entertain the vacationers by playing "amateur" basketball at night.

Rubin knew both Howard Garfinkel and Walter November. He would take Miller to Madison Square Garden to watch St. John's or NYU play, and those guys would always be around. Garfinkel got Miller an offer from coach Tom Blackburn at the University of Dayton, and that's where Miller wanted to go. Dayton was a basketball power at the time and well known in New York, having been to the NIT finals five times in the previous ten years. But Walter November put George Ireland on Miller's trail and Ireland did his thing. As far as Miller could remember, Ireland never saw him play in person; he was acting solely on November's say. But he was the only coach who came to Miller's home.

"He walked in like he was in charge. As soon as he walked through the door, it was like Ronnie Miller, nice to meet you. And my mother came out and he went straight to my mother, almost passed me to talk to my mother, and he was there less than 30 seconds and he was complimenting her on how clean the place was, how orderly everything was. My mother had a cake. He ate the cake and he said this cake brings tears to my eyes. This is the best cake I've ever eaten. And he said to her I can tell you that every kid who comes to Loyola and spends four years with me graduates, period. There's not one kid who's ever gone four years who didn't have a degree. And what does a mother want to hear? It's like we're gonna take care of your son. And that was pretty much it. I said Mom, I really like the University of Dayton. And she said no, I like that George Ireland man."

A few months later Miller was in Chicago. He still wanted to go to Dayton.

"I remember when Frank Hogan, who was my freshman coach, picked me up at the airport and drove me over to the campus. I said, this is it? But then the next day we drift to the gym, of course—because that's the only thing we know: as basketball players in a strange place, what can we do, we can go to the gym." Seeing his teammates roused Miller's enthusiasm. "Once I saw everybody it was like, oh boy."

Miller didn't really have a position. In high school he had played with his back to the basket, but he was not going to be a center on the same team with Les Hunter and Vic Rouse. He would have to learn how to play guard, and he set to it with a determination that impressed his teammates. They all had memories of coming into practice and seeing him already there, working on his shot and his dribbling.

Ireland was fond of practice gadgets. He had ankle weights that his players could wear to improve their jumping. A few years later he had a contraption that would feed a ball from the basket back out to the floor, so a player could practice shooting by himself. On the side baskets he had installed inner rims that made the hoops smaller and forced shooters to use a higher arc. Miller shot at those baskets every day before practice, 75 or 100 shots, trying to imprint his release and arm angle permanently into his muscle memory. Before that he would dribble 20 or 30 minutes: left hand, right hand, left to right,

right to left, running full speed, pulling up. At night he sat on his bed with a ball in his hands and practiced his release over and over.

His teammates thought he was unusual. A little detached. He was competitive, he wanted to win, but his devotion to basketball seemed somehow incomplete. He didn't dive for loose balls; Egan would never understand that. When the team became the toast of the town, Miller didn't see what all the fuss was about. When the black guys wanted to goof off or go out to party, he would stay in the dorm and study, or hang with his geeky white friends. He talked about a woman back in New York, but his teammates came to suspect that she was fictional, an excuse for him to stay in. "We believed that there was something mysterious about Miller, in his life, that he never shared with us," Harkness recalled. It's not that he was antisocial. He got along with everybody. That was one of the most unusual things: he got along with everybody. Later he would marry a white woman. And when they divorced, after about 15 years of marriage, he'd marry another white woman. He didn't seem to relate to basketball or to race the same way the other guys did. He had a different attitude and evidently sent out different signals.

When I interviewed Miller at his home in El Cerrito, California, he showed me a family picture that looked like a soft drink ad—a multigenerational group of smiling blacks, whites, Asians, and shades in between. "My oldest daughter, Lisa, who's 40, is married to a Danish guy, Jan, the nicest guy in the world. She spent ten years in Denmark after she finished at Cal, she has a PhD in psychology that she got in Denmark. She has two kids who are the weirdest thing, I didn't know this was possible, her two kids are as white as you are. My second daughter, Michelle, is married to a black guy, Russell, they live here in Berkeley; his father, Bob Bloom, is Jewish. My son Jonathan, his wife is Filipina. Alex, my son, his wife is a mixture of Spanish and white. People would come to parties and they said I've never seen anything like this."

Miller traced it all back to his grandmother, who was very fair but lived as a black. "My grandmother was Irish," he told me. "She looked just like you. Her mother was mixed, coming out of the slavery thing. Her mother was never married to my grandmother's father. He was the white guy who had businesses in the town. But my grandmother was treated as black, because they knew her mother was black. Now in that same town there was another lady, who looked like my grandmother, who was white, who lived uptown. This lady always used to come by to see my grandmother. And in those days in the South, if you were talking to a white person, everything was yes ma'am, no ma'am. But they would sit in the room, they would talk and laugh. You could hear 'em all the time. I never knew their relationship. When my grandmother died, this lady was at the funeral, and she was sitting with my uncle. I said to my uncle what is her relationship? And he said to me, 'Well, actually it's your grandmother's sister.' But she lived as a white woman."

For Miller, the lines between races were always broad and crossable. "And that's how our family is now. We've always had this mixture of things where color and race has never been a factor in anything. I believe on one level that for me personally it came from my exposure with my grandparents very young. And then going to Columbus, probably my high school coach was the next person who showed me that there's really no difference."

Also on that freshman team were two players who would not stick— Nick Pallotta, a white forward from Canton, Ohio, and Floyd Bosley, a black center from Chicago. And two who would stick, Chuck Wood and Rich Rochelle. Wood was from St. Catherine High School in Racine, Wisconsin, about an hour north of Chicago; he was recruited through an older high school teammate and would become the sixth man on the 1962–63 team. He was 6-3 and white, but not afflicted with what players sometimes call white man's disease. In other words, he could jump. Rochelle was a big black man, 6-9 and 230 pounds, from Evanston. He would become backup center but would spend most of his career on the bench. The team was loaded. Frank Hogan, the freshman coach, recalled that only one team gave them a game the whole year, the Jamaco Saints, a semipro team that included former Loyola captain Art McZier. The freshmen lost to the Saints by three points but rolled over the rest of their opposition; they won 12, lost 1, and averaged 96 points a game.

The varsity, meanwhile, improved instantly with the addition of Jerry Harkness. Having finished with a disappointing 10–12 record the year before, they were 15–8 in 1960–61, including a dramatic 83–82 upset of the University of Detroit, a highly regarded team led by future NBA star Dave DeBusschere. Harkness quickly surpassed Clarence Red as star of the team, with a season shooting percentage of .497 and an average of 22.6 points per game. But for a loss to Xavier in their final game, they would have received an at-large invitation to the NCAA tournament.

Just before the end the season, the university athletic board entertained the idea of a freshman-varsity exhibition game to raise money for the Monogram Club. Ultimately they decided against it. According to the minutes of their meeting, "It was the consensus of the Committee that the ill feelings that might be engendered and the embarrassment that might be caused the University would not justify conducting this particular game."

It was the consensus of the committee, in other words, that the freshmen might clean the varsity's clock.

CHAPTER 11: CINCINNATI
Jucker's Surprise

In 1960–61, his first season as Cincinnati's head coach, Ed Jucker finished the regular schedule with a string of 18 straight wins. He won the championship of the tough Missouri Valley Conference, toppling the team that had been ranked number two nationally at the start of the season. By the end of the season, it was Jucker's team that was number two. And he got there with a completely new system installed after the loss of the great Oscar Robertson.

That's what Cincinnati sportswriter Wally Forste was thinking when he wrote that Jucker should be named coach of the year. But Forste had to know it wasn't going to happen. That's probably why he wrote it. He had to know that the honor would go to Fred Taylor of Ohio State—as it eventually did. Everyone knew that compared to Cincinnati, Ohio State was bigger and better in every way.

The year before, Cincinnati had reached the final four, but Ohio State had won the tournament. This year Cincinnati had climbed from nowhere to number two by the end of the season, but Ohio State was number one and had been all year long. Cincinnati had an 18-game win streak, but Ohio State's streak was 29. They hadn't been beaten since February of the previous year. And while Cincinnati's most famous player was the one who was no longer there, Ohio State had two players who would later join Oscar Robertson on the list of the 50 best in NBA history: center Jerry Lucas, one of the most celebrated college basketball players ever, and forward John Havlicek, who was overshadowed by Lucas in college but would have an extraordinary pro career with the Boston Celtics. (He is the highest-scoring white player in NBA history.) They also had All American Larry Siegfried, who would play nine years in the NBA and win five championships with the Celtics.[19]

If Cincinnati's fans felt a rivalry with Ohio State, it was unrequited. Though the campuses were little more than 100 miles apart, Cincinnati hadn't appeared on Ohio State's basketball schedule since 1922. But as the brackets filled in for the 1961 NCAA tournament, with the two schools on opposite sides of the draw, the Cincinnati press began looking forward to an all-Ohio final. A Buckeye partisan dismissed their enthusiasm with a warning painted on Cincinnati's fieldhouse door: "OSU eats little schools like U.C."

In 1961 the tournament was still a modest affair compared to the drawn-out extravaganza it would later become. Twenty-four teams competed—17 conference champions and 7 independents chosen at large. Ohio State and Cincinnati each had a close game in the opening rounds of the tournament. In the Mideast regional, Ohio State beat its first opponent, Louisville, by a single point, 56–55; Havlicek made the winning basket, a 20-footer, with 6 seconds left. In the Midwest, Cincinnati had a tough game against Kansas State, coached by Tex Winter, who later became known as Phil Jackson's longtime colleague, architect of the famous "triangle offense" that won six championships for the Chicago Bulls and five for the Los Angeles Lakers. Winter's Kansas State team led Cincinnati by seven points in the second half, but the Bearcats came back to win 69–64.

In the final four, played at Kansas City Municipal Auditorium, the Ohio teams sailed through the semifinals on Friday night. Ohio State beat St. Joseph of Philadelphia 95–69, and Cincinnati dispatched Utah 82–67.

---

19   And they had a 6-5 reserve forward named Bob Knight.

"The 'dream game' is a reality," announced the front page of the *Enquirer*. But to everyone outside Cincinnati it looked like a pipe dream. The consensus view had been expressed by none other than Adolph Rupp, after his Kentucky team lost to the Buckeyes by 13 points in the Mideast regional: "That team is truly great," Rupp told a writer from *Sports Illustrated*. "They're going all the way." A few days before the championship game, Ohio governor Michael DiSalle issued a proclamation naming Ohio State team of the year, Fred Taylor coach of the year, and the members of the Ohio State team "All-Americans-of-the-Century." As though Cincinnati were in some other state.

But low expectations may have worked in Cincinnati's favor. In retrospect, they look like the looser team. According to the custom of the time, the main event on Saturday night was preceded by a "consolation" game between the two teams that had lost in the semifinals. That game went to four overtimes before St. Joseph finally beat Utah 127–120. Meanwhile the Ohio State and Cincinnati players waited, and waited, for their game to begin. Cincinnati assistant coach Tay Baker remembered that wait more than anything else about the game. "We played in that old auditorium in Kansas City, it could only seat about 5,000 or 6,000. They had a basketball floor in there but it was more of a theater, an auditorium for operas and things like that. Those locker rooms were like dressing rooms, with big old tables with all these big old lights along there, and it was hotter than hell in there and that consolation game went four overtimes. Our guys said hey, can we go out and watch the finish of the game? We said sure, why not? And Ohio State stayed in their locker room the whole dag-gone time. It had to be miserable in there. It's gotta sap you a little bit physically. But what are you *thinking* about when you're sitting in there? Our guys are sitting out there watching two other teams play basketball. And they're in there, what are they doing, what are they thinking about for 45 minutes or what the heck ever it was?"

Cincinnati senior guard Carl Bouldin, a cocaptain of the team, said, "We're down in the locker room, and we had walked by their room and they're yelling and hollering. And we got in there and Jucker said I don't know if you guys ever saw this, and he rolled the ball down his sleeve, did some tricks with the ball. Just made a loose atmosphere. And I think that's what was needed at the time."

Earlier in the day Jucker had told Dick Forbes of the *Enquirer*, "If we can hang in there in the first half, stay even with them, we'll win it." When the game finally started, both teams played what Forbes giddily called "one of the most brilliantly played first halfs in national championship history." At the intermission Ohio State led by one, 39–38.

In the second half, Bouldin came out firing. He was not normally a big scorer for Cincinnati; that wasn't his role. But this tournament would be the end of his basketball career. After graduation he'd be pitching in the Washington Senators organization. He decided to go out in a blaze of glory. He hit a long jumper, he hit another, and he kept shooting until Ohio State's defense came out to stop him. By that time he had sunk five straight to put the Bearcats ahead 52–46 with about 12 minutes to go in the game.

As Bouldin remembered it, the big difference in the game was his fellow cocaptain, senior forward Bob Wiesenhahn, who was revved up before he got to the arena. "They didn't have locker facilities at the fieldhouse," Bouldin said. "They had a locker room but no lockers in there, just hooks, so Jucker said we're gonna change our clothes at the hotel, we're gonna walk over, it's only two blocks. So Wiesenhahn and I were roommates, and while we're getting dressed in the hotel room, we're listening to the radio, and the Ohio State announcer is saying, we see the matchup with Mel Nowell and Tony Yates pretty even, Bouldin and Larry Siegfried pretty even, and then even Hogue and Lucas fairly even, little edge to Lucas. But the big difference we see in this game is UC's big bear, Bob Wiesenhahn, their hatchet man, against the great Hondo, John Havlicek." In the view of this announcer, that's where Ohio State was going to clean up. "Wiesey was pulling up his pants," Bouldin said, "and he looked up and his face just got red from the neck up. He said, I'm gonna kill him."

Wiesenhahn, 6-4 and 220 pounds, was a very physical forward with wide-swinging elbows. "Bob was a gorilla," said Tay Baker. "He was just the most ferocious player that we ever had at UC, the most determined athlete you'll ever see in your life." His teammates knew how to motivate him. Tom Thacker said, "You'd tell Wiesenhahn, 'That's the guy who was talking about you, Bob.' That man was dead. That guy's gonna get no rebounds, would not get close to Wiesenhahn. We told Wiesenhahn, 'This boy Havlicek is gonna kill you, man.' Newspapers were saying Bob Wiesenhahn doesn't have a prayer. Well he got psyched, his eyes started getting big and spinning around like a weirdo."

Wiesenhahn scored 17 points that night and took 9 rebounds. Havlicek had four points and four rebounds.

"It was just tit for tat the whole game," Baker recalled. "Back and forth, a very well-played game. There were like five turnovers in the whole dag-gone game. I think they had three and we had two. [Actually Ohio State had eight and Cincinnati had three.] It was just one of those things that whoever had the ball last was probably gonna win."

The game was tied with 56 seconds left to play. Cincinnati went into a stall, playing for one last shot. Thacker took it with three seconds to go, but he missed. Lucas got the rebound and called time with two seconds left. When play resumed, Larry Siegfried heaved the ball downcourt to Havlicek, who caught it and called time again with one second left. "Never was there such drama in a tournament," Forbes wrote. Ohio State tried to lob the ball inbounds to Lucas, but Hogue grabbed it and the game went into overtime.

In the overtime period, Yates converted three free throws, Hogue two, Wiesenhahn hit a layup, and Thacker took a long jumper at the horn. "I can hear them now," Thacker said 50 years later. "Don't shoot! Don't shoot! Bang. Oh, good shot!" The final was Cincinnati 70, Ohio State 65.

Lucas was gracious in defeat. Cincinnati athletic director George Smith, who had tried to recruit Lucas when he was head coach, presented the runner-up awards to the Ohio State players. He reported that Lucas gave him a smile and said, "Congratulations, I guess your boys just wanted it more than we did."

On Monday morning, the *New York Times* headline read: "N.C.A.A. Defeat of Ohio State Stuns Basketball World." Gordon S. White Jr. quoted Ed Jucker's thickly veiled postgame dig at the basketball establishment: "No All-Americas, just a great bunch of defenders, shooters, hustlers." Translation: you treated us like nobodies all year, and we just beat your golden boys.

But then Jucker admitted that he was surprised himself by the way the season unfolded: "I would have settled for 15 victories—really, I would have. I kept saying to myself—well, we'll lose the next one. We'd win and I'd think, 'Well, the next time.' We just kept winning and pretty soon I was convinced myself."

The *Times* noted that each team would have three starters returning next year. "Could this Cincinnati-Ohio State game be repeated? Possibly. The teams well could meet in next year's championship game."

On Monday night, students scaled the famous monument in Cincinnati's Fountain Square and hung Governor Michael DiSalle in effigy.

CHAPTER 12: MISSISSIPPI

Is there anything wrong with five white boys winning the national championship?

―――――

After Bailey Howell graduated and went off to the NBA, Mississippi State's basketball fortunes dipped predictably, but not for long. They lost more than they won in 1959–60, but in that year's freshman class Babe McCarthy had the core of a new team, and he hadn't gone too far to get it. Joe Dan Gold, a 6-5 forward, came all the way from Benton, Kentucky, about 260 miles north. The rest were Mississippi boys: Bobby Shows, a 6-7 center, from Brookhaven; Red Stroud, a 6-1 shooter, from Forest; and Leland Mitchell, or Mitch, a 6-4 forward from Kiln. Mitchell, who grew into the most formidable player of the bunch, wasn't really recruited by McCarthy; it would be closer to the truth to say that McCarthy was recruited by him.

Kiln is on the Gulf Coast, where life is loose and hardscrabble compared to the northern parts of the state. Mitchell was one of ten kids raised by their mother and her parents. He had some rough edges. He told me his family didn't have electricity until he was four or five; didn't have an indoor bathroom until he put it in himself at age 14 or 15. His first hoop was a wire coat hanger nailed to an oak limb. His first basketball was a crumpled Pet milk can. You couldn't dribble it, of course, but you could move, defend, learn to use your body.

Unlike some of his teammates, Mitchell remembered playing baseball and basketball with black kids, and hanging around with a black friend whose father owned a honky tonk, made moonshine whiskey, and kept thick stacks of money, wrapped and tied, at home in a safe. Mitchell and a friend made some moonshine of their own one summer. They had about 300 gallons—$900 worth—hidden in the woods, but a crew of pipeline workers came through and they ran over some of the barrels and drank what was in the rest. One of the crew was friends with one of Mitchell's sisters, so Mitchell and his partner got their $900, whereupon they decided to leave the whiskey business to pursue other opportunities.

Mitchell played high school ball through his junior year, then as a 12th grader transferred to a local junior college and played for their junior varsity. That took him off the recruiting radar, but he knew he could play for a big-time college. The summer after 12th grade, he worked with his brother in a carnival that traveled through the upper Midwest—Minnesota, Iowa, North and South Dakota. They ran a basketball stand. "We had two goals and you'd come in and pay 50 cents or 25 cents to shoot, and if you made all three shots you'd win a bear. The goals were regulation height and they were regulation goals, but we had taken an inch or two out of the rim, cut the size down, to make it a little harder. And I shot there all summer. And a couple of basketball players from Ohio State came by there, and nobody could outshoot me, 'cause I was shooting five or six hours a day. If a good player came there, he would win a teddy bear—two was his limit, he could win two—and then I'd challenge him to shoot me. And you know I could make 50, 60 in a row, so I'd make 'em when I wanted to, and I'd miss a few if I needed to, and after I'd win some money off of them they'd quit. I knew I could compete with those players. At least I felt like I could."

At the end of that summer, Mitchell returned to the Gulf Coast too late to re-enroll at the junior college. He wanted a bigger school anyway. He knew a guy who knew a guy who knew his way around Mississippi State, and they drove up to Starkville to meet Babe Mc-Carthy. According to NCAA rules Mitchell couldn't try out, exactly, but he and Bobby Shows, the tallest of McCarthy's new recruits, worked out in a high school gym while Shows's father, a former high school coach, looked on. He asked Mitchell if he could make ten free throws in a row. Sure he could. And could he touch the rim ten times in a row? Mitchell, who was 6-4, could do that too. Somehow, word of this little pickup session reached Babe McCarthy, and soon Mitchell had a basketball scholarship to Mississippi State.

He and his mates ran over their competition. Playing as freshmen in 1959–60, while the varsity stumbled to a record of 12–13, they rattled off a perfect season of 21 straight wins. When they moved up to the varsity as sophomores, Mississippi State basketball entered its brief golden age. In 17 of the 26 years since the founding of the Southeastern Conference, Adolph Rupp's Kentucky Wildcats had won or tied for the conference basketball championship. But now the "Baron of the Bluegrass," as Rupp was called, had to move over for the young Babe McCarthy. In 1960–61 his Mississippi State Bulldogs won their second SEC title with a record of 19–6. In 1961–62, they went 24–1 overall and 13–1 in the SEC, sharing the conference title with Kentucky and finishing the season ranked fourth in the nation.

With each championship came a brief flurry of speculation about the NCAA tournament. In 1961, Mississippi governor Ross Barnett, a stubborn segregationist, spoke up against participation, invoking the primal fear at the root of the race-mixing issue. According to an article in the *Jackson Daily News*:

> Barnett said any integrated team which played against the Maroons in the playoffs would feel it had the right "to come down here and play."

> "If there were a half dozen Negroes on the team, where are they going to eat? Are they going to want to come to the dance later and want to dance with our girls?" he asked.

Again, Babe McCarthy toed the line, though a sympathetic reader might detect a hint of disappointment:

At Starkville, Coach Babe McCarthy said there apparently is no chance the team will go to the playoffs because of the state's policy against integrated athletics.

The coach said, "We aren't counting on playing in the tournament. There hasn't been any talk of it."

The following year was different, but only a little. In March 1962, just before the end of Mississippi State's 24–1 season, an AP story published in the *Jackson Daily News* reported there was "quite a bit of behind-the-scenes maneuvering" to get approval for going to the tournament. Alumni groups, the SEC, and even some politicians were agitating, albeit carefully and quietly, for a change in policy:

Rep. Flavous (Butch) Lambert, who has been a basketball and football referee in the Southern Conference for nine years, said he had talked with other legislators at the request of SEC commissioner Bernie Moore.

Lambert said Moore wasn't trying to run Mississippi's business, but merely was interested in seeing the SEC champion represent the conference in the national playoffs....

"It seems foolish to pass up national honors when not playing in Mississippi...," Lambert said.

"Is there anything wrong with five white boys winning the national championship?"

But this potato was still too hot. Representative Lambert said the state board of higher education would have to decide the matter. Some members of that board said the new president of the university, Dean W. Colvard, should make the decision. Colvard (who had replaced Ben Hilbun in 1960) told the AP he didn't "know who'd made the decision last year, and I don't think I will be the one this year." Meanwhile, the article concluded, "Head basketball coach Babe Mc-

Carthy has repeatedly refused to comment on the suggestion. He says his primary object is to win his final game."

In mid-February, Mississippi State had upset Kentucky, then ranked number two, on Kentucky's home court. About a thousand fans came to the airport to yell "We're number one" and welcome the team home. MSU basketball had "certainly hit its peak," proclaimed a jubilant McCarthy. And now, two weeks later, it hit its nadir. For the second straight year, and the third time in four years, the Mississippi State Bulldogs stayed home while Kentucky took their place in the national tournament.

In the finals of the Mideast regional, Kentucky played (and lost to) Ohio State. Two Mississippi State players, Joe Dan Gold and Jack Berkshire, drove to Iowa City and saw the game. "That's the first time I really understood," Gold remembered. "We could have been there. We deserved to be there. And certainly when you're setting up in the stands watching them play, you realize what you're missing out on."

Doug Hutton, who was also on that thwarted team, recalled that he and his teammates accepted the situation without complaint. "I can't remember us even bringing it up. We were 24–1. We would have got to play against Ohio State, the Big Ten champions. We would have got to play against John Havlicek, Jerry Lucas, Bobby Knight. When we saw who Kentucky was playing I'm sure we all thought, boy, what a treat that would be, to see how good we were compared to them. But when you grew up in the South, you respected authority and just never really questioned it."

But the ground was shifting. Governor Barnett was about to make a serious tactical blunder. Mississippi State president Dean Colvard was about to find his courage. And Babe McCarthy, who had abided the bitter disappointment of Bailey Howell, the best player he ever coached, was not about to let it happen again.

INTERLUDE: LOUISVILLE, MARCH 23, 1963
Keep Shooting

Though George Ireland could be withering in his criticism of players, and sometimes seemed to enjoy humiliating them, he kept his cool during the championship game. At the half, down by eight points, he told his team not to panic. They were getting good shots. The ball wasn't falling, but it would. The game was winnable. Their spurt would come.

Now with less than 13 minutes left, down by 15, his message was similar. The game was not lost. They were capable of reeling off 10 or 12 points in a hurry; they'd done it many times before. The previous night, in their rout of the Duke Blue Devils, they'd scored 20 points in less than four minutes. They could come back. But soon Cincinnati would begin their stall. The Ramblers needed to take some chances now. Risk a foul, slap at the ball, leave your man and try to steal a pass.

Harkness came out shooting. Not scoring, just shooting. He missed a layup on a three-on-three break. He missed a jump shot from the corner. He missed another jumper but drew a foul, then missed one of his free throws.

After Thacker missed a shot for Cincinnati, Les Hunter cleared the rebound and Harkness and Egan broke for their basket. Red Rush, the hometown radio announcer, saw the play developing, a flash of the team he knew, and cried out hopefully, "There they go!" Harkness took the outlet pass from Hunter and without dribbling tried to thread the space *between Egan and the lone Cincinnati defender, Tony Yates. He missed. Yates batted down the pass and the ball was picked up by his teammate Larry Shingleton. He returned it to Yates. Then Harkness, aggravating his blunder, fouled Yates trying to steal it back.*

"I'll never forget that," Harkness said 50 years later. "That's normally the way we start everything, that fast break. I saw Egan had a step, I got it ready, and then I didn't lead him enough. I see that play a lot at night. He would have had the layup but I threw it behind and then the guy came up and got it. Oh, man, you talk about something that hurt. Then I foul. That's frustration. I'm out of it."

Harkness was a mix of seemingly contradictory personality traits. He was the guy who didn't go out for his high school team because he didn't think he was good enough. He didn't get mixed up in the point-shaving scandal because he couldn't summon the nerve to approach the player he'd been asked to contact. "Lonely Face." And yet according to many who played with and against him, he had a fierce determination to win. Ron Miller recalled that even when the team was just conditioning, running the cross-country course, if someone got close to Harkness he would press harder and surge ahead. He couldn't stand to come in second. Maybe it was fear of failure.

"I was scared of them," Harkness recalled. "I was scared of Thacker and all of them. Their defense, quickness, shooting. I was an insecure guy, despite all of my accomplishments. I still didn't have the confidence that I should have." So why didn't he fold under the pressure? "I can't do that," he answered. "I had so many people watching me for the first time, all my friends and relatives, and we're on the national stage. My thoughts were that we're not gonna win, but let's make it close. So I gotta score or do some things to make this thing close. I gotta keep trying."

The rest of the team was flailing along with him. They'd show a spark now and then, but they couldn't put a run together. Looking back on it, Egan wondered if their captain's malaise had spread. "Jerry's missing shots that he normally makes. He's sort of demonstrative when you're playing, like 'Oh my God how can this be?', that kind of stuff. Maybe that had some subtle influence, that this is a day unlike other days for us."

Still, Egan and the others knew that they had to keep giving him the ball. And Harkness knew that he had to keep shooting. "If he wasn't taking the shots he was supposed to be taking, that would get you even more discouraged," Egan said.

Cincinnati, meanwhile, was having problems of its own. They'd begun to slow the game down—not to a complete standstill, but to what might be called a semi-stall. They were milking each possession, taking as much time off the clock as possible, moving the ball in and out until they had a sure shot. But when they took those sure shots they missed. They turned the ball over. Thacker and George Wilson got into foul trouble. Ron Bonham, who'd hit three in a row early in the half, missed one and barely touched the ball again. Cincinnati had 45 points with more than 13 minutes left in the game. Eight minutes later they'd added just three more. It was a sloppy game all around, but quietly, almost imperceptibly, Loyola was clawing its way back. Miller made a short jumper. About two minutes later, Rouse hit a 13-footer. Hunter made two key free throws. Cincinnati's lead shrunk to 13, to 11, to 9...

With Thacker in foul trouble, Jucker had shifted his defense to keep him in the game. Now Yates was guarding Harkness. It gave him a subtle lift: "I thought, I got another guy on me. Maybe I can get this Yates."

With five minutes to go, Cincinnati leading 48–41, Egan took the ball up the right side. As he crossed center court he pointed toward his left and Harkness, in the right corner, broke along the baseline toward the basket. Egan passed to Ron Miller on his left. Miller passed right back. Harkness turned north and ran up into the paint, through the "back door," as he would say later, stopping just short of the foul line and extending his arms to receive the pass that Egan was about to throw. Yates was on his back—"where I wanted him," Harkness said. He caught the ball, turned to his left, and without dribbling or hesitating rose up. Yates started to go up with him but then held his hands back to show the refs he wasn't fouling. "It's too late. He's beaten," Harkness said, explaining why Yates laid back. "Plus, I been missin' all day. Let him shoot."

The ball arced up and then down and fell through the net. It was a cathartic moment for Red Rush, the radio man. "Egan, into Harkness.

Turnaround jumper's good! Jerry made his first basket! He made it! He might do it." On the bench, Rich Rochelle had the same notion. *"When he finally hit that first shot, we just felt like: it's on."*

On the inbounds play, Thacker brought the ball up against Loyola's full-court press. Ron Miller was guarding him on his right and Egan was a few feet downcourt with Cincinnati guard Larry Shingleton. Thacker made a fancy turn to spin Miller around to his left. Egan left Shingleton and ran up to double-team Thacker on his right. This was classic Loyola. They'd done it a thousand times. Feeling the pressure, Thacker passed the ball across the center line and suddenly Harkness was streaking the other way. By the time he intercepted the pass he was almost in full stride. Thacker went to the basket with him but with four fouls he had to let Harkness go up. Red Rush was beside himself. *"Here's Thacker with that ball. Passing down. Intercepted by Harkness! Here goes Jerry! Lays it up...and he scores! Harkness scores! Jerry Harkness scores! He scores! Jerry Harkness. Beautiful. Beautiful. Bee-yootiful!"* With 4:24 remaining in the game, it was Cincinnati 48, Loyola 45.

Though Cincinnati's commanding lead was gone, they didn't seem to know how to get out of the stall. Loyola fouled intentionally twice and Cincinnati obliged by missing key free throws. Harkness also missed a free throw. Cincinnati lost the ball under the Loyola basket. Hunter put up a shot and George Wilson slapped it on its way down—goaltending, two points for Loyola. 51–50. Finally Cincinnati began to attack. Thacker took a long inbounds pass from Shingleton and scored on a two-on-one break. Hunter missed a shot and Cincinnati broke again. Thacker fed to Tony Yates, who shot a jumper from the corner. Vic Rouse slapped it off the backboard—also goaltending, but the refs didn't call it. With 19 seconds left, Harkness missed a layup but it was tipped in by Hunter. 53–52 Cincinnati. As soon as Shingleton took the inbounds pass, Harkness fouled him intentionally.

Shingleton, a lefty, went up on his toes and sank his first free throw, which gave his team a two-point lead. Twelve seconds on the clock. Bonham and Wilson raised their fists in the air. Thacker clapped his hands. One more point would put the game out of Loyola's reach. If Shingleton *made his second free throw, Cincinnati would become the first team ever to win three consecutive national championships.*

Shingleton was still talking about that shot almost 50 years later. People wouldn't let him forget it. In the living room of his home in Cincinnati, there was a framed newspaper clipping topped by a photo taken from under the basket just after he put it up. "When I look at that picture I can instantly see why I missed the free throw. I'm left-handed, I flip the ball and I finish this way," he said, holding his hand over his head to illustrate. "You'll see in that picture my hand is kind of like this." Pushing off to the side. "So the ball came off the left side of my hand and it hit the left side of the rim."

It bounced up and fell down and Les Hunter shot up out of the scrum and took the rebound just below the rim. As he came to the floor and rocked back on his heels, he looked to the side for Miller. They knew what to do. Get the ball! Get it out! Get going! Hunter's pass led Miller downcourt. Miller took it on the run and dribbled full speed down the left side. His stride stuttered once. Some would claim later that he traveled, and Miller would admit it, but there was no call. Just as Miller crossed half court he pushed a chest pass to Harkness, who was on the left side about even with the foul line. As Harkness took the ball his back was to Cincinnati's Tony Yates. Eight seconds. He dribbled once with his left hand and lifted off, turning in midair to face the basket squarely. Yates came up to meet him but his feet stayed on the floor.

The freeze frame shows them on the left side of the key, about six feet from the baseline. With his left-handed shot, Harkness is virtually shooting from the side; if he misses, there's no backboard to help him with a lucky bounce. Cincinnati's George Wilson is coiled under the basket, well positioned to take the rebound. Loyola is not likely to get a second shot. Harkness, having raised the ball over his head in both hands, has removed his right hand and holds the ball high in his left.

"I didn't feel this shot," Harkness told me as we watched the film. "When I made my first shot of the ballgame, I turned around and let it go, and I felt it. You can always feel it. Oooo, that feels good. Oh yeah, that's it. Let it go. I did not feel this one at all. If it would have been a

brick I wouldn't have been surprised. I didn't know how much push I had on it, I didn't know what was going on, I just looked at the basket and let it go. It's almost like I didn't put it in."

The ball fell right through, a clean swish. For the first time all night, the Loyola Ramblers were not losing.

Under the basket, Cincinnati scrambled to make an in-bounds pass. Three seconds on the clock...two...one...

Overtime.

Mississippi governor Ross Barnett. He and President Kennedy agreed that James Meredith could be registered quietly in Jackson. But then Barnett went to an Ole Miss-Kentucky football game and backed out of the deal.

One of the messages received by Mississippi State president Dean Colvard after he announced that he would send the team to the NCAA tournament.

A

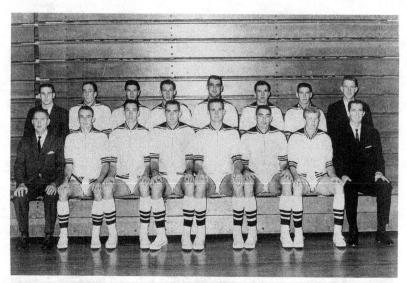

Mississippi State Bulldogs, 1962-63. Front row, coach Babe McCarthy, Doug Hutton, Stan Brinker, Joe Dan Gold, Bobby Shows, Leland Mitchell, W.D. (Red) Stroud, assistant coach Jerry Simmons. Back row, manager Jimmy Wise, Don Posey, Larry Lee, Jackie Wofford, Howard Hemphill, Billy Anderton, Aubrey Nichols, freshman coach J.D. Gammel. Not shown, Richie Williams.

Mississippi State coach Babe McCarthy, aka "Magnolia Mouth," holds court for the press before the NCAA Mideast regional in East Lansing, Michigan. A week earlier he'd seen Loyola play and said, "Nobody can beat a team like that."

B

Mississippi State's Leland Mitchell drives on Loyola's Ron Miller. Jerry Harkness is in the backcourt. "This was not we had murdered somebody and the law was after us," Mitchell said of the team's flight. "This was more like a wedding. Everyone was for it."

Bobby Shows (left) and Don Posey of Mississippi State. Though the Jackson *Clarion-Ledger* feared trouble when the team arrived in East Lansing, in fact they were greeted warmly. Shows said, "We were the sweet babies, I reckon."

Cincinnati Bearcats 1961-62: Kneeling, Larry Shingleton, Tony Yates, Larry Elsasser, Tom Thacker, Tom Sizer, Jim Calhoun. Standing, assistant coach Tay Baker, Bill Abernathy, Fred Dierking, George Wilson, Ron Reis, Paul Hogue, Dale Heidotting, Ron Bonham, head coach Ed Jucker.

D

Mississippi State captain Joe Dan Gold. He had watched from the stands a year before when Kentucky played Ohio State in the NCAA tournament. "That's the first time I really understood. We could have been there. We deserved to be there."

Cincinnati head coach Ed Jucker. According to Tom Thacker, "He disrobed very quickly. Highly intense guy....He'd get wound up tight, he'd go off, and we'd say 'Juck, take it easy!'"

Top, Courtesy Mississippi State University Archives,
Mississippi State University Libraries
Bottom, Courtesy Archives & Rare Books Library,
University of Cincinnati

E

Loyola Ramblers 1962–63: Standing, Jerry Harkness, Jack Egan, Chuck Wood, Vic Rouse, Les Hunter, Rich Rochelle, Jim Reardon, Dan Connaughton, Ron Miller, manager John Gabcik, assistant manager Fred Kuehl, trainer Dennis McKenna. Kneeling, head coach George Ireland, assistant Jerry Lyne.

Cincinnati's Tom Thacker (25), George Wilson (32), and Tony Yates (20), three black players who were not named AP All Americans in 1962. Ed Jucker said, "You look at that list and it almost makes you sick to your stomach."

Loyola's basketball program was developed primarily by Lenny Sachs, a manically active athlete and coach who died of a heart attack at age 45.

Ron Miller, Jack Egan, George Ireland. The coach told them not to panic. The game was winnable. Their spurt would come.

Two seconds: Vic Rouse shot up over Thacker and took the ball in two hands. He didn't tip it, he said later. He was taking no chances.

Photos Courtesy Loyola Athletics

H

PART TWO:
COLLISION COURSE

CHAPTER 13: CHICAGO
Off-Court Adjustments

Despite their success on the basketball court, life could be difficult for Loyola's black recruits. Most difficult, perhaps, for Les Hunter. Though he would turn out to be the most accomplished player on the team, the one with the most successful pro career, he was probably the least self-assured as a freshman, and the most sensitive to slights and insults. Like Jerry Harkness before him, he decided at one point to give it up and go home.

Before arriving at Loyola, Hunter had spent lots of time on the campuses of Fisk and Tennessee State. He thought he knew what college looked like. It was a fun, stimulating world, teeming with spirited and purposeful young black people. He knew he'd signed up for a "white" college, but he didn't really know what that meant until he saw it. In the course of a week, he recalled, he might see only 10 or 12 blacks, not counting other athletes. Everyone knew why he was there—you could tell by looking at him—but once in a while he had to ask himself: what am I doing here?

On campus he felt safe and accepted, if painfully conspicuous. Off campus he was just conspicuous. Rogers Park, the lakefront neighborhood that surrounded the university, was cut off from it psychically as well as physically. The residents were overwhelmingly white and did not identify with the school or its athletic ambitions.

Blacks were not welcome in the bars or on the beaches. They could get a pizza at Cindy Sue's Rambler Inn, which was just off campus on Sheridan Road, but as they crossed the street they might have to endure a racial epithet from a passing car. At the barber shop on Sheridan, there was no one who knew how to cut their hair. Some of the players resented that, some excused it, some noted the irony a few years later when their championship trophy was displayed there.

Of course there were virtually no black girls on campus, and white girls were considered off limits. All the black players remembered the story of the "mixer" where Pablo Robertson danced with a white girl. Robertson was a flashy New York player who came to Loyola as a freshman in 1961. He was a life-of-the-party type who knew (too well, it turned out) how to have a good time. Where his teammates might be inclined to sit in the corner and watch the girls and talk about basketball, Pablo had nerve enough to ask a white girl to dance—and when she agreed, a priest came over to tell the couple that "intermingling" was not allowed.

One night the boys wandered over to a party at Mundelein College, a Catholic women's school adjacent to the Loyola campus. (It has since been absorbed into Loyola.) As Harkness remembered the story, a reserve player they called "Drip," because there was often some saliva on his lips, became too insistent in his attempt to chat up a Mundelein girl. "He just didn't act right. He wasn't thinking. The girl didn't want to talk to him. These girls, some of them, didn't have many experiences with black guys. He scared her." In short order the Sisters of Charity of the Blessed Virgin Mary protested to George Ireland and he had to give his black players a pep talk on race relations. "He brought us all in and he asked us what happened," Harkness recalled. "We told him and he said well, people are not ready for that. One of these days, 10, 20, maybe 30 years from now, it'll be different, it's going to be OK for those things. But not now."

George McKenna, a grad student and teaching assistant who hung out with the ballplayers, told me that Ireland once asked him to find some black girls to come to the dances. McKenna was shocked. "I said, 'Are you serious? I'm not a procurer.'"

McKenna, who was working on a master's degree in math, was from New Orleans. He was black but he looked white. He saw and heard things that the black basketball players did not. Harkness recalled that he would give the players tips on which professors to seek out and which ones to avoid.

"I would sit in the lunchroom when the players weren't around and people would say things," McKenna remembered. "There were a lot of biases and prejudices. I don't think it was malicious as much as it was just the white people's culture about black folks. You know, Loyola hadn't had a whole lot of black players in the past. It was kind of an adjustment for them to come out and cheer for black athletes."

McKenna knew how the players felt. "I had something in common with them; they were the only friends I had. They were younger than me but I didn't know anybody at Loyola. I was living alone in a room in somebody's house." Grad students were not allowed to live in Loyola's one dorm. "I ate my meals and I hung out in the dorm with the guys, in the rec room, played cards with them and talked trash and stuff like that."

The racial environment on campus was calm, McKenna said, but black students were isolated. Where could they feel comfortable? Whom could they hang with? "I didn't see them affiliating with any of the white ballplayers in their spare time. I mean when we played cards together, none of the white guys came over to play."[20]

To find their fun the black guys had to travel into Evanston and to Chicago's black neighborhoods. On the South Side there were hotel parties and clubs on 47th Street and Provident Hospital, home to many black nurses and nursing students. Up in Evanston was a guy named Doc who could cut their hair. The black athletes from

---

20   McKenna earned a doctorate in education and became a teacher and administrator in the Los Angeles public schools. His success in turning around a failing inner-city school, George Washington High, was the subject of the 1986 TV movie *The George McKenna Story*, starring a young Denzel Washington. When Washington became more famous the film was rereleased on video under the title *Hard Lessons.*

Northwestern would also go there. They could hang out at Doc's house and shoot the breeze without worrying if they were breaking some kind of rule.

But the players had to be careful even in black neighborhoods. They could be challenged walking off the El. Who are you? Where you from? What are you doing here?

Like the night they went to a party in Evanston and Vic Rouse was stabbed.

Rouse was by all accounts the most sophisticated of the black guys. He was focused and intelligent. "He'd speak up a little bit more. He wasn't a take-the-back-seat-of-the-bus kind of guy," George McKenna recalled. And he was sharp. He wore nice clothes. Had his shoes shined. He enjoyed the company of women and they enjoyed him. "He thought of himself as a debonair kind of fellow," McKenna said. "Which I think is probably what got us in trouble over in Evanston."

"The girls started giving us a lot of attention," Harkness recalled. "And the local guys got upset. I've seen it happen in the projects. And then these guys went and got knives I guess. They left, they came back, and they came after us. And we ran."

As Hunter remembered it, four or five cars returned to the party just as the "college boys" decided it was time to leave. Rocks and bottles started flying and the chase was on. Hunter and Henry White, a friend from the track team, went one way. The other guys went another. Each group feared that the other had been caught, but they all arrived safe—armed with sticks and rocks, just in case—on the Howard Street El platform. It was like a scene from the Walter Hill movie *The Warriors*. On the train, someone noticed that Rouse's jacket was torn and wet. The wet stuff was blood. In an adrenaline fog, Rouse hadn't realized that he'd been wounded by a thrown knife.

"They didn't know who they were messing with, 'cause Ireland had a fit," Harkness said. "You don't mess around with my boys."

"Ireland pulled his muscle then," Hunter said. "They had the police out there, and they rounded up some people and brought them down to the dorm. Then the police told Rouse, regardless of the one we bring in front of you, you say he's the one who stabbed you." The police brought Rouse a suspect and Rouse performed as instructed. "Rouse said yeah, that's the motherfucker there, that's him," whereupon the chump suspect immediately spilled the name of the real perpetrator, as the officers had intended. "He ratted the guy out right there," Hunter said. "The guy went straight to reform school."

———————

Hunter was no fan of Ireland's. The day he went to pack his bags, he called the coach a prejudiced motherfucker.

It was his freshman year. Ireland had Floyd Bosley at center on the freshman team. He started Chuck Wood at one forward spot and had Rouse and Hunter competing for the other. Though they'd come to Loyola as a twosome, Rouse and Hunter had a complicated relationship. In high school they hung out together after practice and before games, but they were not close confidantes. Rouse, fresh off the streets of East St. Louis, was smooth and assured. He was also more mature as a ballplayer. When he came to Pearl High as a junior, he and Hunter competed for the starting center job that Hunter thought would be his. Rouse won it; Hunter did not start at Pearl until their senior year. There was an edge on their friendship, and when they began as Loyola freshmen Hunter thought Ireland was making it worse. Why did he have to compete with Rouse for a starting position? Why didn't Chuck Wood have to compete for his job? Hunter was sitting on the bench and he thought he knew why: he was black, and Ireland didn't want too many blacks in the starting lineup.

His frustration spilled over one afternoon at practice, when he started mixing it up with a junior on the varsity team, John Crnokrak. "Crno," as they called him, was a hardhead. The grandson of Serbian immigrants, he'd come up on the racially mixed playgrounds of Gary, Indiana. He was a physical player who liked to talk trash and intimidate. The following year he'd be a cocaptain of the team but riding the bench.

"Crnokrak was kind of a bad ass," Hunter said. "He had been like a star in high school, and then he was a starter on the varsity, and then here come all these freshman guys who were jumping higher and blocking shots and stuff, and he was getting kind of mad and rough. So he and Vic were roughing it up, and I think Vic threw an elbow or something at him, and Ireland sat Vic down and brought me in. Well as soon as I came in I started roughing it up with Crnokrak, because you know, I gotta support my guy. And Ireland told me to sit down. I said you prejudiced motherfucker, I'm going home. I'm not getting to play anyway. So that's when I left."

It wasn't just Ireland, it was everything. Hunter's grades were bad. He was disappointed with the social life. Back at the dorm, he tried to find a janitor to get his trunk out of the storage room. Before he could, a black friend persuaded him to stay. "He said think about your parents and all of that. I know you can do the work, you gotta make some decisions. How you gonna feel if you go back home and people say hey, man, you didn't make it? He told me don't throw your career away in the heat of the moment. After that I never had another failing semester."

Ireland could be a forgiving soul. Some of his players would come to believe that the more valuable the talent involved, the more forgiving he was inclined to be. "The next day I called Ireland, apologized," Hunter said. "He made me sit out one freshman game, but after that I came back and I started getting to play quite a bit. Go figure!"

CHAPTER 14: CINCINNATI
Defending National Champions

Carl Bouldin and Bob Wiesenhahn graduated from Cincinnati in spring 1961. Bouldin went on to baseball, and Wiesenhahn to a brief pro career with the Cincinnati Royals. As the 1961–62 season began, Jucker had Tom Thacker and Fred Dierking at forward, Paul Hogue at center, and Tony Yates and Larry Shingleton at guard. Three juniors and two seniors, three blacks and two whites. Waiting in the wings were two sophomores who needed some seasoning. One was Ron Bonham, a 6-5 shooter from Muncie, Indiana. He was Indiana's Mr. Basketball in 1960, but his defensive game needed work. The other was George Wilson, 6-8, who had been a center and a prolific scorer at Marshall High in Chicago. Wilson could not play center on the same team with Hogue, and his scoring wouldn't be needed. He'd have to learn a new position and a new defensive focus.

By midseason—game 16, as Shingleton recalled—both sophomores had been promoted to the starting lineup. Bonham replaced Dierking at forward. Wilson played the other forward, and Thacker moved out to guard, replacing Shingleton. If Jucker had ever cared about the unwritten racial quota, he had ceased caring by then. The defending national champions had four black starters.

Wilson's story was a lot like Ron Miller's. Shortly after he was born—in 1942, in Meridian, Mississippi—his father went to war. When the war ended his parents went separate ways. George and his father went to California, along with his father's parents and numerous aunts and uncles who found work in the defense plants there. Young George wound up living in LA with his grandparents. Meanwhile his mother moved to Chicago and remarried.

When George got to be six years old and too much for his grandparents to handle, a family friend who worked as a Pullman porter brought him to Chicago on the Super Chief. It was an adventure for the boy. He enjoyed being on his own in a cozy sleeping compartment. Then "I got to Chicago and saw my mom for the first time in a long time. I could tell it was my mom because she had the same green eyes."

Wilson's new family lived on the West Side of Chicago in the Francisco Terrace Apartments, an 1895 building designed by Frank Lloyd Wright. Originally meant as one of the first "projects" for low-income families, it had been converted to co-op apartments in the 30s. George's stepfather, "Mr. Henry," worked in the parking lot of the Conrad Hilton Hotel downtown. "He was from Alabama, so he had that—he had that segregation in him. He just thought white folks ruled and he couldn't say nothing or do nothing. He was the greatest guy. He always had wisdom for you. He always used to tell me be ten minutes early. You look at my watch, my watch is always early. My clocks are always ten to fifteen minutes early. I got that from Mr. Henry.

"I was always a young man that listened to my elders and did what they told me," Wilson said. He never missed a day of school. He always had a job. He remembered the name of every boss, every coach, every person who ever gave him a tip or a break. At age 69 he still remembered how the white workers at the downtown Walgreens treated him when he was 12 or 13.

"My buddy Phillip Stone, he was an only child and I'm an only child, so we were running buddies. When we were in the eighth grade we used to go downtown to State and Lake. Go to downtown Chicago, 1954, '55, '56—you see what I mean?" What he meant was that downtown Chicago was still pretty white. "And we would see the movies before they came to the inner city. So we could tell our friends, oh yeah, man, you're gonna like *Davy Crockett* when it gets out here, you're gonna like *The Ten Commandments*, you know. This was our thing once a month. Phillip and I would go downtown, we'd come out of the movie, we'd walk down the street and go to Walgreens and we'd sit at the counter. What did I do? Did I integrate Walgreens on State and Lake? We didn't see any other black people there except us.

"I'll never forget, to this day, I always had ham salad on toast. I had a strawberry shake and Phillip had a chocolate shake. And we'd share one piece of apple pie. We were gentlemen. We were just as neat as could be. We'd finish our shakes and put 'em there, put our forks and our spoons together and count our little money. So guess what happened? After a while, all the waitresses and the managers at that Walgreens, who were all white, they would look forward to us coming in, sitting there, and they would ask us questions. How did it go this month? How are your classes? How are your grades? And that one piece of apple pie kept getting bigger and bigger. I don't know what went on in those people's minds, but I guess they figured if these two little brothers come in here and know what they're doing, let's see what happens. Instead of prejudging us as two little black fellas who are gonna come in here and steal everything, or throw everything around, just let us prove how we're gonna be. You know, they treated us like their sons. That's why I love Walgreens to this day."

Wilson started playing basketball at age ten, at a newly opened Boys Club a few blocks from home. At first his mother wouldn't let him go. She thought it was a gang. He had to collect some literature and bring it home for her to read. Of course he had his own money to pay the membership. A coach there, Will Bonner, saw him throw a basketball through a hoop. "They were starting a Chicago Boys Club league. I was tall, he thought I was too old. He asked, how old are you? Ten? Ten! Come over here, let me talk to you!"

By the time he was a sophomore in high school, Wilson was 6-6 and leading Marshall High to a perfect 31–0 record. That year they became the first Chicago high school ever to win the Illinois state tournament. They won again in 1960. And three years in a row they won the hotly contested Chicago city championship, played at the Chicago Stadium between the winners of the Public and Catholic leagues. In 1960 *Scholastic* and *Parade* magazines named Wilson (and future teammate Ron Bonham) to their high school All American teams.

Wilson grew two more inches in high school and received at least 50 college recruiting letters, he recalled. "I'm sure some of the schools weren't even integrated, they'd just invite me anyway." He planned to attend the University of Illinois, but thought better of it when he got a letter from George Smith, visited Cincinnati, and met his hero Oscar Robertson. He liked that the Missouri Valley Conference was more basketball-minded than the Big Ten, and not so white. But the biggest reason he chose Cincinnati, he said, was that it made Champaign-Urbana look like a small town. "I grew up in LA and Chicago, I don't know nothing about no little town. Go down to Champaign, man, it's about this big." He was holding his hands together, making a small circle. "And you know, we're talking the end of the 50s, those little communities outside of Champaign—you know what I'm talking about." He was talking about the way a 6-8 black man might feel or be treated in downstate Illinois.

———————

One can't delve too deep into the history of Loyola basketball before learning that the 1962–63 team was extraordinary for having four black starters. But the fact that Cincinnati had four black starters the year before never seems to come up. Perhaps as a smaller and more southern city, Cincinnati was more polite than Chicago, or more repressed. Perhaps, as George Wilson suggested, Chicago blacks felt freer to express their racial pride. Whatever the reason, Wilson said that people in Cincinnati didn't talk about it. Black fans would talk about the team that had Thacker, Yates, Wilson, and Hogue. Their color was understood. (White fans talked about the team that had Bonham, Thacker, Yates, Wilson, and Hogue, in that order, Wilson said.)

Within the team, it was not an issue and was never expressed, according to all the participants I talked to. Larry Shingleton, the player who was benched when Wilson became a starter, said, "There's no question that the five that ended up the year, they were the five best players," and that's all anyone would admit to caring about.

It was a tight group. Before the 1961–62 season began, the State Department sent them on a goodwill trip to the Philippines, where they played industrial teams and the Philippine Olympians. They lived together for nearly a month, Shingleton said, and there was nothing to do but play basketball and ping-pong. On a bus they took to singing "When the Saints Go Marching In." Fifty years later, most of the players still lived in the Cincinnati area and still gathered for lunch regularly in a downtown hotel. They invited each other to their children's weddings and had begun to attend each other's funerals.

Of course winning is a great promoter of harmony and cohesion, and by the second half of the 1961–62 season Cincinnati was beating everyone. In many ways that season was a replay of the year before. First the Bearcats dug themselves an early hole in the Missouri Valley Conference. In December they barely escaped Drake, winning 60–59 away as the excitable Jucker drew two technical fouls from referee Jack Fette. A few nights later, at home against Marshall, Fette T'd Jucker twice more. "If he's assigned to work this Wichita game, I'll walk off the floor," Jucker said. Fette wasn't assigned to that game, but Cincinnati lost it 52–51 when Wichita State guard Lanny Van Eman sank a 20-foot jump shot with three seconds on the clock. That was the end of a 27-game win streak. Dick Forbes of the *Enquirer* wrote that Jucker was "practically inconsolable."

Three weeks later, in January, the Bearcats lost again to Bradley in the Snake Pit, 70–68 in overtime. This time Jucker was "shell-shocked." Just like the year before, Cincinnati now had two losses in the MVC and Bradley had none. Forbes reported, "Somehow it seemed like sentences repeating themselves, one year later, when Jucker declared, 'It's all up to somebody else now. We'll have to have some help.'"

But as they had the year before, they bounced back from their loss to Bradley by beating Dayton in the Cincinnati Gardens, and from that point on they were unbeatable once again, running off 13 consecutive wins to finish the regular season at 24–2. The help they needed came from Wichita State, which beat Bradley 89–88 in late January. Bradley and Cincinnati both ended the season with MVC records of 10–2, so they had to meet in Evansville, Indiana, to compete for the conference berth in the NCAA tournament. Cincinnati easily won that game 61–46 and kept rolling through the NCAA regionals, defeating Creighton by 20 and Colorado by 27. Their defense was stifling. Three games in a row they held their opponents to 46 points. With Wilson, Hogue, and Bonham in the frontcourt, this was the tallest and by most accounts the best team Cincinnati had ever had. Their only close call came in the final four, facing UCLA in the semifinal on Friday night, March 23.

UCLA, coached by John Wooden, was making its first appearance in the final four, just two years before starting a legendary streak of 10 championships in 12 years. They were "pesky gnats," in the words of *Sports Illustrated*'s Ray Cave, a small, fast-breaking team including future NBA all-star Walt Hazzard. "[E]verybody knew Cincinnati would crush them," Cave wrote, and everybody seemed right when Cincinnati got off to an 18–4 lead. But then UCLA started coming back. By halftime the game was tied, and it was tied again with ten seconds left to play. As Cave told it, Jucker then called time out and ordered a play for Hogue, who had scored Cincinnati's last 14 points. But Hogue's teammates couldn't get the ball to him. The final shot was taken by the unabashed Tom Thacker. Dick Forbes of the *Enquirer* saw it as a 12-foot jumper. Howard Barry of the *Chicago Tribune* called it a 20-footer. Ray Cave saw a 25-footer, just the kind of low-percentage shot that drove Jucker crazy.

What made the shot crazier was that Thacker had not made a basket all night, having missed on six consecutive attempts. Three seconds remained on the clock. "I never had a fear of shooting," Thacker understated. "I figured the next shot was going in." It did. The final was Cincinnati 72, UCLA 70.

Earlier in the evening, Ohio State had defeated Wake Forest to earn a place in the final. (Billy Packer, who later became famous as a TV announcer, was on that Wake Forest team.)

Jucker and Cincinnati now had what they had been hoping for all year—a rematch. For them, it was a grudge match. Though they had beaten Ohio State a year ago, they felt they were still being treated as losers.

CHAPTER 15: CHICAGO
Racial Peace Prevails

———

In 1961 George Ireland hadn't read John McLendon's book *Fast Break Basketball*. It wasn't published until 1965. But when the '61 season opened and Loyola's fabulous freshmen came up to the varsity, Ireland installed a style of play that came straight from McLendon's playbook. Perhaps "installed" is not the right word. It might be more accurate to say he let it happen.

Ireland had been a high school coach for 15 years and had amassed a record of 262 wins and 87 losses. As Les Hunter pointed out, it would be hard to do that without drawing a lot of Xs and Os. In the late 50s, according to Art McZier and Clarence Red, the Ramblers played a relatively conventional structured offense. Red's teams would run, he remembered, but then they would set up at half court. A squib in a 1958 issue of the Loyola student newspaper said that Ireland's teams played "a slow style...with an occasional fast break."

But in '61 Ireland had players who could get the ball, get it out, and get going. Harkness, Egan, and Miller were fast and had quick hands. They could slap at the ball and gang up on an opponent to force a hurried pass. Hunter and Rouse ran well for big men and were excellent rebounders who knew how to make an outlet pass to start the fast break. They had trained in McLendon's three-on-three sweatbox academy at Tennessee State.

"The best play for us," Miller recalled: "Les gets the rebound, to me to the side, to Jerry, score. Or out to me, to Jack, score. That's us at our best." Take it off, kick it out, and run. "We played very aggressive the whole game. We pressured the ball. We wanted to score, we wanted to run. That's what we wanted every single time." As McLendon would later advise in his book, Ireland started the season with cross-country running. He was a fanatic for conditioning; he wanted his team to run their opponents ragged. Miller said, "I remember Ireland saying in practice: 'Run run run run run run. Run run run run.'"

Of course they had an offensive play they could use when they had to. They called it "the pattern." It was a series of moves and passes meant to deliver the ball to Hunter, posting up near the free-throw line, who would then dish it off or put it up according to what the defense was doing. They also had a clearout play, in which everyone would try to draw his defender to one side to clear the way for Harkness to play one-on-one. But with this team Xs and Os were mostly beside the point. "My high school coach did more actual technique or strategy coaching than Coach Ireland," Hunter said. "His whole idea was, you got the better athletes, jump all over them and press the whole game, and get into your motion offense and that'll suffice."

In early December the *Chicago Tribune* published a Sunday magazine story for the beginning of Loyola's 1961–62 season. The headline invited readers to "Meet a Very Unusual Coach. He Says: 'MY TEAM IS GREAT!'" The writer, Tom Fitzpatrick, had Ireland defying the unofficial rule of the unofficial "basketball coaches union" by claiming that "the current Loyola team is a great one—the best I've had in 26 years of coaching....Why shouldn't I admit it if it's true?"

As the season began Ireland had Harkness and Rouse at forward, Hunter at center. The starting guards were two Irishmen from the Chicago Catholic League: Egan and Mike Gavin, a 6-0 senior. One senior, one junior, three sophs; three blacks and two whites. As the season progressed Ron Miller got a lot of playing time, but he didn't start until the last game. Floyd Bosley was Hunter's backup but flunked out after the first semester.

They came out strong—but then Loyola usually did, thanks to Ireland's early season scheduling. They won two of their first three games by 50 points or more, three of the first four by more than 40: they defeated Assumption University of Windsor, Ontario, 95–44 ("a mild case of murder" according to the *Sun-Times*), South Dakota 104–63 ("oppression of the downtrodden"), Wayne State 93–43 ("Loyola Coasts"), and North Dakota 96–73 ("Rips"). But if Ireland was not ashamed to schedule such "warmup" games, as the *Tribune*'s Richard Dozer called them, he was not afraid to take on bigger challenges. Next up would be an away game at Western Michigan, which had beaten Loyola home and away the previous year and had just added Manny Newsome, a sophomore star from Gary, Indiana, who would hold WMU's all-time scoring record for 46 years. After that came another away game against the almighty Ohio State.

At Kalamazoo the Ramblers led by 13 points at the half, but Western Michigan surged in the second half and took an 80–78 lead with 45 seconds to go. Harkness drew a foul and made two free throws to send the game into overtime. With seconds left in the overtime period, the score tied again at 85, the ball was in the hands of Ron Miller. Playing in place of Vic Rouse, who had broken his nose against North Dakota, Miller was having a good night. He had 22 points. He launched a 20-foot shot that bounced off the rim. With one second left, Floyd Bosley tipped it in to give the Ramblers an 87–85 win.

Three nights later, when they faced Ohio State, the *Columbus Citizen Journal* called it a "Battle of Unbeatens," but there wasn't really much suspense. Loyola, despite their prodigious early season scoring, was an unknown team that had barely beaten its one serious opponent. Ohio State, the team of Jerry Lucas and John Havlicek and coach of the year Fred Taylor, had been at the top of the AP basketball poll since the beginning of the previous season.

Loyola scored first, but the Buckeyes took the lead at 5–4 and never gave it back. At halftime, with Ohio State leading 45–31, the *Chicago Tribune* presented Lucas with its silver basketball trophy for being the most valuable player in the Big Ten the year before. Loyola came within nine points in the second half, but then Havlicek led a charge that put the game out of reach. He scored 30 points on the night, Lucas 20. They took 32 rebounds between them, more than Loyola had as a team. The final was Ohio State 92, Loyola 72.

It didn't hurt much. The Ramblers left feeling they had hung tough through three-fourths of an away game against everybody's number one. They bounced back with wins over four respectable opponents—Ohio, Colgate, Indiana, and Detroit—before falling to Marquette, 63–60, just before semester break. They had a frigid night shooting. Harkness scored 24 points, hitting 10 of 20 shots from the floor, but according to Dozer of the *Tribune,* "the rest of the Ramblers' beleaguered forces made only 16 of 58 shots—many of them from close enough range to embarrass a grammar school offense."

After semester break (and the loss of Bosley), Loyola rolled over Memphis State 100–76. Mike Gavin shot 10–14 from the floor and scored 22 points. John Crnokrak, coming off the bench, scored the 100th point with nine seconds left. Halfway through their regular season, the Ramblers were 10–2 and scoring an average of 88.5 points per game.

Then came a road trip to Loyola of New Orleans, sometimes called Loyola of the South. This turned out to be one of the high points, or low points, of the season, for reasons that had nothing to do with basketball.

———————

Two years before, in 1960, Loyola had played in New Orleans with an integrated team including hometown boy Clarence Red. Though that was the city's first public integrated sporting event since such things had been banned in 1956, it came off without incident. But the climate had changed since then.

In December of 1960, the Supreme Court decided a case called *Boynton v. Virginia,* which ruled that a bus terminal restaurant was an integral part of interstate travel and therefore could not discriminate against or segregate black passengers. In May 1961, the first Freedom Riders set out for New Orleans from Washington, D.C., hoping to use that ruling as a way to challenge discrimination in the South. Their buses never arrived in New Orleans. They were intercepted by arrest (Charlotte, North Carolina), firebombing (Anniston, Alabama), and a vicious attack by a club-wielding mob, as police stood by (Montgomery, Alabama). The South was seething with racial feeling. When the Ramblers arrived in New Orleans to play basketball in January 1962, the city was mere days away from a mayoral election in which race policy was a prominent issue.

Segregation then was not just a matter of keeping blacks away from whites; it was about preventing the mixing of the races. Blacks couldn't stay in a white hotel and whites couldn't stay in a black one. According to contemporary newspaper accounts (whose main source seems to have been George Ireland), the Loyola team planned to stay at Xavier University of Louisiana, an all-black school with strong ties to Chicago.[21] But the day before the team was scheduled to leave, Ireland called the black players together and told them that the Xavier plan had fallen through. According to the *Sun-Times,* he said arrests had been threatened if Loyola's black and white players stayed together. Ireland told the team they would have to split up in New Orleans. The white guys would stay at the Sheraton. The blacks guys would stay in Algiers with Clarence Red's family and another nearby.

Ireland told the press that he put it to a vote and the team decided to go anyway, but that's not how the players remembered it. Ron Miller recalled that the meeting was black players only and that Harkness, their leader and spokesman, was visibly shaken by Ireland's plan. "He kept saying it's not right, it's not right. We're a team. We shouldn't have to do this, we can't be doing this. And he got Ireland defensive. Ireland was saying, I didn't know, Jerry, I will never let

---

21   Xavier was founded by Mother (now Saint) Katharine Drexel, a Philadelphia heiress who established a religious order, the Sisters of the Blessed Sacrament, devoted to serving blacks and Native Americans. She and her order also established and operated the Chicago high school that became St. Elizabeth. Before integration, Xavier was a destination for black Chicago high school athletes, including Nat "Sweetwater" Clifton, one of the first black players in the NBA.

this happen again. They told me one thing and broke their promise." Harkness said they should cancel the game and stay home, and at that point Ireland started talking fast, Miller said. "He's gotta get away from that, no way in hell is he gonna have a discussion on that. So you know, you talk through it—like, I can get through this if I just keep talking."

Harkness: "He thought we'd say well, we're ready to go, but we said no, if this is the situation, we don't have to go. So then he changed it. We sat down and he changed his whole approach. He made it as if we *should* go, this would be good for integration: 'I understand what you're saying, but I think we shouldn't back down. We gotta hit this thing straight on and it'll be good, it will bring it to the forefront. Let's be brave. And then we can play them and beat them,' something like that. And then that changed my mind, when he took that approach."

In New Orleans, a few hours before the game, Ireland spoke by speakerphone to a group of sportswriters meeting back in Chicago. The next day's papers were full of his outrage. The *Tribune* reported that he "tossed a segregation bombshell" into the meeting, charging that his team had been victims of "unrelenting segregation" since they'd arrived in New Orleans. "It's been so bad that this will probably be our last trip down here," he said. Notre Dame coach Johnny Jordan was at the meeting and praised his former teammate for having the nerve to "go on a crusade like this."

Fifty years later Harkness was still not sure about the coach's motives. "I truly believe that Ireland wanted a controversy," he said. "I think Xavier was ready, willing to take us in. I heard that all of a sudden Ireland changed his mind."

Why would he want a controversy? Was he really trying to strike a blow for integration? Did he want to draw attention to himself or his virtue? Was he trying to motivate the team with an us-against-the-world story?

Maybe all of that, Harkness said. And maybe he was motivating himself. "He was different. A hardhead. He liked to dig on people.

That's the kind of guy he was: 'Let's show 'em.'" Later, on the banquet circuit, Ireland would let it be known that other coaches liked to crack wise about the composition of his team. "Unfortunately George Ireland couldn't be with us tonight, he's in Africa, recruiting," stuff like that. "I don't like that stuff," Harkness recalled him saying. "Let's show 'em."

Ron Miller thought Ireland was naive about the state of race relations in New Orleans, and surprised by what he found there. "When we got to the airport, and we got into the cab, the sign on it was 'colored.' So I think it was myself and Vic and Les, we get into the cab. Ireland gets in the front of the cab, and the cab driver says 'I'm sorry sir, I can't take you.' And Ireland said, 'These are my players, I want to go with you.' And the driver said, 'You don't understand sir, I'll get fined.' And Ireland said, 'I'll pay the fine.' And the driver says, 'No sir, you will not, I'll go to jail. I cannot drive you.'"

Rich Rochelle, the backup center—who disliked Ireland profoundly—remembered this incident differently. Like Harkness, he thought Ireland was being deliberately provocative. "Black people could only ride in cabs that were painted black, and driven by black drivers. Whites could ride in any cab that was not black and was not driven by a black driver. So the cabs come, two black cabs and two white cabs. We think Ireland is going to get in the cab and go with the white boys. No. He jumps in the front seat of one of the cabs with the black ballplayers, sticks his arm out the window, and grabs the top of the cab. And the cab driver said, 'I can't take you.' Ireland said, 'I'm going with my guys. These are my ballplayers and I'm going with them,' or something like that. And the driver said, 'I can't do it, I'll get a ticket.' And Ireland said, 'I'll handle any tickets that you get. Don't worry about it.' Now he sticks his arm out the window of the black cab, with a black driver, he has on a white shirt, his big white arm holding on to the outside—to draw attention from a cop. Cop stops us, writes the ticket. Ireland said, 'I'll take care of that.' We get over to Algiers, the cab driver drops us, Ireland tears the ticket up and throws it away. I watched it. The driver took him, knowing that he was going to get stopped, and thinking that Ireland was going take care of it. That's the way I remember it. I remember the arm out the window, I'm not going to forget it. He knew what was about to happen."

Les Hunter did not recall any of this except driving away in separate cabs. "We were going down the same highway and then the white guys and the coaches went off to the right—the fork in the road—and we went off to the left. That may have been symbolic." Hunter was not alone in remembering that the black players got the better end of the deal. They were treated like visiting dignitaries in Algiers. There were parties, girls, home-cooked food—and no bed check. One of the neighbors had a Pontiac dealership, Rochelle recalled. He gave Rouse the keys to a black Bonneville and Rochelle got a blue and white Star Chief. While the white guys were with the coaches in the Sheraton downtown, the black guys rode in style. Hunter laughed at the memory: "We had a tremendous, tremendous time."

The tension in New Orleans was palpable, but for the players it was an opportunity to give each other shit. Jack Egan remembered walking down the street with his teammates and hearing the song "Bye Bye Blackbird" coming from a PA truck. It was the campaign song of one of the mayoral candidates.[22] Egan was always alert for an opportunity to poke a stick. "I said Jesus, that's a catchy number! What is this song? I love this song," he recalled, his eyes twinkling.

The team gathered for a pregame dinner in a private room at Dooky Chase, a black-owned restaurant where civil rights leaders sometimes met. Chuck Wood remembered arriving with the white guys: "We go around to the back door, we go in, we see the guys, we're giving them a hard time. Hey, can't stay in the hotel, eh boys? Just giving them shit. And they say yeah, well we're living like kings, 'cause we're staying with private people and they think we're the greatest thing since sliced bread. And so we're jawing back and forth and the owner opens up the door and says hey guys, keep it down.

22   Art McZier remembered being treated to the same tune by the Kentucky band when Loyola played at Lexington in the 50s.

OK, why do we have to keep it down? We weren't really loud, we were just having a good time. And he says if the whites find out I got whites in my building, or if the blacks find out I got whites in my building, they'll burn my building down."

That night, according to the *Times-Picayune*, about 2,000 came to see the game, including about 75 blacks. A black boycott had been threatened to protest the segregated seating. (Two years before, 500 blacks had come; the seating had been segregated then too, but the climate was different now.) Bill Jauss of the *Chicago Daily News* reported that Loyola's three black starters were booed as they came onto the floor, but that Vic Rouse was cheered when he went off. Buddy Diliberto of the *Times-Picayune* wrote that the crowd watched in "stunned disbelief" as the Ramblers rolled up a 30-point halftime lead. Jack Egan recalled that Ireland kept his starters in the game too long. Egan felt bad for the bench guys and at one point told Ireland he was tired and wanted a blow. Ireland said no, stay in. He wanted to make a statement.

Harkness scored 29 points, Hunter 24, and Rouse 24. Together they took 47 rebounds. The final score was 96–73. The Chicago papers picked up Ireland's statement and rubbed it in. "Three Negro Stars Score 77 Points In Ramblers' Win," proclaimed a subhead in the *Chicago Daily News*. *Chicago's American* said "Racial Peace Prevails; Loyola Wins."

———————

Whether or not the Ramblers were motivated by George Ireland's segregation theater, their 96 points against Loyola-New Orleans made them the highest scoring team in the country, with an average of 89.1 points per game. They beat their next ten opponents, scoring 90 or more in seven of those games. Then came a tough trip to Ohio. In Cleveland, John Carroll University played a slowdown game and held the Ramblers to 67 points. It almost worked, but Carroll's last shot, with four seconds left, rolled off the rim and Loyola escaped

67–66. Two nights later in Cincinnati, in their last regular season game, Rouse, Hunter, and Egan fouled out and the Ramblers lost to Xavier 96–89.

But by then Loyola was tournament-bound. In February they had been offered spots in both the NIT and the NCAA tournament. Though the NCAA was by this time the more prestigious of the two, Ireland chose the NIT. Not because playing in Madison Square Garden would be good for New York recruiting; nor because the NIT would be easier to win, Ireland said. It was because playing in New York would give Harkness and Miller a chance to visit with their families. "Jerry deserves to go home...and Miller too. They didn't get home for Christmas. And we will miss less school playing in the NIT."

Besides, Loyola would have another chance at the NCAA next year. All the starters were returning except Mike Gavin, and he was replaceable.

———————

At the beginning of the 1961–62 season, Gavin's role was unquestioned. He was a solid player, the only starting senior on a very young team, and Ron Miller, his closest rival for the job, was still working on his ballhandling and learning to play guard. But by the end of the season Miller was playing significant minutes and scoring significant points. He had 19 against St. Norbert, 22 against John Carroll, and 20 against Xavier. Les Hunter recalled that as the season progressed, he and some of his teammates thought that Miller should be starting—and Hunter thought he knew why he wasn't. Miller remembered that at some point Ireland tried to explain it to him. "He said I can't play you. I can't have four on the court."

He said that explicitly?

"It was code. Totally code. I cannot play you and you know why. I don't even think he said 'You know why.' Because I knew why. And I didn't even think of making a stink about it or being upset about it. You know, that's just how it was and you kind of accepted how it was. That's what was so bad to me about the 50s and 60s and all that period before, you had to accept things like that. And that's why the whole movement was so important. You don't have to accept things like that anymore."

Ireland wanted Miller to play in the NIT for the New York fans, especially for Walter November and his playground prospects. But instead of starting Miller in Gavin's place—which would have meant four black players on the floor—he did an elaborate shuffle, putting Miller at forward, moving Vic Rouse to center, and dumping Les Hunter on the bench. Hunter was still stewing about it 50 years later. The lineup worked fine in Loyola's first tournament game against Temple. Miller led the team with 19 points and they won easily, 75–64. But next up was Dayton, whose sophomore center, Bill Chmielewski, was 6-10 and 235 pounds. Flanking him at the forwards were Garry Roggenburk, 6-6, and Harold Schoen, 6-7. Miller was an extraordinary leaper and had experience in the frontcourt, both in high school and occasionally with Loyola, but he was 6-2 and 190 pounds. Against Dayton's front line it didn't make much sense to start him instead of Hunter (6-7, 212).

As it turned out, Hunter played a lot of the game and ended his evening with 19 points. But with or without him, Loyola had no answer for Chmielewski. Earlier in the week Ireland said that Loyola could afford to let Chmielewski score 25 if they could hold his teammates down. Chmielewski scored 27 points and Gordon Hatton, Dayton's 6-1 left guard, scored 33. (His brother Tom, also 6-1, played right guard.) Loyola's hope for a NIT championship went down 98–82.

The next night, Loyola played in the consolation game against Duquesne. This time it was Gavin who sat on the bench as the game started. Maybe Ireland had seen the error of his ways. Maybe he had crossed some kind of psychological threshold. Or maybe in his mind the loss to Dayton was the end of the 1961–62 season, and now it was next year. Whatever his reason, the Ramblers' starting five that night was Harkness, Hunter, Rouse, Miller, and Egan—four blacks and one white, the same as it would be for the whole of 1962–63.

"Ireland was created after that loss to Dayton," Les Hunter told me. "That's when he became George Ireland. Prior to that, he was just a coach."

CHAPTER 16: CINCINNATI
Two Flukes in a Row

Meanwhile, the NCAA tournament had come down to the final four, which was held at Freedom Hall in Louisville, capacity about 18,000. The Cincinnati Bearcats looked like a juggernaut going in, but they could not win for winning. Nothing they could do, it seemed, would earn them the respect of the basketball opinion leaders. Despite being the defending national champions, despite having defeated Ohio State head to head in the 1961 final, they were also-rans in the eyes of the sportswriters and coaches who voted in the national basketball polls. The experts had put Ohio State at the top of their preseason lists and kept them there throughout the year. The message received by Cincinnati players and fans was that they hadn't deserved to win that title game; their championship was a fluke.

The afternoon before they beat UCLA in the 1962 semifinal, at the awards luncheon of the National Association of Basketball Coaches, Jucker watched as Fred Taylor was named coach of the year for the second straight season. A week earlier UPI had also named Taylor coach of the year, and Jucker didn't even come in second: the runner-up in that poll was Adolph Rupp of Kentucky, who lost to Ohio State in the Mideast regionals. In the national team rankings, meanwhile, every one of the 35 coaches who voted in the UPI poll gave his first-place vote to Ohio State. In the AP poll, 38 first-place votes went to

157

OSU, two to Cincinnati. Ray Cave previewed the final four for *Sports Illustrated*. After detailing Cincinnati's many strengths and the improvements they had made over the previous year, he predicted that the oddsmakers would favor them to win the tournament. Then he made his own prediction: "Favored or not, our choice is Ohio State."

Jucker boiled over shortly after the close of the regular season, at a weekly luncheon for Cincinnati boosters and press. He couldn't complain about being ranked behind Ohio State—coaches are always saying the rankings don't matter—so he focused on the AP All American list, which had just been announced. Fifteen players were named as first- second-, or third-team All Americans, and another 41 received honorable mention. Paul Hogue, who was placed on the third team, was the only Cincinnati player included. A story by Dick Forbes in the *Enquirer* quoted Jucker calling it "an insult both to the city and the University of Cincinnati."

"You don't get ranked second in the country without good players," Jucker said. "How can they leave Tony Yates off that team, to name just one? He's the best guard in the game. He has had 115 assists, but he didn't get a mention.

"I'm tired of reading about Cotton Nash and some guy named Kirvin at Auburn.[23] Who are they? You look at that list and it almost makes you sick to your stomach. Something should be done about checking on the persons who picked that team. It's a positive disgrace."

Was Jucker sick to his stomach simply because Yates was not recognized, or did he have something else in mind? Forbes's story does not touch on the matter of color, but the players Jucker was tired of reading about were white, and blacks were conspicuously scarce on the AP's three All American teams. The first team included Chet

---

23   Cotton Nash was a much-hyped sophomore from Kentucky. I could not figure out who or what Jucker (or Forbes) meant by "some guy named Kirvin at Auburn." Layton Johns of Auburn was an honorable mention that year, but I could not find anyone named Kirvin, or anything close, on the AP list or the Auburn roster. Jucker may have been thinking of Billy Kirvin, a guard at Cincinnati's crosstown rival Xavier, or he may have been using "Kirvin" like he used the name Joe when he said "two guys named Joe" beat Cincinnati in St. Louis in 1959 (Chapter 8).

Walker of Bradley and Billy McGill of Utah. Hogue was the only other black among the 15 players chosen.

Hogue also had a few words for the press—not on the subject of the All American teams, but more generally on the presumed superiority of Ohio State. "People said we were lucky when we won last year. We're going to show them who is boss."

Now it was a rivalry: overlooked Cincinnati starving for attention, haughty Ohio State hungry for revenge. Ohio State fans wore bibs that urged "Go Go Ohio." Cincinnati fans wore buttons that said "Hate State." Freedom Hall was sold out; the tournament chairman said he could have sold 100,000 seats if he'd had them. According to the press there wasn't a hotel room to be had within 40 miles. A "veteran room finder" said it was worse than the Kentucky Derby.

The game was anticlimactic. Tay Baker, Cincinnati's assistant coach, recalled that the year before, "Ohio State was better than we were, but we got them to an overtime and happened to beat them. The second year it was a no-doubter. We were a much better team than they were." At one point Cincinnati led by 19. Paul Hogue, the third-team All American, had 19 rebounds and 22 points. Jerry Lucas scored only 11 points; his left leg was heavily taped because of a knee strain he had suffered the night before against Wake Forest. The final score was Cincinnati 71, Ohio State 59.

"The second the buzzer went off," Ray Cave wrote, "Ed Jucker leaped from his chair and flung his hand skyward time after time with a single upraised finger showing the magic No. 1. Within minutes he was clutching the gigantic championship trophy to his chest while both he and the trophy were being held high by Paul Hogue....

"'Does this prove it?' he was saying a minute later. 'Aren't we the best? They can't overlook us anymore. They can't overlook the national champions two years in a row.'"

Jerry Lucas, ever the gentleman, swore that his knee did not bother him or affect the outcome of the game. But the coaches gathered in Louisville for the weekend saw otherwise, Ray Cave wrote. "They had seen Lucas start to limp late in the first half, and had seen the things he couldn't do—the drives, the cuts, the fierce rebounding that has made him college basketball's best player. And they saw he scored only 11 points."

Still, Cave concluded, "The real heart of the matter is, could Cincy have won anyway last Saturday night? The answer is yes. Ed Jucker's team is rightfully No. 1."

CHAPTER 17: MISSISSIPPI
Civil War Redux

On January 20, 1961, John F. Kennedy began his presidency by exhorting his fellow Americans to "ask not what your country can do for you—ask what you can do for your country." The next day his call was answered by James Meredith, a 28-year-old black Mississippian just honorably discharged after nine years of service in the U.S. Air Force. What Meredith could do for his country, he believed, was provoke an armed confrontation between Mississippi's tradition of racial apartheid and the military power of the U.S. government. He would do this by breaking the color line at the University of Mississippi, the beloved Ole Miss. On January 21, he wrote for an application.

Segregation had been crumbling in the South, slowly, since 1954, when the U.S. Supreme Court outlawed the charade of "separate but equal" schools in the landmark case *Brown v. Board of Education*. By 1960 most states in the old Confederacy had begun to desegregate, but Mississippi, Alabama, and South Carolina continued to defend their "way of life." Mississippi was arguably the hardest case of the three. One of the richest of states before the Civil War, it now had the lowest per capita income and the highest proportion of blacks (43 percent) in the nation. Half its adults had fewer than nine years of education. In the wake of the Brown decision, the state abolished its compulsory education law in hope of avoiding forced school integration: if blacks and whites had to go to school together, better they shouldn't go at all. The legislature also passed a resolution directing state officials to prohibit the "implementation of or compliance with the Integration Decisions of the United States Supreme Court."

Meredith's application to Ole Miss was a deliberate challenge to this system. Years later, in an interview with William Doyle, he said he'd been inspired by the integration of Central High School in Little Rock, Arkansas, in 1957. President Dwight Eisenhower had sent Army paratroopers to Little Rock to control an angry mob and escort a group of nine black students into the school. "Little Rock was a very, very big factor in my whole desire to break the system of white supremacy," Meredith said. "I genuinely believed that the only way we would get our rights of full citizenship was to get a greater military force on our side than Mississippi had, and there was only one force in the world bigger than that, and that was the U.S. armed forces... that's what my objective was in the whole Mississippi scheme."

Meredith was an odd duck. Many years later he would wind up on the staff of North Carolina senator Jesse Helms, a frank segregationist. Historian Arthur Schlesinger found him a "lonely, taciturn, and quixotic man of purpose and courage." He was acting on his own initiative. "Nobody handpicked me," he said later. "I believed, and believe now, that I have a Divine Responsibility to break White Supremacy in Mississippi, and getting in Ole Miss was only the start." When he filled out his application, he flagged it with a note stating, "I am not a white applicant. I am an American-Mississippi-Negro citizen....I certainly hope this matter will be handled in a manner that will be complimentary to the University and the state of Mississippi."

But he expected no such thing, and he'd planned his campaign carefully. He'd discussed his scheme with Medgar Evers of Mississippi's NAACP; he introduced himself at the FBI field office in Jackson, the state capital; he wrote to ask for legal help from NAACP attorney (and future Supreme Court justice) Thurgood Marshall in New York. So he was ready when, on February 4, he received a telegram from Ole Miss advising him not to appear for registration. His game was on. On May 31 he filed suit in U.S. District Court, and for the next 16 months he and his lawyers patiently plowed through a series of obstacles placed in their path by U.S. District Judge Sidney Mize and Court of Appeals Judge Ben F. Cameron. Finally, in September 1962, as the academic year began, the U.S. Supreme Court ordered his admission.

Now the drama shifted to a much bigger stage and more prominent actors. On one side were President Kennedy and his brother Robert, the U.S. attorney general. They were not eager for this fight, but Meredith was forcing them to assert the primacy of federal law. They hoped to do so without a show of federal force such as Eisenhower had made in Little Rock.

On the other side was Mississippi governor Ross Barnett. He wanted a show of force.

Barnett was an unabashed racist who had once been arrested for raising a stink in a restaurant because a black man was dining there. In Connecticut. He had run for governor three times and finally won election in 1959. He liked to strike a defiant pose against integration and the federal government's interference in affairs that should, according to southern orthodoxy, be left to the states.

Three days after the Supreme Court ordered Meredith's admission to Ole Miss, Barnett threw down a remarkable gauntlet. In a speech broadcast across Mississippi on radio and TV, he said, "I speak to you now in the moment of our greatest crisis since the War Between the States....We must either submit to the unlawful dictates of the federal government or stand up like men and tell them 'Never!' The day of reckoning...is now upon us....I repeat to you tonight: no school will be integrated in Mississippi while I am your governor!"

Barnett privately admitted that his legal theory of states' rights was bogus, and he surely understood that in the hundred years since the South had tested that theory, the federal government's forces of compulsion had only multiplied. So what was he thinking? He must have imagined that he was going to outsmart those impudent young preppies in Washington, D.C. And Mississippi's segregationists egged him on. As the congratulations and thanks began to pour in, the *Clarion-Ledger* of Jackson proclaimed, "Place Assured In History For Fearless Ross Barnett."

For a while Barnett seemed to relish the role he'd cast himself in. On September 20, the day Meredith first tried to enroll, Barnett got himself appointed special registrar of Ole Miss, ensuring that he personally would star in any confrontation. When Meredith and his escort of federal marshals arrived, Barnett turned them away reading grand officialese from a sealed proclamation. "Pursuant to the authority...for the protection of all citizens...you, James H. Meredith, are hereby refused admission...Great Seal of the State of Mississippi" and so on. The second time Meredith came to enroll, five days later, 2,000 people and national TV cameras were looking on. Barnett greeted him and his coterie of white escorts with a joke: "Which one is Meredith?"

But Barnett's fun did not last long. That night he had a telephone conversation with Attorney General Robert Kennedy. According to William Doyle,[24] the governor expected that the matter would now go to a "prolonged legal phase," but Kennedy told him he intended to send Meredith to class the next day. Now Barnett started to squirm.

The next day—Wednesday, September 26—Barnett's lawyer called Kennedy's assistant to suggest a photo op: Meredith's escort of federal marshals should physically move Barnett out of their way, so the governor could claim that he'd stood firm against integration until push came to shove. But when Kennedy and Barnett spoke soon after, the governor seemed unable to stifle his inner rebel and they failed to come to agreement. That same day, a third try to enroll Meredith was turned away by Lieutenant Governor Paul Johnson.

The next day Barnett proposed a better photo: the U.S. marshals should draw their guns on him, then he would step aside. He was insistent, though, that guns had to be drawn by all the marshals, not just their chief. "We got a big crowd here," he told Kennedy, referring to his entourage of highway patrolmen and county sheriffs. "If one

---

24   Doyle's book *An American Insurrection* was indispensable to this chapter. See Notes and Sources.

pulls his gun and we all turn, it would be very embarrassing." Kennedy agreed to this scenario and sent Meredith and the marshals into Oxford for a fourth try. But by then the situation was spinning out of control. As Meredith's caravan of federal cars made its way from Memphis, other cars and trucks were already arriving in Oxford. Good old boys in Mississippi and across the South had heard Governor Barnett's stirring words of defiance, and they were fixing to fight the Civil War all over again.

Groups like the Ku Klux Klan were spreading the word that a states' rights showdown was coming in Oxford. Edwin Walker, the former Army general who had led the federal troops in Little Rock in 1957, had confessed on a radio show that he now saw the error of his ways and called on his fellow patriots "to make a stand beside Governor Ross Barnett....Bring your flag, your tent, and your skillet." FBI field offices across the South and as far away as California were getting tips that volunteer insurrectionists were headed toward Oxford with guns and makeshift weapons. "There were people strutting with guns in the streets," William Doyle wrote. "Twenty-five hundred people swarmed around the campus and nearly one thousand students were massing at the campus gate....Teams of civilian snipers were rumored to be lying in wait on the outskirts of the city to ambush Meredith."

Now Barnett faced the consequences of his bluster. If Meredith and the marshals arrived on this twitchy scene, he feared, there might indeed be a day of reckoning. He begged Kennedy to turn the federal vehicles back toward Memphis, and after a couple of hours Kennedy relented. Later they arranged instead to register Meredith quietly in Jackson, 170 miles away, the following Monday morning. President Kennedy himself got on the phone to close the deal. But that night Barnett went to a football game and the agreement fell apart.

Forty-one thousand fans attended the Ole Miss-Kentucky game in Jackson on Saturday night. They cheered the Ole Miss football team, called the Rebels, and the Ole Miss band, which dressed in the uniforms of Confederate soldiers, and the Ole Miss majorettes, who waved Confederate flags. At halftime they called their brave governor onto the field with chants of "We want Ross." Barnett waved and gave a passionate 15-word speech: "I love Mississippi! I love her people! Our customs. I love and respect our heritage." That was all he had to say. The fans cheered wildly and waved their Confederate flags. After the game, Barnett called Robert Kennedy and begged off again. The president, despairing of a resolution, ordered 500 soldiers from Fort Hood, in Texas, to a staging area near Memphis, about 80 miles from Oxford. Around midnight, he signed an order federalizing the Mississippi National Guard.

The next afternoon, Sunday, September 30, Barnett was back on the subject of photo ops. The Kennedys now intended that Meredith would register in Oxford on Monday morning. Barnett proposed an alternate scenario: he wanted to stand firm at the gates of the university before an unarmed force of about 500 Mississippi highway patrolmen and various county sheriffs and deputies. He would deny admission to Meredith, the marshals would draw their guns, and he would reluctantly yield to the oppressive might of the federal government. He told Robert Kennedy, "I have said so many times that we couldn't have integration and I have got to do something. I can't just walk back....I have to be confronted with your troops."

But Barnett himself had canceled a similar plan just two days before, claiming it was too risky. And the tension around Oxford had only increased over the weekend. Robert Kennedy would have none of it. That night, he said, the president was going on national TV to speak about the crisis. Since Barnett had reneged on the agreement to register Meredith in Jackson, the president would have no choice but to reveal the governor's dirty secret: that while he had been posing as the heroic protector of Mississippi sovereignty, he had quietly been negotiating the terms of his surrender. Panicked, Barnett said, "Why don't you fly him in this afternoon?" He added quickly, "Please let us treat what we say as confidential."

Everyone was expecting Meredith to arrive on Monday morning; maybe sneaking him onto campus Sunday afternoon would let some air out of the crisis. Barnett would save face by claiming that the

Kennedys had tricked him. After Meredith was installed on campus, the governor would feign surprise and "raise Cain about it." Kennedy agreed, and Meredith was rushed in from Memphis. He was driven onto campus by a side entrance and placed in a dormitory with a few men to guard him. Very few people noticed.

But by that time it didn't matter.

Around 4:00 PM, a group of about 170 U.S. marshals had arrived on campus. They hadn't expected to be there until the following morning, but when the decision was made to rush Meredith in, they were rushed in as well. Lacking a convenient place for them to assemble, the man in charge, Deputy Attorney General Nicholas Katzenbach, lined them up around the university's administration building, where Meredith's registration would take place. The symbolism couldn't have been worse. The Lyceum, as the building was called, was a postcard from the Old South, a Greek revival structure of pink brick with a portico of white columns. Completed in 1848, it was the university's first building and had been used as a hospital during the Civil War. Geographically and spiritually, it was the center of the campus. Now it was surrounded by a hastily gathered group of men dressed not in uniforms but in street clothes, carrying billy clubs and teargas guns, wearing helmets and vests. They looked ragtag but menacing, both vulnerable and insulting.

A crowd began to gather around the Lyceum—mostly curious students at first, but as afternoon wore into evening it grew in numbers and in daring, slowly evolving into an angry mob. They began to insult the marshals, then to throw pebbles and cigarette butts and eggs and burning newspapers. The marshals stood their ground and did not retaliate, which only seemed to encourage more abuse. Around dusk, as photo flashes started to pop, the crowd took to attacking reporters and smashing cameras.

Soon gunfire was added to the volatile mix. Dan Rather, then a young reporter for CBS News, later wrote, "Whenever anyone turned on a light—which meant every time we needed to film—one or more bullets would attempt to knock it out. We had to film and move. Film and move. After a while we worked out a pattern: turn on our battery-powered, portable light, film for fifteen seconds by actual count, turn off the light—if we didn't get hit—and then run, because we were bound to catch gunfire or bricks or both."

A Molotov cocktail landed at the marshals' feet and burst into flames. The marshals readied their teargas guns and put on their gas masks, then took them off for fear of inciting the mob further. A TV truck from Memphis, abandoned by its fearful crew, was tipped and burned. Still the marshals stood stoically against what *Time* magazine called a "deadly arsenal—stones, clubs, iron bars, bricks from construction sites, jagged hunks of concrete from smashed-up campus benches, gasoline bombs made of Coca-Cola bottles and paper wicks, shotguns, pistols, and rifles."

Around 7:30 PM Governor Barnett, miles away in Jackson, took to the airwaves and announced that Meredith had been installed on campus. The governor hadn't had his photo op, but his speech contained the double-edge imagery he was after: the defiant man of principle, confronted by illegitimate federal force, stands down in order to prevent tragedy. He said, "Surrounded on all sides by the armed forces and oppressive power of the United States of America, my courage and my convictions do not waver. My heart still says 'never,' but my calm judgment abhors the bloodshed that would follow." He went down swinging, with words that were addressed to his federal tormentors but fraught with meaning for the armed roughnecks who were now converging on Oxford. "To the officials of the federal government I say: Gentlemen, you are trampling on the sovereignty of this great state and depriving it of every vestige of honor and respect as a member of the United States. You are destroying the Constitution of this great nation. May God have mercy on your souls."

The riot began in earnest around eight that night—probably as President Kennedy spoke to the nation. A marshal was struck and felled by a section of metal pipe, and the order was given to fire the teargas. Having withstood hours of abuse, the marshals pushed back aggressively, shooting gas canisters directly into the crowd. Now the protesters were screaming instead of taunting, fleeing the Lyceum rather than pressing in. Retaliating, they commandeered a fire truck and drove it toward the line of marshals; later they did likewise with a bulldozer. Snipers shot out many of the lights; in some places the only illumination came from a burning car. Around the Lyceum, the vehicles and bricks and bullets came at the marshals out of the smoke and fog of their own teargas. One of them was hit in the throat by a gunshot; his jugular vein severed, he was dragged into the building, which was filling up with lame and bleeding men. Some of the rioters broke into the chemistry building and found a new weapon to hurl at the marshals—acid.

"[T]he entire operation had the feel and mood of combat..." Rather wrote. "One sniper had positioned himself on top of the Science Building, across the way [from the Lyceum]. Shots were coming from other rooftops, classroom windows, and even trees. But the most dangerous area was on the periphery of the Lyceum, in the shadows, where the bushes and trees provided a natural cover between the buildings. There were groups of twos and threes, hiding in ambush, taking shots or whacking people in the head and knees with clubs."

In Washington, President Kennedy completed his television address without knowing that the riot had erupted. Soon after he was on the phone with Barnett, who saw one last chance to emerge a hero: he was trying to talk Kennedy into pulling Meredith off the campus. Kennedy replied that it would be unsafe to move Meredith from his dorm. "I hear they got some high-powered rifles up there that have been shooting sporadically," the president said. "Can we get that stopped?"

Crucial to the events of the night was the profound ambivalence of the Mississippi Highway Patrol. In the runup to the crisis, as Meredith had repeatedly tried to enroll, the Highway Patrol had stood with Barnett, representing the state of Mississippi against the forces of federal incursion. That's where their loyalty naturally lay. But tonight they were expected to change sides—to help the marshals keep the peace, according to a promise the Kennedys had extracted from

Barnett. Not all the patrolmen warmly embraced this duty. Some were seen watching and chuckling as the rioters made their mayhem. To make matters worse, some patrolmen were hit and one was seriously wounded when the marshals opened fire with their teargas, which reinforced the patrolmen's feeling that they and the marshals were on opposite sides of the conflict.

Around 7:30 the Highway Patrol began withdrawing from the campus. Then they returned. Then shortly after 9:00 they withdrew again, ending what the *New York Times* called their "half-hearted" efforts to control the rioters. When they abandoned their posts at the gates of the university, Klansmen and yahoos from off campus and out of state came streaming in with their shotguns, squirrel rifles, and, eventually, automatic weapons.

Gathering in a parking lot at the edge of the campus, the Highway Patrolmen heard a false rumor that the federal marshals had killed one of their comrades and had arrested their commander, Colonel T.B. Birdsong, and Lieutenant Governor Johnson. Years later, William Doyle talked to several patrolmen who said they were getting ready to go back to campus and fight on the side of the rioters. "Almost all the patrolmen were going back to fight and shoot," one said. Fortunately, at that moment Johnson and Birdsong pulled up and turned the patrolmen back.

Confusion, error, miscommunication—the fog of war had descended; the night was tipping into chaos. Around 10:00 PM, Nicholas Katzenbach called in the National Guard, and President Kennedy gave the order to mobilize the U.S. Army.

The first reinforcements were only minutes away: the Oxford contingent of the Mississippi National Guard. Many had doubted that the Mississippi guardsmen would be willing to confront their neighbors in support of a federal policy that most of them detested, but they took their places beside the marshals and performed effectively and with discipline. Eventually they were joined by National Guard units from more distant towns, some of which had to fight their way onto campus through bullets and Molotov cocktails and mobs of rioters swinging pipes and baseball bats. According to Doyle, all of Mississippi's 11,000 National Guardsmen reported for duty that night, including the governor's son, Ross Barnett Jr.

The Army, bogged down in chain of command and communications snafus, took much longer to act, but they began to arrive from Memphis a few hours later. Unlike the marshals and the National Guard, the Army force included black soldiers, which inflamed the rioters. The troops were challenged as soon as they set foot on campus, first by highway patrolmen, who were quickly brushed aside, and then by the rioters, who showered them with bricks and Molotov cocktails and ignited two sheets of gasoline flames in their path. But this was a company of riot control specialists, MPs trained to march and thrust their bayonets rhythmically in an intimidating display of force and cohesion. Several witnesses marveled at their discipline as they stepped in cadence through the flames. The first group on campus numbered fewer than 120 men, but they sent a strong signal: the U.S. Army had arrived. The rebellion was finished.

Eventually the federal force grew large enough to take the offensive. They pressed outward in all directions from the Lyceum, scattering the rioters and pushing them off campus. By dawn it was mostly over, even as federal troops continued to pour into Oxford. Later that morning, James Meredith registered and attended his first class. Having enrolled as a transfer student from all-black Jackson State, he graduated from Ole Miss in 1963 with a degree in political science. He later received a law degree from Columbia University in New York.

———————————

The incident at Oxford was well covered in the regional and national press but is not well remembered today. Other key confrontations of the civil rights movement were captured in photographs and news films that were seen around the world and down through the years—the dignified young girl in Little Rock, the dogs and firehoses of Birmingham. But as Doyle has pointed out, because the Oxford uprising happened mostly after dark in a fog of smoke and gas, and perhaps because the crowd attacked photographers early on, there are no iconic images to commemorate that night.

Nonetheless, it was certainly the most violent and constitutionally significant moment of the civil rights era. In the end, more than 30,000 federal troops were mobilized in the incident. A lot of those were overkill, and the trouble was over before most of them arrived, but nearly 12,000 Army troops and 2,700 National Guardsmen wound up in or close to Oxford. More than 200 federal troops were wounded, 30 by gunfire. Two people were killed: Paul Guilhard, a reporter for Agence France-Presse, was shot in the back, apparently from no more than a foot away. Ray Gunter, a 23-year-old jukebox repairman from nearby Abbeville, was shot in the forehead. Having come to campus with a friend to see what all the excitement was about, he was probably struck by a stray bullet.

It had to be impossible to know how many people participated in the riot, but news accounts numbered them at 2,500. Some 200 people were arrested: about three dozen were students of Ole Miss and other nearby colleges; the rest, according to *Time*, were "pretty seedy specimens...intruders who had nothing to do with any university," from Georgia, Alabama, and Texas among other places.

Some of the troublemakers came from Mississippi State. Bobby Shows, who would play center that season for Babe McCarthy's Bulldogs, was just beginning his senior year. He later remembered that "carloads and carloads" of boys made the 100-mile trip north from Starkville. "Everybody had their radios on, and these rumors got out that students were getting killed and they were raping all the girls up there. A lot of bad rumors, and they weren't true at all, but that fired us up. And the Ku Klux Klan and the White Knights were offering money for anybody who would get a carload of boys to go over there and take their guns with them."

His teammate Don Posey recalled, "You'd look out on the highway and there were just taillights all you could see. Coach McCarthy called us together as a team and said keep your ass in Starkville. Do not go."

McCarthy feared the events unfolding in Oxford, but in a way they worked in his favor. Because of what happened that weekend and in the weeks before, Mississippi State would finally get its chance to go to the NCAA tournament, where it would play an historic game against a team with four black starters.

CHAPTER 18: CHICAGO
Collision Course

———

The Loyola Ramblers were mostly ignored by the national polls in 1961–62. The season was nearly over when they broke into AP's top ten, and they quickly dropped off after losing to Xavier in their last scheduled game. But the secret was out. At the start of the 1962–63 season, the poll ranked Loyola fourth in the country, behind Cincinnati, Duke, and Kentucky. With four starters returning and Ron Miller replacing Mike Gavin in the fifth spot, they'd lost nothing to graduation. Indeed they may have gained: because Miller could play forward, Harkness could drift to the backcourt on defense, where he could try for steals and lead the fast break. And there were two new faces up from the freshman team: Ed "Billy" Smith and Pablo Robertson, both Walter November kids from New York.

Smith had played center for the High School of Commerce in Manhattan. In his junior year he scored 88 points in a single game. He could rebound too. "He was 6-5 but played like 6-8," Ron Miller recalled. "A Charles Barkley type, not afraid of anybody." He grew up in Harlem, the fourth of ten kids. His father worked for the Pennsylvania Railroad. His mother made sure her children saw how the other half lived. She knew how to get them free summer camps and family vacations out of the city. Billy learned to like rye bread and lox, to play soccer and catch butterflies. He even learned to square dance.

Like Jerry Harkness, he remembered Walter November as a generous man who cared about him and his future. November did not pay him to play, Smith said, but did provide financial support when it was needed. "I got hit by a car one time, needed some extra money, and he advanced me the money. I gave it back to him when my insurance came in. If there was something he could do for you—we're not just talking about being a ballplayer. Sometimes you'd sit down and talk to him about other things. What would be beneficial for you as a young man to try and get forward?" Smith could tell that November liked to watch basketball and hang around with young basketball players. "If I had a picture, I would always remember him with—not so much a smile, but his face had a certain ambience to it. And you'd look at it and say, ah, he's all right. He's always looking out for you. You don't meet many of them, you know?...He was a saint."

Smith said that when he decided on Loyola, he did not know Harkness, had only heard of Miller, and was not aware that November had sent the two of them to Loyola before him. But he was tight with the other prospect November was working on that season. He and Pablo Robertson came up together in Harlem, went to college together, and flunked out together.

By all accounts Pablo was a comedian—"all jokes all the time," as Les Hunter put it. When Pablo was around, everybody had a nickname, everybody was laughing. He had that New York sense of humor. "He was chesty," said George McKenna, the grad student who hung out with the team. "He could talk trash, he could play the dozens, talk about your mama. You didn't want to get into it with him because he would have you laughing and crying at yourself."

He was also a Harlem playground legend. When he played at DeWitt Clinton High, the *New York Times* called him a "vest pocket dynamo." At 5-5 he was "a long way from the basket," Robert Lipsyte wrote, but he was a crowd-pleasing dribbler and ballhandler. Pete Axthelm wrote that Robertson was "hailed as one of the great 'fancy players' of all time, a guard who could ignite playground crowds in a way that no bigger man could match. One observer after another tells his own favorite story of Pablo 'shaking' defenders, weaving around and through entire teams and then flipping behind-the-back or between-the-leg passes to teammates who were waiting for easy dunk shots."[25]

"He could pass as well as anyone I had seen," Jack Egan said. "He did some things with the basketball that were really unbelievable. I loved Pablo. He knew how to win, and he was a teammate. He wasn't a showboat just to show off, there was a reason for all the stuff he did."

"Pablo was a fantastic guy for feeding people," Billy Smith said. "If you ran and could shoot, Pablo would make sure you got the ball." Eddie Bowen, who played with Harkness at Clinton High and with Robertson in the Rucker tournament, learned it was risky to turn his back when Pablo had the ball. "He would throw the ball, put the ball in motion, and call you." You had to pay attention. If you didn't turn when he called your name, the ball would hit you in the back of the head. If you didn't turn quickly enough, it would hit you in the face.

By the time he got to Loyola, Robertson was listed as 5-9. He roomed with Ron Miller his freshman year. Miller remembered, "Fun guy, nice guy. Heck of a ballplayer. Great ballhandler. Great passer. And he would see it. He'd be dribbling downcourt and then bam! Over his shoulders to Les underneath the basket. How the heck did he make that pass? I didn't even see the guy. Crowd favorite. Fans wanted him to start instead of me. He had that style, showmanship. Not a great shooter, but boy he could make it happen. On the fast break there was no such thing as him not giving the ball to the right person."

Pablo moved up to the varsity in 1962–63. It didn't take him long to make an impression. In the second game of the season, Loyola crushed North Dakota 110–56. Robertson got in the game and scored ten points. Les Hunter scored 25. The story in the next day's *Daily News* was all about Pablo. "What wonders he can work with his hands!" gushed writer John Kuenster. He "had the crowd yelling for more of his razzle-dazzle ballhandling."

25   Axthelm went on to elucidate the in-your-face ethos of New York playground ball: "To 'shake' a man is not merely to elude him, but to tantalize him, to throw him off balance and leave him helpless as you drive by. The ultimate 'shake' was performed on a drive along the baseline: nothing humiliated a big man more than a little man who could challenge him underneath the basket and execute a move that would 'shake him into the pole.'"

The story sketched in some biographical details. It said that Robertson grew up watching the Globetrotters and playing on a court at 135th Street, right across the street from Bill Russell's home. He sometimes practiced with Russell and other older players. "If Robertson could add six more inches to his lithe frame," Kuenster wrote, "he'd be a hot prospect for the Harlem Globetrotters." In fact he didn't grow any taller, but he did later play with the Globetrotters and even became a character in *Harlem Globe Trotters*, a Saturday-morning cartoon show that ran for a couple of years on CBS.

Kuenster wrote that the North Dakota game was dominated from start to finish by Les Hunter, but that news didn't come until the very last sentence of his piece. Decades later, Hunter could recite the headline from memory: "Loyola Fans Grin When Pablo's In."

"I think that bugged me a little bit," Hunter admitted.

————————

Loyola started the 1962–63 season scoring more than 100 points in each of its first five games. The first four were warmups, including a team from the University of Wisconsin's Milwaukee outpost, "one of the cruelest mismatches ever offered as a college basketball game," according to the *Tribune*'s Richard Dozer. The fifth game was a "step up in class" against Western Michigan. Rather than slowing the fast-scoring Ramblers down—which is how many teams tried to beat them—Western Michigan opted to run with them and scored 102 points. But that was 21 fewer points than Loyola scored.

It was a "rough contest that saw two near outbreaks of fisticuffs," Dozer wrote. Smith, "who may qualify as the Ramblers' next hatchetman," drew five fouls in nine minutes. He was "an innocent bystander, however, when chunky John Egan and the Broncos' Ajac Triplett...almost tangled late in the game. Smith tried to break this one up but got a midcourt tongue-lashing from Ireland, who didn't see Egan slip nimbly from the scuffle."

Slipping nimbly from scuffles was an Egan specialty. Here's how he told the story: "There's a guy on their team name of Ajac Triplett, who I had never particularly liked. We're beating them by 20 points, the game's almost over, and he's getting a breakaway layup, OK? I could let him just have it, you know—he was a big guy, and I'd probably have to foul him or something—but I didn't want to just give him a basket. So I caught him and wouldn't let him get the ball in the air. [This is an Eganesque euphemism for some sort of mayhem.] So now he's so pissed off he has to be restrained by all his teammates. And Smith, he is now pushing Triplett back away from me. Nothing happened.

"So we're in the shower after the game is over, and I think it was my roommate, Chuck Wood, who says to me something to the effect, why'd you do that? And I said, I don't like Triplett, OK? And I said what's the difference, I got Smith fighting my battles! Smith's standing right next to me [Egan is laughing now], and he was so pissed off that he had interceded in my behalf.

"That I enjoyed."

After Western Michigan came Loyola's first serious test, an away game at Indiana University. Coach Branch McCracken had a formidable starting five that year. All of them were Indiana boys, all of them were white, and all would later be drafted by professional teams. They included the Van Arsdale twins, Dick and Tom, from Indianapolis (24 years combined in the NBA); Jon McGlocklin from Franklin, Indiana (11 years); and Indiana's Mr. Basketball of 1959, Jimmy Rayl, the "Splendid Splinter" from Kokomo, a two-time All American who had scored 56 points in a college game, an Indiana record, and would do it again two months later.

Ron Miller associated Indiana and the Van Arsdales with a mental image he had of Les Hunter psyching up before big games. "Les would be almost like in a trance, just like this"—fists clenched, hunched over, breathing deep—"kind of anxious. Whenever you saw that you knew it was gonna be a good game for him."

"I'd talk to myself a lot," Hunter said. Later, as a pro, he would earn the nickname "Big Game" Hunter. "I don't know whether it was a ritual, but I'd try to remind myself of what I had to do, and how I had to go about it. And probably—some embarrassing things to say—a lot of macho things: you're the man, you know you're the man, stuff like that."

He was the man that night in Bloomington. Indiana led by 11 at one point and held a 44–42 lead at the intermission. The game was tied at 63 with about 12 minutes to play, and then Loyola went into another orbit. It was a script that would be repeated many times in the weeks to come: a couple steals or intercepted passes, a couple easy layups, the opponents would get flustered, and then the Ramblers would pour it on. In the next six minutes they scored 23 points to Indiana's 8. Hunter had 17 in the second half, 27 overall, with 19 rebounds. Billy Smith came off the bench and chipped in 12 in the second half, 14 overall. Harkness had 24 on the night, Miller 17. The Hoosiers were crushed, 106–94.

It was the sixth time in a row the Ramblers had scored more than 100 points and the most points ever scored against Indiana on their home court. Those who wondered what would happen when Loyola played a really good team now had their answer: the Ramblers were for real.

They proved it again three nights later against a higher-ranked team, in a doubleheader at the Chicago Stadium. Playing Seattle University, ranked number ten by the AP, the Ramblers scored fewer than 100 points for the first time that season and lost most of a 22-point lead. But they spurted with 90 seconds left and got away with a 93–83 win. Egan had a good night, with 10 points from the floor and 10 of 11 free throws, and Harkness played good defense against Seattle's star Eddie Miles.

From there it was on to a holiday tournament in Oklahoma City, where Loyola dispatched Arkansas, Memphis State, and Wyoming in rapid succession. The most memorable event of that trip—an historic event, as it turned out—was Egan's ejection from the final game. The *Daily Oklahoman* reported that "Jack Egan, Loyola's fiery guard, was ejected with 7:45 remaining after brawling on the floor with the Cowboys' Bob Hanson going for a loose ball." Of course Egan's version contains a few extra details.

"I remember this very well," Egan said. "One of the referees was a guy named Conway, who was a showboat. And in the second half, we sort of had the game in hand. There was a loose ball on the floor and at that time you jumped after every held ball. [There was no "possession arrow": if two players tied the ball up there was a jump ball.] So their guy had the ball and I'm attempting to tie him up. I get my hand on the ball—he's on the ground sort of, and I'm sort of over him with my hand on the ball. And I'm not really doing anything to the guy but holding the ball to make sure they call a jump ball, and then he throws an elbow at me or something like that, some stupid thing. Nothin'. And I'm thinking to myself, why is he doing this? And so rather than get up off him, I stay on him a little longer as he's trying to get up. And so now he has got to be restrained by his teammates. Now, I may have said something to him. It wasn't bad, whatever I said wasn't bad. I probably swore at him, 'asshole' or something, I don't know. So we go to center court for a jump ball. And as I said, the referee was a showboat. And he says to the Wyoming guy, 'Number 35, I don't want any more...' He's giving him a lecture. Now the person in the first 15 rows can hear it—and that's why the referee is doing it, I think. 'I don't want any more of that, do you understand me?' Yes sir! Then the ref says to me, 'Number 11, I'm tired of this, I'm telling you right now, blah blah blah blah blah. Do you hear me?' And so I can't believe some guy is asking me whether or not I can hear, OK? And so I don't really answer him, I just look at him. And now he takes the ball back down, he says 'I'm talking to you number 11.' I say, 'Throw the ball up, just throw the ball up will you?' He says, 'You're out! You're out of the game!' So when I walk to the bench Ireland says to me, 'What did you say to him?' 'I said nothing to him. Go ask him what I said, I said nothing.' Ireland says 'You're lying.' I say 'Go ask him.'

"So we win the game, and the presentation of awards is right afterwards. And the referees are walking out to go to the locker room. And I'm all the way at the end of the bench [Egan can barely restrain his gleeful laughter], and as he's walking by me I said, 'You chickenshit dog.' I said, 'Your colors ought to be yellow and white you chickenshit.' Oh! He went into a tirade. He's screaming at me. I have now turned my back on him and I'm standing there looking at the presentation of awards. He's screaming back there, he's saying, 'I got you three more times in the [Chicago] Stadium Egan—I got you three more times.' All of a sudden Ireland hears him threatening me, he said 'What!' I said 'He's still upset.' He lived in Milwaukee. He was getting a ride back on the plane with us. Ireland said to Conway, 'You don't have him any more times, you're off!' And he didn't get a ride back with us either."

When Egan was ejected, Ireland put Pablo Robertson in the game. According to the NCAA records book, it was the first time any major college basketball team had five black players on the floor at the same time.

––––––––––––

The Ramblers Express rolled on through January. By the end of the month, when they played Santa Clara at the Chicago Stadium, they were 17–0, ranked second in the nation by AP, and averaging an eye-popping 97.7 points per game.

Loyola played most of its home games on campus in Alumni Gym, a 3,000-seat fieldhouse built in 1923. But several times a year they played at the Chicago Stadium, in a double- or sometimes triple-header organized by a promoter named Art Morse. On January 26, 1963, the stars aligned for Morse: he had scheduled a doubleheader pitting Loyola against Santa Clara, a respectable if unspectacular matchup, and Cincinnati against Illinois. As the date arrived, Cincinnati was ranked first in the country and rolling on a 32-game win streak; Loyola was unbeaten, 17–0, and ranked number two; Illinois was unbeaten in the Big Ten and ranked third. According to the *Tribune*, some 23,866 spectators paid their way in, which would have made it the biggest crowd ever, anywhere, for a college basketball program. But the official count was announced as 20,867, probably to square with city fire regulations.

Loyola and Santa Clara played first. Santa Clara was tall and Ron Miller was nursing a sore ankle, so Billy Smith got a chance to start and performed admirably, with 18 points and 14 rebounds. Santa Clara hung tough for the first three-fourths of the game, but in the last ten minutes Loyola surged to a 92–72 final.

In the second game, Illinois came within four points with about a minute left, but Cincinnati held them off 62–53. Loyola's players were able to watch much of that game—with more interest, evidently, than the Cincinnati players had watched them. Les Hunter remembered sizing up Cincinnati and concluding that the Ramblers could take them. He knew he could handle George Wilson. In a letter to his girlfriend Betty (later his wife), he wrote that Loyola and Cincinnati were on a collision course.

Ron Miller recalled having a few words with Tom Thacker between games. "I said I guess we'll see you in Louisville." That would be the site of the NCAA final four. "He laughed and said I tell you what, we'll be there; the question is will you be there?"

Thacker has no such memory. He was shy and quiet, he told me; he didn't usually talk to people. And the Loyola team "were the least likely people I would see meeting up with in Louisville. I know they were ranked up there, but they still didn't faze me as an opponent. They were nowhere on my radar screen."

CHAPTER 19: CHICAGO
Four Blacks and an Albino

Sometimes Jack Egan had to wonder what his black teammates made of him. Did they think he was the token white guy?

His friends back in Marquette Park knew his role on the team. As the only white starter and the playmaking guard (nobody used the term "point guard" then), Egan was obviously the brains of the operation. According to the stereotypes then in fashion, the black players would run wild if he weren't there to channel their brute athletic ability. Egan was amused by such thinking and liked to confound it. He told his buddies that Hunter, the biggest and most athletic of the starters, was actually the mastermind.

But he wondered what his teammates thought. Nobody understood what was going on in Ireland's mind, but everyone on the team knew that the Man was at least aware of the unspoken racial quotas. Did they think that Pablo Robertson, who in some ways epitomized the flash and athleticism of black basketball, deserved to be starting ahead of Egan? Fifty years later they were firm and unanimous in the conviction that Egan was the best man for the team. Robertson was a marvelous passer and ballhandler, but he didn't have much of a shot. Egan was better at the harassing defense the team specialized in, and he was a leader. Of course Egan thought he was the better fit. It was not in his nature to think otherwise. But he liked Robertson and admired his skills. How did the other guys see it? It wasn't the sort of thing they discussed, at least not in mixed company.

The question became moot when first-semester grades were posted. Pablo Robertson and Billy Smith had flunked out. Egan recalled that Pablo got four Fs and a D. He exited joking. "He said he put too much time into that one subject."

Robertson went back to New York, played with the Globetrotters, and according to some stories helped to save the Hall of Fame basketball career of Nate "Tiny" Archibald. Archibald had been cut from the team at DeWitt Clinton High School, the alma mater of both Robertson and Jerry Harkness. He got a second chance at the urging of Robertson and community coach Floyd Layne, one of the CCNY players stung in the basketball scandal of 1951. Archibald, listed at just 6-1, went on to become a six-time NBA all star and was named one of the 50 best players in NBA history. In 1972–73 he led the league in both scoring and assists, the only player ever to do so.

According to Billy Smith, Pablo Robertson was drafted into the Army in the mid-1960s and went to Vietnam. In college, a few teammates recalled, he was already overfond of alcohol and reefer. The war undid him, Smith said. Robertson told him about being so scared in a firefight that he jumped on the back of another soldier and tried to use him as cover. "By the time he finished with Vietnam, his whole mind had seeped out. I mean you deal with that kind of stress, you take to the bottle, you take to this that and the other, and he was no longer the same person. A lot of guys who didn't die over there were killed psychologically." Robertson did play for the Globetrotters after the war, but "something was wrong," Smith said. "They'd look at him and say he's well—no, no, he wasn't well. You come back from that stuff and your whole persona's gone. You can tell the difference if you know him."

Robertson died at age 46. An upbeat obit in the *Amsterdam News* said the cause of death was "walking pneumonia," but at least one of his college teammates heard it was booze; another heard it was drugs.

Billy Smith fared a little better. After flunking out he enrolled in junior college, worked on his studies, and within two years clawed his way back to Loyola. In his first game back, in January of 1965, he scored 38 points in a 93–92 overtime upset of Wichita State, then ranked third in the country. In 1966 he finished his basketball eligibility about 18 credits shy of a degree. The Cincinnati Royals took him in the ninth round of the NBA draft, but he didn't make the team. Then the U.S. Army took him in their draft. He didn't go to Vietnam but served mostly in Germany. After his discharge, he worked for many years at a topless nightclub; he hinted darkly at having spent some of his younger days at the outer edges of legitimacy. When we spoke, he was living with his mother in New York and had become something of a philosopher. I asked if he regretted missing the second half of Loyola's 1962–63 season and all that went with it. "No, no," he said. "With life comes a package, right? These are your mistakes, these are your consequences. Hold them, they're yours."

————————

When Smith and Robertson flunked out, Ireland announced that Earl Johnson, a sophomore reserve from Cleveland, would be promoted to sixth man. About three weeks later, Johnson quit school because of "financial problems," according to the *Defender*. Having started the season with 12 players, Ireland was now down to 9: the five starters plus Chuck Wood, Rich Rochelle, Jim Reardon—a 6-4 forward from Leo High School of the Chicago Catholic League—and Dan Connaughton, a 6-1 guard from Xavier High School in Cincinnati. Ireland was not inclined to trust the reserves. In the weeks to come the starters would earn the reputation of an "iron-man" team, five guys who went 40 minutes.

Looking back on it, none admitted to being concerned, but the record suggests they were sputtering. Their first game after semester break was at the Stadium against Marquette, a team they had whipped 87–68 earlier in the season, on Marquette's home court. In Chicago they just eked out a win in overtime. Three starters got in foul trouble early, but Ireland would not substitute for them. Les

Hunter had a bad night; Ron Miller picked up his slack with 28 points. But it took six points from Harkness in the last 1:15—two free throws, a steal and a layup, and another layup off a feed from Egan—to close the game out at 92–90. Harkness was carried off the court by his relieved teammates. Loyola was 21–0 and ranked number two.

But their undefeated season didn't last any longer. A few nights later they traveled to Ohio to face a Bowling Green team that was loaded for upset.

A year before, the Bowling Green Falcons had come into Alumni Gym at the top of the Mid-American Conference and ranked number seven in the AP poll. They were led by the inside-outside team of 6-11 Nate Thurmond at center and 6-1 Howard "Butch" Komives, a formidable shooter, in the backcourt. Both would shortly be named as first-teamers on their respective NBA all rookie teams (1964 and 1965).

They arrived as basketball fever was peaking at Loyola. The gym was sold out and an overflow crowd of students listened to the game in the union building. The Ramblers won 81–68. Afterwards, George Ireland appeared at the union to accept the cheers of his now adoring public. "Just two years ago," he said, "a dummy was hanging on that flagpole out there, and that dummy was me."

Roy Damer of the *Tribune* wrote that Loyola's win could be traced back to Ireland's fall conditioning drills: the Ramblers "simply wore down Bowling Green, keeping the pressure on...until the Falcons finally broke in the last 10 minutes." But as Ron Miller remembered it, the Bowling Green players thought they'd been jobbed by local-leaning refs.

Now, in February 1963, the teams' positions were reversed and the Falcons were looking for revenge. It was homecoming weekend at Bowling Green. Egan remembered helicopters. "This was a big-time celebration when we were coming in there. The place was packed, the gym was really rocking." The sellout crowd was chanting, "We want Loyola."

"They wanted to beat the hell out of us," Miller said. "And they did." Bowling Green ran off nine points before Loyola scored one. Komives had 23 in the first half; when the Ramblers came out to cover him, Thurmond had 18 in the second. "It wasn't really a contest," Egan recalled. "They beat the crap out of us," Hunter said. "They were just rabid." The final was 92–75.

That same night, in the Missouri Valley Conference, a sophomore named Dave Stallworth led Wichita State to a one-point upset over top-ranked Cincinnati. Stallworth, who would later play with the legendary 1969–70 New York Knicks, accounted for 46 of his team's 65 points and singlehandedly overcame a six-point deficit in the closing seconds, scoring the last seven points of the game. It was the first time Cincinnati had lost since January of 1962, the end of a 37-game win streak. That afternoon there had been two undefeated teams at the top of the rankings. Now there were none.

After Bowling Green, the *Tribune*'s Richard Dozer speculated that the loss of Pablo Robertson and Billy Smith "might convince Ireland and Loyola's athletic board that an adventure into the National Invitational Tournament in New York would be wiser than a trip to the N.C.A.A. meet." But the day his story appeared (February 18), Loyola accepted an at-large spot in the NCAA. That night, they took an easy game on St. John's home court in Queens. St. John's, which did not have a very good team that year, tried to slow the pace, but the Ramblers led all the way and buried their opponents with a 21–5 spurt in the second half. Three games remained on their regular schedule, but the Ramblers could now take a deep breath and relax.

A few days later they flew to Houston, where they encountered the most hostile crowd any of them would be able to remember.

It wasn't just that the Ramblers were coming in as a highly ranked team, a scoring juggernaut, and that Houston was fighting for a bid to the NIT. "It was very personal," Ron Miller recalled. "It was very personal because we were black."

The University of Houston had begun in 1927 as a community college founded by Hugh Roy Cullen, an oilman, who once vowed that "no nigger will ever set foot on this campus." But in early 1963 history had made a liar out of him. The school was in the process of converting from a private institution to a fully funded part of the state university system. It had recently admitted a few black graduate students, and in the fall it would be officially desegregating the entire campus. Not all of Houston's fans were ready for the transition.

This was Loyola's first time playing in Houston. The team was surprised by their reception. Hunter and Harkness both recalled coming onto the floor through a tunnel in the stands. People were leaning over the railings into their faces, booing and gesticulating and yelling insults. They called the black players niggers. They called the white players albinos. They chanted, "Our team is red hot. Your team is all black."[26] They spat. They threw stuff—popcorn, ice, pennies. At one point, Ron Miller remembered, Chuck Wood got hit with a piece of ice and for a moment thought he had been shot.

Cincinnati had been treated to this hospitality the year before, after one of Houston's players got his face in the way of Bob Wiesenhahn's elbow. "The fans got so outraged they started throwing cups of ice and money and popcorn and hot dogs and everything they could find," Tom Thacker recalled. "They called us sambos and everything. They stopped the game and we had to go in the locker room until they cleaned the floor. We didn't come back out until about 25 minutes later. They were threatening to clear all the people out and play the game without the fans."

This intensity of feeling was not entirely new to Les Hunter, who had grown up in Tennessee. He remembered just wanting to get through the tunnel. He'd feel safe once he was out on the court. But Harkness, the New Yorker, was taken aback. "I felt the pressure," he said. "Are these people gonna come down on us—come out of the stands, during the game? That's what I felt. I was worried."

Houston, playing a full-court press and a slow, controlled offense, took an early lead. Loyola replied with a spurt and led 27–25 at half-

---

26   Inspired, possibly, by the 1957 rockabilly hit "Red Hot" by Billy Lee Riley. The famous chorus went, "My girl is red hot, your girl ain't doodley-squat."

time. At the start of the second half they stole several passes and put on another run, but they couldn't quite shake the Cougars. They ended up with a narrow win, 62–58, and their lowest point total of the season.

The following year, Houston coach Guy Lewis brought on two black recruits, Elvin Hayes and Don Chaney. In the 80s his "Phi Slama Jama" teams, led by Hakeem Olajuwon and Clyde Drexler, became nationally famous for their high-flying, fast-breaking, slam-dunking style of play.

CHAPTER 20: MISSISSIPPI
Come Hell or High Water

Two days after the Loyola-Houston game—February 25, 1963—Babe McCarthy was in New Orleans, on the radio, trying to close the sale of his life.

McCarthy was about to be named SEC coach of the year for the third straight time. He had become a formidable figure in Mississippi, popular with the press and beloved by the public: their natty, sweet-talking Babe had pushed Adolph Rupp aside and made Mississippi State the king of the southern basketball hill. Now four of his five starters—Leland Mitchell, Red Stroud, Joe Dan Gold, and Bobby Shows, the players who had made him famous—were coming to the end of their senior year. This was their last chance to play for the big prize.

And maybe his.

In years past McCarthy had made no secret of his desire to play in the NCAA tournament. He always deferred to Mississippi's unwritten rule, but he seemed to grow less deferential with each successive SEC championship. After the 61–62 season, he stepped up his lobbying. As Rupp prepared for the third time to take McCarthy's place in the tournament, the *Jackson Daily News* published a column that could have come straight from the mouth of Babe—and possibly did. Headed "Maroons Not Quite Satisfied After Season's Accomplishments," it described "the discontent of being left at home while all other conference champions...prepare for NCAA tournament competition." (The sports sections of the Jackson papers had always shown more enthusiasm for the tournament than the editorial pages.) The column quoted a prepared statement that was typical of McCarthy's postseason comments: "As basketball coach, I think that the boys should be allowed to play against integrated teams away from home. However, I will abide by the decision passed down by those that I work for." But this time McCarthy went a bit further, adding, "I feel that the majority of the people in Mississippi would favor our playing integrated teams out of the state."

The column, by sports editor Lee Baker, explained in considerable detail how the Mississippi policy was hurting McCarthy's efforts to recruit talented players. It ended by asking "Will Babe Keep Up the Struggle?...Can Maroon fans expect a man of McCarthy's drive and ambition to accept the year after year of staying home while the likes of Kentucky goes off to represent the SEC in NCAA play?...Babe has had offers in the past. As one of the nation's foremost coaches, he will get them in the future." One can almost see the coach whispering in the sportswriter's ear, laying the groundwork for his final appeal.

Not all the players remembered it the same, but some recalled that the following season, 1962–63, McCarthy promised it would be different. Bobby Shows told me, "Sometime towards the early part of the year—before the season or after we had played a little bit, I don't remember exactly the timing on it—Coach McCarthy made a statement: you know, we didn't get to go the last two years, and his expression was 'come hell or high water' we were gonna go this year." Jimmy Wise, the student manager of the team, said, "When we came back for our senior year Coach McCarthy had a team meeting and he said, 'Guys, I'm gonna make a promise to you. If you win the championship again this year, I'm gonna do everything in my power to get us to the tournament.'" Looking back on it, most of the players believed their coach was quietly lobbying the university president, Dean Colvard, and working his contacts among businessmen and politicians.

The players didn't get their hopes up. "To be honest with you, we really didn't give it a second thought," Jimmy Wise said. "We said well, he's gonna try, but it's not gonna happen." In mid-February, with the end of the season just two weeks away, their pessimism was justified: Mississippi State athletic director Wade Walker, operating no doubt on automatic pilot, said the school would again abide by the unwritten law.

But Babe wasn't done yet. On February 25, in the second-to-last game of the regular season, Mississippi State earned another tournament invitation by beating Tulane in New Orleans. On the postgame radio show, Magnolia Mouth laid it on thick for the audience back home. "It makes me heartsick to think that these players, who just clinched no worse than a tie for their third straight Southeastern Conference championship, will have to put away their uniforms....I do wish by some means that these boys could have the opportunity to play."

That night in Starkville, a few hundred students gathered outside the president's residence, chanting, "We want to go." President Colvard came out on the porch to talk with them. He made no commitment, but according to his memoir he had already made up his mind.

Colvard was in his third year as president of Mississippi State. He saw himself as an institution builder and the university as a "sleeping giant," a land-grant school that was ready to move beyond its roots in agriculture science and mechanical arts. Previously he had been dean of the agriculture school at North Carolina State, which had admitted its first black students in 1953. As the first "outsider" to lead what was now Mississippi's largest university, Colvard was wary of the state's racial history, and acutely aware of his place in it. He kept a detailed diary and meticulous files, on which he based a memoir titled *Mixed Emotions: As Racial Barriers Fell—a University President Remembers*.

Colvard wrote that when Mississippi State confronted the tournament issue in 1961 and '62, he would have been inclined to challenge the unwritten rule, but the question hadn't reached his desk: the athletic department had reflexively rejected the NCAA's invitations. "This was probably fortunate," he wrote, "because the only decision I could have made would have been contrary to tradition, and I had not become well enough established to weather the storm that would have been created." But by 1963 he felt the time was right to take a stand. If Babe McCarthy helped him arrive at this position, Colvard didn't mention it.

Much had changed in the preceding year. Most obviously, James Meredith had crashed through Mississippi's color wall in higher education. Though many refused to believe it, the battle was over; no longer could a basketball game be condemned as the first step down a slippery slope to race mixing. The majority of the public was ready for change. Students, alumni, and sports fans, aware that a window of opportunity was closing, had begun to write letters and circulate petitions in favor of sending the team to the tournament. The sports director of a Jackson TV station took a postcard poll of viewers and reported that 85 percent of them were in favor of it. The only groups still firmly opposed were the rabid segregationists and the politicians who cynically stoked their hatred—and the politicians' stock had declined significantly after the mess they'd made at Ole Miss.

Perhaps none of these broad changes was more significant than a tactical blunder made by Ross Barnett in the heat of the Meredith affair. On the day before Meredith's first attempt to enroll at Ole Miss, Barnett barged into a meeting of the state board of higher education (officially, the Board of Trustees of the Institutions of Higher Education of the State of Mississippi), which had constitutional authority over all the state's public four-year colleges. By this time the federal courts had ordered Meredith's admission. Defying the order would mean contempt of court, and conceivably jail. Some of the trustees were wavering in their segregationist resolve. Barnett came to buck them up and he made a good show of it, shaking his fist in the face of one board member and calling him a "yellow-bellied dog," whereupon the fellow promptly suffered a heart attack. The next day, less than an hour before Meredith arrived in Oxford, the trustees washed their hands of the matter, passing a resolution that transferred to the governor all authority to act—not to mention, and they didn't, all culpability for the consequences. Thus empowered as a special registrar of Ole Miss, the governor went forth to meet his enemy.

Barnett's bullying attracted the attention of the Southern Association of Colleges and Schools (SACS), the institution responsible for accrediting colleges in Mississippi and ten other states. The state board of higher education was supposed to operate independently, by academic lights, free from political interference.[27] After the dust settled on the Meredith affair, the SACS sent a warning to Governor Barnett and put Mississippi's state schools under "continued and careful observation" for a year. In effect, they were on probation.

To all but the most fervent separatists, disaccreditation was unthinkable. For one thing, it would sorely embarrass a state already seen as backward. "This was a time," Colvard wrote, "when Mississippians traveling in other states were tempted to rent cars rather than drive their own cars with license plates that identified them." Moreover, disaccreditation would probably provoke a faculty exodus and cripple the colleges. Perhaps worst of all, it would taint the degrees of Mississippi's upper crust and their offspring. So when the basketball issue surfaced a few months later, Barnett was hogtied. He opposed participation in the tournament and everyone knew it, but he made no public comment. It was the board's decision, and he could not afford to be caught interfering again. That was the opening Dean Colvard needed to challenge the unwritten law.

Colvard felt he had two options. One, he could make his recommendation to the board and ask them to ratify it. In that case, the board would vote on the question of whether or not the team should participate—a vote Colvard was not sure he could win. He astutely chose the second course. On March 2, a few minutes before

---

27   In fact the board was the upshot of a previous accreditation incident. In 1930, Governor Theodore G. Bilbo fired three college presidents and dozens of faculty members who did not support his politics. Several accrediting agencies, including SACS, delisted Ole Miss, Mississippi State, and two other Mississippi colleges. A constitutional amendment enacted in 1944 created the board to prevent such political interference in the future.

Mississippi State's traditional season-ending game against Ole Miss, he released a lengthy written statement whose gist was this: "I have decided that unless hindered by competent authority I shall send our basketball team to the NCAA competition." Now the question before the board was a stickier one: was Colvard acting within the scope of his authority? More to the point, did the board members have the guts to reverse his decision?

Colvard's announcement—followed quickly by the news that Loyola would likely be State's first opponent in the tournament— provoked two weeks of heated debate and political maneuvering. Colvard received letters and telegrams from both sides of the issue. One anonymous mailing contained a card that said, "I have contributed $1.00 in your name to the NAACP. Congratulations...you are now an HONORARY NIGGER." This was accompanied by a crudely copied flyer showing a photo of five black people armed with rifles running toward the camera. A large caption beneath the photo said, "Join the NAACP Today!"

A letter from a concerned mother spoke on behalf of the Mississippi State basketball team: "For a coach to insult those white boys by asking them to play against negroes is most disgusting. If my son was playing on the team he would be removed by his parents and the coach be fired." Another letter warned: "A defeat at the hands of this team would only prove the superiority of the Negro over the white man." A recurrent variation on this theme was expressed by a New Orleans lawyer who wrote: "Here's hoping the niggers—pardon, I suppose you and the Board will insist I say negroes—beat Mississippi State by a humiliating score."

But messages like these were the minority. Colvard carefully filed the correspondence and in his memoir tallied more than 300 messages pro, about 100 con.

Among elected officials the reaction was different. One lonely sentence at the very bottom of an article in the Jackson *Clarion-Ledger* stated that "Sen. Sonny Montgomery endorsed Colvard's action," but if Mr. Montgomery had any company among his colleagues they seem to have kept it to themselves. State Senator Billy Mitts, who had been a cheerleader at Mississippi State and president of its student body, called Colvard's announcement a "low blow to the people of Mississippi." As a remedy he proposed a substantial decrease in funding for his alma mater and for "every university of this great state that encourages integration." (He added that only native sons of Mississippi should be hired as university presidents so as to avoid "a similar tragedy of this sort in the future.") Another legislator, Representative Walter Hester, phoned Colvard's office and asked his secretary to provide a list of all the people who had written in favor of playing integrated teams.

The controversy appeared almost daily in the two Jackson newspapers, which were owned by the same company and shared the same editorial perspective. To their credit, they tolerated some dissonance from their letters and sports pages. *Clarion-Ledger* sports columnist Carl Walters called Colvard's announcement the "biggest and best sports news" of the weekend. The next day brought a letter from a "humble scribbler" who wondered what all the fuss was about:

> Only yesterday I saw a Negro maid walking down the street with the hand of a white child in each of her hands. I wondered just how much more bodily contact she could have had with these children who were in her complete care while their parents were away at work....

> In professional basketball, baseball and football Mississippi boys play with and against Negroes. Just how much will it hurt them to play against a Negro or two in the NCAA playoffs.

But such reasoning was shouted down by the editorial writers. One loopy argument in the *Clarion-Ledger*, the lead editorial of March 6, starts with a letter from a brigadier general that points out, "The proponents of integration take advantage of every turn of events to edge in just a little closer and to get just one more small concession.

Each concession leads to another, until all guards are down." From here the argument moves to William F. Buckley, who in a recent column had found it "interesting, and depressing, to note the acquiescent reaction to James Baldwin's explosive indictment of white society." (Baldwin had recently published *The Fire Next Time.*) Next our essayist pays a visit to civil rights activist Daisy Bates, who had admitted in a memoir that "her girlhood was embittered by hate of the white, and at the age of eight, she slapped a white playmate only because her little friend was white."

Having laid this logical foundation—some blacks are angry at whites!— the editorialist then intones,

> There are those who would have us bare our unprotected breast to the darts and arrows of a people who are preaching hatred of the whites and overthrow of the white people and their government.
>
> The college board needs to take a long look before it lowers a barrier or opens a door that cannot but mean deterioration in our present preferred position.
>
> If Miss. State U plays against a Negro outside the state, what would be greatly different in bringing the integrated teams into the state? And then why not recruit a Negro of special basketball ability to play on the Miss. State team? This is the road we seem to be traveling.

The *Clarion-Ledger* was Jackson's morning paper; it was sober and reflective compared to its afternoon sibling, the *Jackson Daily News*. The editor of the *Daily News*, one Jimmy Ward, observed the following on March 6:

> When a basketball player "shaves points" for the benefit of gamblers it is an act of lowest sportsmanship and a case of soul-selling.

To "shave points" off the state's unwritten law is diluting a principle that wise men of Mississippi inaugurated years ago for valid, tested reasons, and all the hysterical harping over a crack at a mythical national championship isn't worth subjecting young Mississippians to the switchblade knife society that integration inevitably spawns.

Ward suggests that his readers contact members of the state college board, helpfully providing their names and hometowns, and then ends on this ominous note:

The first likely team to be faced by the Maroon basketball club...has a first string that is all Negro. It would be most unfortunate if friction developed during this sports contest.

The following day, Ward had to apologize for a factual error: Loyola's first string was not all Negro, as he had said:

An Associated Press Wirephoto straight out of Chicago within recent hours gives the latest information on this subject...

Presumably only four of the starting five are Negroes. If the *Daily News* said all five were Negroes it was an honest error based on the best sources of information then available. Or maybe a lucky white boy finally graduated to the first team.

Ward published the photo across five columns, with a caption headlined "Mississippi State's Possible Opponent At NCAA Tourney." It's a staged action shot of Loyola's starting five, showing Egan in the center flanked by his taller teammates. All five are in practice clothes; each is dribbling a ball and coming toward the camera. In the context of the *Jackson Daily News*, the photo is uncomfortably reminiscent of the picture of five armed blacks sent to Dean

Colvard's office. Ward thought his readers might want to clip it and send it to the college board.

The board had been called to a special meeting on Saturday, March 9, to decide the question. The game was scheduled for the Friday after that, March 15. On March 6, Ross Barnett broke his silence with a prepared statement against participation. He was careful to say that the decision was the board's to make, but said, "Personally, I feel that it is not for the best interest of Mississippi State University, the state of Mississippi, or either of the races." He was sending a signal to his appointees on the board.

The newspapers predicted a close vote. Georgia Tech, runners-up that year in the SEC, waited hopefully in the wings and reserved hotel rooms in East Lansing, Michigan, where the final rounds of the Mideast regional would be played. But the special meeting of the board was short and anticlimactic. M.M. Roberts, the Barnett loyalist who had called the meeting, moved to keep the team out of the tournament. The motion was defeated 8–3. He then moved that the board request Dean Colvard's resignation. That motion failed for lack of a second. Then the board gave Colvard a 9–2 vote of confidence. That motion was made by Tally D. Riddell, the "yellow-bellied dog," who had recovered from the heart attack he'd had in September.

"There was much happiness on campus," Colvard wrote. That night, he and his wife went to a student ball.

> When we were introduced, we were given an enthusiastic ovation. The students had watched their president lay his job on the line, and this group was expressing its enthusiastic support. Some people thought it was an act of courage. I thought it was simply doing what needed to be done....
>
> On the afternoon of March 13, I went to the gymnasium to wish the team and the coaches well. They were scheduled to leave for East Lansing, Michigan, the next morning....My message was simply that I was supporting them and wished them well as they represented Mississippi State.

He was walking back to his office around 4:30 PM when a university PR man found him and told him the news: State Senator Billy Mitts, the former cheerleader, and an accomplice named B.W. Lawson had obtained an injunction ordering Colvard and other university officials to refrain "from allowing any athlete enrolled in Mississippi State University to compete in any athletic contest against members of the Negro race."

That afternoon in Atlanta, a Georgia Tech booster told the *Jackson Daily News* that the Yellowjackets had been "practicing like mad," just in case.

CHAPTER 21: CHICAGO
The Greatest Fast Break Team Ever

Having escaped unmolested from Houston, the Loyola Ramblers came home to finish their 1962–63 schedule in friendlier surroundings. On February 27 they faced Ohio University in Alumni Gym. For a while it looked like another upset. Ohio hit 10 of their first 11 shots and seemed to have cracked Loyola's press. They led 54–47 at the half. But the Ramblers opened the second half with a nine-point spurt and the gym started rocking. They scored 67 points in 20 minutes and finished with a 114–94 win.

It was Jerry Harkness's last game in Alumni Gym. With about a minute and a half to go, he scored his 585th career field goal, tying a Loyola record held by Jack Kerris (1945–49), who had played four seasons of varsity ball to Harkness's three. Ireland took Harkness out of the game so the crowd could show its appreciation. After the buzzer they carried him off the floor.

It would have been a fitting finish to the regular season, but unfortunately the Ramblers had one game left—at the Stadium, against Dave Stallworth and Wichita State, who had knocked Cincinnati off their 37-game win streak just a couple of weeks before.

Wichita State's athletic teams were called the Shockers, short for Wheatshockers, and this year their basketball team was living up to the name. Though they came into Chicago with seven losses, they

were ranked eighth in the nation and had earned a rep as giant kill-
ers. Not only had they upset top-ranked Cincinnati, they had also
defeated fourth-ranked Arizona State and fifth-ranked Ohio State.

The game at the Stadium, before a crowd of more than 18,000,
was a back-and-forth affair that turned on fouls and free throws.
With about six and a half minutes to go and Loyola leading by one,
Les Hunter fouled out, and half a minute later Vic Rouse joined
him. Loyola was now severely handicapped underneath. Stallworth
was 6-7 and his teammate Nate Bowman was 6-10. Still Loyola was
able to keep the lead, and even increase it to two points. But then,
according to the *Tribune*, Stallworth completed a three-point play
after a "questionable" foul called against Harkness.[28]

The clock wound down. Loyola trailed by one. But Jack Egan had
a plan.

Drawing fouls was an important part of Egan's game. He liked to
drive his stocky 5-10 body into the lane against much taller players,
daring them to foul him and send him to the free-throw line. On
defense, with his quick feet, he was expert at drawing charging fouls:
he could move into the path of an oncoming player and establish his
position so quickly that his opponent couldn't help but slam into
him. If the occasion called for drama, Egan was not above what today
would be called flopping—crashing to the floor on impact, just to be
sure the referees noticed the hit.

With about a minute left before the buzzer, Egan went to work
on Wichita State guard Ernie Moore. "He was fast, shifty," Egan
recalled. "I had guarded him most of the game, and I didn't really
attempt to do much with him other than just guard him. Not attempting to make steals from him, not attempting to get charges
from him. But now at the end of the game, we need the ball. He has
the ball and now I'm guarding him a little bit closer, and I'm trying
to get a charge on him. I've been watching him the whole game and

---

28   A player fouled in the act of shooting was awarded one free throw if he made the basket
despite the foul. Before the establishment of a three-point line, this was the only "three-point
play."

I know exactly what he's gonna do now. He is going to make a fake to his left, and then he's gonna go right on me. So now he makes the fake to the left, and I feign like I'm going to go to his left, and I move right back to the right. And he plows right into me. He gets me with his shoulder in my chest area, stomach area, and I said oh man, I got him. At home, I really got him!"

Years later, Moore told Les Hunter that Egan not only went to the floor for the ref's edification, he also grabbed Moore's jersey and pulled him down too. Egan did not remember that specifically, but he did allow that the move was in his repertoire. Anyway, he felt sure he would get the hometown call.

But he didn't. "They call it the other way! Right in front of our student body. I forget who the referee was. He makes that call, I said oh, you gotta be shittin' me. Oh! It was just a bad call. And Moore had to know it, too, he just got faked out and came right into me. But they called it the other way. I remember my older brother Jim was at the game and he's up out of his seat, and friends of mine are up out of their seats screamin': 'Oh shit, how can they do this to us?'"

Moore made his free throws and Wichita State won the game 73-72. Dave Stallworth led all scorers with 28 points. Jerry Harkness had 17, including the 586th field goal of his varsity career—the only Loyola scoring record he didn't hold already. But the Ramblers' regular season ended on a sour note. According to Bill Jauss's story in the *Daily News*, a few Loyola fans expressed their feelings about the officiating by spilling onto the court as Wichita State walked off. "The angry young men wanted to belt the game officials."

In retrospect, at least, the Ramblers looked wobbly. John C. Thomas, who 40 years later wrote a game-by-game recap of the season for the web site Ramblermania.com, pointed out that after the loss of Pablo Robertson and Billy Smith, Loyola's scoring average plunged from 97.9 over their first 20 games to 80.8 over their last six. Loyola players fouled out five times in those six games, and their bench replacements contributed a total of only 15 points. How could they hope to survive in the NCAA tournament?

Luckily, the first round of the draw gave them a warmup game.

———————

Six teams received bids for the Mideast regional part of the tournament: Notre Dame, Bowling Green, Loyola, Tennessee Tech, Mississippi State, and Illinois. The winner would go to the final four. The teams from the Big Ten and the SEC had byes in the first round. Loyola's opponent was Tennessee Tech, an all-white team that had squeaked into the tournament by beating Morehead State in an Ohio Valley Conference playoff. The game was a mismatch and the first-round venue made it worse: Northwestern University's McGaw Hall, about five miles north of Alumni Gym. It was virtually a Loyola home game.

It was played on Monday night, March 11. Loyola was heavily favored. Egan was in rare form. Tennessee Tech's center, John Adams, had been a teammate of Egan's at St. Rita. When they met at the arena, it was clear to Egan that Adams wanted no part of him. So Egan followed him into the Tennessee Tech locker room. Don't worry, he said, it will all be over quickly.

Did he do this to get inside the guy's head? To gain some advantage? Or just to be a pain in the ass? "Maybe they were the same to me," Egan said. "If he'd have been friendly to me outside the locker room, I wouldn't have gone in with him. That's what probably bothered me more than anything, OK? And then the more I thought about it as I was going in there, I thought good. His teammates will get pissed at him for talking to me.

"It just seemed like the right thing to do."

The two teams traded baskets and then it was over. The *Daily News* reported: "Egan stole the ball. Miller blocked a shot. Harkness, Miller, and Hunter made steals. Miller blocked another one. Harkness stole again and it was 16–2 Loyola." After 11 minutes the score was 40-11.

At the half, Egan saw an opportunity to make the evening more interesting.

"It was such a slaughter. For whatever reason, it all made sense to me at the time, it makes no sense now, but things couldn't have been going any better. 61–20 at the half? And I'm thinking that when we go in the locker room, Ireland's got nothing to bitch about. And I wanted to hear him bitch about something. I really did. They have these oranges, cut in half or in quarters, that's your nourishment at halftime. Sometimes you eat them and sometimes you don't. But the guys on the bench are doing nothing, and they're looking for something to do, and they always get the oranges first. So when Ireland comes in there—and I gotta wait till he gets there—I say something like jeez, you'd think they'd save a couple of oranges for the guys who are playing. And Ireland takes off on the poor guys on the bench. You orange-eating sons of bitches! Most coaches would say oh, shut up. To me. But he takes it seriously, like we need oranges at halftime and these guys are doing nothing, they're eating all the oranges! I mean that's the way his mind is working. And the other thing is, the guys on the bench know that's the only reason I'm saying it. And they look at me, you asshole!"

In the second half, Ireland forgave the greedy scrubs and put them in the game, but the slaughter could not be stopped. Tennessee Tech was stunned. They shot 18 for 82, or 22 percent from the field. The final score was 111–42. The 69-point margin of victory remains an NCAA tournament record.

Among the spectators in McGaw Hall that night were Mississippi State coach Babe McCarthy and assistant coach Jerry Simmons, there to scout the opposition. The winner of this game would be their opponent next weekend when the Mideast regional moved to East Lansing, Michigan. They too were stunned, or at least they pretended to be. Student manager Jimmy Wise recalled that when the coaches returned to Starkville, McCarthy gathered the team at midcourt to tell them about the quickness and athletic ability he had just seen in Evanston. "He had a circle of players around him, and he was in the middle of the circle, and he had a basketball, and he dropped it, and he said, guys, if just one member of the Chicago Loyola team is in this circle and we drop that basketball, they got it and they're gone with it." Leland Mitchell thought this was just bullshit, motivational coachspeak. Jackie Wofford, a sophomore reserve, recalled that McCarthy thought they could win and communicated as much to the team. But their teammate Doug Hutton wasn't so sure. It hadn't sounded like coachspeak when McCarthy talked to reporters after the game. Robert Marcus of the *Tribune* quoted him calling the Ramblers "the greatest fast-break team I have ever seen." He said, "I wish I'd stayed home. It was useless to come here. Nobody can beat a team like that."

CHAPTER 22: MISSISSIPPI
Cloak and Dagger

———

Dean Colvard said he would send Mississippi State to the NCAA tournament "unless hindered by competent authority." Evidently his idea of competent authority did not include the Chancery Court of Hinds County, Mississippi. That's where Jackson, the state capital, is located, and that's where State Senator Billy Mitts and B.W. Lawson got their last-minute injunction forbidding the team to participate. When he heard the injunction was on its way, late in the afternoon on Wednesday, March 13, Colvard called an impromptu meeting with Babe McCarthy, athletic director Wade Walker, and a few other people, including a local attorney. That evening, he and a colleague drove east about 140 miles to spend the night at the Air Host Motel in Birmingham, Alabama, beyond the reach of Mississippi lawmen. McCarthy and Wade Walker drove north, into Tennessee.

According to Colvard's memoir, the attorney at the meeting suggested that the team leave also, but Colvard was not comfortable with that; he gambled that not even a Mississippi politician would try to arrest or serve papers on a group of handsome young men in their 20s who happened to be three-time champions of the SEC.

Mississippi State students heard on radio newscasts that officers from Hinds County were on their way to Starkville with the injunction. At a pep rally they strung up effigies of Billy Mitts and B.W. Lawson. Campus police cut the dummies down before they could be torched.

The players didn't know what was going on. They all lived on the second floor of Memorial Hall, the athletes' dorm, and they wandered in and out of each others' rooms as the news dribbled in by radio and rumor. Most of them didn't know exactly what an injunction was, but they understood that politicians were trying to keep them from going to Michigan. At one point Leland Mitchell said, "To hell with this, let's get in our cars and drive up there right now." But they were a disciplined team and accustomed to following orders. They'd been told to keep to themselves and be ready to go Thursday morning right after breakfast, dressed in their gray slacks and maroon blazers, same as any travel day. They were scheduled to leave by charter flight at 8:30 AM.

It's not clear when they learned that their coach had skipped town, but in the morning assistant coach Jerry Simmons told them about a change in travel plans—a "Cloak and Dagger Trek Unprecedented in History," as it was later described by the *Jackson Daily News*. Just in case there was any attempt to stop them from leaving, a "decoy" team of scrubs and nonstarters was going to the airport with trainer Dutch Luchsinger. The rest of the team—the starters and the first three subs—were staying behind on campus. If the decoy team was intercepted at the airport, the starters would drive to Columbus, where a second plane waited to spirit them away if necessary.

Colvard's memoir credits this plan to Jerry Simmons, but Leland Mitchell thought it had Babe McCarthy's fingerprints all over it. "See, Babe was a real strategist. He was a snooker player. Snooker is a game where when you miss, you need to leave the other guy a real hard shot so he'll miss. I'm sure he came up with that idea."

The teammates joked with each other about who was a real player and who was a decoy. At least one of them, sophomore Don Posey, was a trifle concerned that the plan made them fugitives from the law. "If they catch us," he remembered thinking, "what are they going to do to us? Are they going to take us back to the dorm, or lock us up?" Mitchell, on the other hand, was confident that everyone but the politicians wanted the team to go. "This was not we had murdered somebody and the law was after us," he said. "This was more like a wedding. Everyone was for it." The only concern for most of the players was whether they would make it to the game. Aubrey Nichols, the sixth man, recalled, "It was sort of a cat and mouse game, you know? It was fun. We were kids!"

As it turned out, the second plane was not needed. According to Colvard's memoir, the officers serving the papers from Hinds County were supposed to be accompanied by the sheriff of Oktibbeha County, where the university is located. The sheriff was ill, or too smart to get involved, so the duty fell to Deputy Sheriff Dot Johnson. Various stories are told about Johnson's attempts to serve the papers and prevent the team's escape. Colvard wrote that the night before, Johnson did escort the Hinds County officers, but was "not too helpful in leading them directly and promptly to Coach McCarthy's home." On Thursday morning, according to one tale, the deputy let it be known that he had every intention of getting out to the airport—as soon as he finished his coffee. Perhaps this story goes with another in which the deputy roars through the airport gates just as the plane lifts off the runway. In still another version, he arrives at the airport and finds that the charter has been delayed by weather in Atlanta, so he leaves. Whatever the case, he did not complete his mission. Though the Hinds County court had enjoined the state board of higher education and all its "agents, servants, and employees," Johnson's marching orders consisted of a summons that explicitly named two people, Colvard and McCarthy. Plenty of people were at the airport—players, coaches, reporters, photographers, and assorted well-wishers—but Colvard and McCarthy were not among them. Case closed. Dutch Luchsinger phoned back to the dorm to say the coast was clear. The starters hurried out from campus to join the decoy team. The plane arrived from Atlanta, the flight took off, the players cheered, and the legend of Dot Johnson was born: he was a deputy sheriff who tried to do his duty, but not too hard.

Babe McCarthy and Wade Walker were waiting in Nashville. The plane stopped there to pick them up, then flew on to East Lansing. Meanwhile the Loyola team, accompanied by cheerleaders and fans, motored from Chicago in a bus with "Loyola Ramblers" painted on the side. Back in Mississippi, a justice of the state supreme court dissolved the injunction, ruling that it was issued "without authority of law." In East Lansing, fans and tournament officials waited, wondering if Mississippi State would show up. The plane was late. They were hearing rumors. Had the team been arrested at the airport? No, a single carful of players had escaped the state. No, their plane had taken off but was turned back in midflight.

That afternoon in the *Jackson Daily News*, editor Jimmy Ward, or someone who had mastered his style, pronounced it a great day—with heavy irony. A Gulf Coast newspaper had outrageously predicted that Mississippi State's participation in the tournament "one day will be regarded as a milestone in Mississippi's progress toward full democracy." Thus provoked, the *Daily News* shot back:

> As was expected, the *Pascagoula Chronicle Star* went goo-goo with glee, gushy with joy, and flumed ecstasy over the decision by the State College Board to permit the Mississippi State University basketball team to soar up to East Lansing, Michigan, to engage in just a little bit of bear-hugging under the wicket with Loyola University's famed, sepia-toned, basket-whisking bucket poppin' quintet....
>
> Yes, it is such an abundant victory. Had the Starkville boys not been granted permission to play in that gosh awfully important tournament, the hysterical liberal advocates of race-mixing would still be in the middle of the street like Chicken Little, screaming in panic that the sky was falling.

When the team's plane arrived in East Lansing, the *Clarion-Ledger* breathed a great sigh of relief. "No Demonstrations Mar MSU Michigan Arrival," its banner headline announced.

"It had been feared," the paper reported, without saying exactly who feared it, "that the team would be picketed due to the furor raised in the state over the Bulldogs playing against racially-mixed teams in the tournament." In fact the team was greeted warmly. Where the *Clarion-Ledger* saw the absence of an angry mob, Charles Love of the Memphis *Commercial Appeal* saw "a delegation of tournament officials and news personnel on hand to greet the team." According to Love, an airline official came aboard the plane and asked Babe McCarthy to get off first, explaining, "There are all kinds of people looking for you out there."

"Yeah," said the Babe. "There were all kinds of people looking for us back where we came from, too."

CHAPTER 23: EAST LANSING
This is history.

———

Leland Mitchell recalled that the Mississippi State team was cheered as the players stepped off their plane in East Lansing. Don Posey swore there was a red carpet. "It was an enjoyable time," Aubrey Nichols said. "I can't remember any kind of situation where there was any confrontation or anybody mistreated us. On the contrary, we were treated like royalty almost." Hardly any Mississippi fans had made the trip—no one could be sure the team would actually play—but Michigan State's team was not in the tournament this year, so East Lansing adopted the other MSU as their own. Bobby Shows said, "We were the sweet babies, I reckon."

They stayed in the Kellogg Center hotel on the campus of Michigan State. Don Posey and his roommate Richie Williams were settling into their room when they heard a thud at the window. Posey said, "We were on the second floor, maybe the third, but it wasn't far to the ground, and we had a little balcony outside. A snowball or two hit our window. I went to the window, and if I'm not mistaken it was three young black girls. And I stepped out on the balcony, and they were kind of smiling, you know, and they said, 'Are you the guys from Mississippi?' And I said, 'Yes we are, we're the guys from Mississippi.' And I don't remember exactly what the young lady said but it was something to the effect of, 'Well, you don't look like a monster to me. You look normal.' And I said, 'Well, we are!'"

When they took the floor for the game on Friday night, the crowd gave them a standing ovation. Forty years later, Bobby Shows was still getting teary when he talked about the welcome they received. He told the producers of the 2002 documentary *One Night in March*, "The most exciting thing about the entire trip was when we started onto the court. Some band, some pep band, played our fight song for us. And we knew it wasn't our band. That still fills me right now, to think that somebody else from another team thought enough of us to play that." When Aubrey Nichols heard it, he felt it was like a home game.

According to a story told by George Ireland's son Mike, the two coaches exchanged a few words and a laugh before the game. "Don't worry," Ireland told McCarthy, "I won't let my black boys sweat on your white boys."

The players were young men in their late teens and early 20s, innocent and full of themselves, and they lived in an athletes' bubble, protected from much of the complicated world outside. They had earned some notoriety by learning to tune out that world and focus on basketball. Years later, they would contend almost unanimously that they did not see this game in the light that history would later shine on it. But that night they knew something was up. "I could feel something different about the game," Egan said. "Ireland seemed a little more tense than normal. And that's why I may have detected something in the players—a certain amount of anxiety, shall I say, from the black players, that this was a real, real important game."

For Les Hunter it was a matter of pride and respect. Finally the guys from Pearl High had been noticed by the Nashville press. "All of that time we won all those black national high school tournaments, the newspapers were giving us a little squib like this"— holding his fingers an inch apart—"whereas the white state champions would get headlines, full pages. But now John Bibb, of the *Nashville Tennessean*, had come all the way up to Chicago to interview me and Rouse about the upcoming tournament and how we felt about the racial issue and all that. That's when I knew it was a big deal."

Harkness remembered being apprehensive. All he knew about the South and southerners was what he had learned in New Orleans and Houston, which was not good, and what he had seen on TV, which was worse: police dogs, fire hoses, white faces twisted with hate. He later told interviewers that he was feeling the pressure from two sides. He'd received a few letters signed KKK. *You're not good enough to beat white boys. Don't show up unless you want your neck in a noose.* At the same time he felt the burden of hope and urgency stirring in Chicago's black neighborhoods and churches. "There was a lot of pressure on us. People were telling us, 'You gotta win!'"

Just before the opening tip, the two captains met at center court for the customary handshake: Jerry Harkness from the Bronx by way of Harlem, and Joe Dan Gold, a Kentucky farmboy. Both of them and many of their teammates have told the story of that handshake. Harkness remembered wondering, "Does this guy really want to be here, or is he just a racist that wants to prove something? You know, a lot of that is going in your mind. But I didn't see any of that. I remember looking him in his eyes and we kind of nodded. I saw a warmth, like hey, I just want to be here to play the game. Almost like it's a pleasure to do this, to take this step with you."

When they reached out to grip hands, the court exploded with photo flashes. Most of them came from an unusually large group of news photographers on the sideline, but to the players it seemed like the whole arena lit up. "Bulbs were just popping all over the place," Harkness said. "It startled me at first. And then it came in my mind that this was more than just a game. This is history."

Loyola came out tight. Or maybe polite. Ireland had promised McCarthy that his boys would be treated with respect in the North, and he instructed his team accordingly. This was not a night for extraneous enthusiasm or for sticking it to the Southern white guys.

He needn't have worried. Mississippi State's Doug Hutton scored first, pulling up for a jump shot on a fast break. Leland Mitchell got a layup, Red Stroud made a free throw, and Mitchell scored again on a drive to the basket. Mississippi State led 7–0.

Babe McCarthy had them right where he wanted them. Like Cincinnati's Ed Jucker, he liked to play slow. And when he got a lead, he liked to play slower. It would be a few years before Dean Smith would make the "four corners" famous at North Carolina, but until 1985, when the shot clock was added to college basketball, the stall was a popular tactic among coaches if not fans. Babe McCarthy used it even back when he had Bailey Howell, a prolific scorer. "We would just stand outside with the ball," Howell recalled. "Our guards would just pass it back and forth out near the center line...which wasn't a lot of fun."

McCarthy's 1963 team was built for the stall: all five starters had good ball-handling skills, and they were obedient Southern boys who did what the coach told them. McCarthy drilled them in the stall and he preached it. "Nothing but layups," he'd tell them constantly. And "Boys"—or sometimes he'd say "Girls"—"they can't score while we have the ball." And, "Give me one point and the ball, and I'll beat you." In the world according to Babe, a game could be won on the opening tipoff.

"We believed this wholeheartedly," Don Posey said. "If we got the tip, we were gonna score, and then we were gonna win the game. When we beat Kentucky earlier that year, 56–52, we got the tip, scored first. Coach McCarthy said, 'It's all over girls, we got 'em.'" So when Posey's teammates jumped out to an early lead over Loyola, he thought the Ramblers were going down. He couldn't see why everyone thought they were so good. "I'm sitting over there thinking, I don't know what they've been talking about. This is over."

McCarthy's players weren't surprised when he called time out and said, "OK, boys, let's put it in the cooler." But some of them were probably surprised by what happened next. "Over the next four minutes," Nichols recalled, "it wasn't in the cooler, it was in Loyola's hands. They were slapping and stealing and making goals, and we weren't shooting."

Leland Mitchell said, "They had such a gambling defense that you needed to punish them when they gambled. You know, if they gambled to get the ball and they didn't get it, then you go in and score." Instead, if Loyola gambled and missed, Mississippi State would return to their pattern and wait for the sure shot. "We wouldn't take anything but a layup," Mitchell said.

Loyola quickly ran off ten points, six of them from Harkness on two three-point plays. Though it took them almost six minutes to score their first point, they tied the game at 12 about midway through the first half. They went into the locker room with a 26–19 lead—an "almost ridiculous halftime score" according to the AP's writer, who reported that the crowd booed sometimes at Mississippi State's slow-down tactics.

In the second half, Loyola twice opened up a ten-point lead, and both times Mississippi State fought back to within three. But they never could get closer. Red Stroud, their shooter, was harassed by Harkness and had a terrible night. As a team the Bulldogs were flailing at the foul line, making only 11 of 20, and were outrebounded by Loyola 48–35.

The game turned on a dunk, Doug Hutton recalled. "Sometime late in the second half, the score was really tight, and for some reason our center dribbled the ball across the center line. When he picked it up to throw it to me, Miller came in between us and intercepted it, took about three or four dribbles, and just stuffed it with both hands. And that just changed the complexion of the game." The SEC didn't have many 6-2 players who could dunk like that. (Though Hutton, 5-10, was one who could.) Don Posey said, "We were all white guys. There wasn't a whole lot of jumping and dunking and that kind of stuff that we were used to seeing. When he went down and slam-dunked it, it was like from that point forward they were back in the groove."

With about seven minutes left in the game, Egan did his thing to Leland Mitchell. "I had the ball at the free-throw line," Mitchell recalled, "I was going toward the sidelines, and Egan I guess he jumped out in front of me, and we had a collision, and it should have been a foul on him, but they called it on me. That was five fouls."

With Mitchell on the bench, Mississippi State was sunk. Vic Rouse scored eight quick points and the Bulldogs couldn't get a rebound. The final was 61–51. It was Loyola's lowest scoring game of the season.

Looking back on it, the Mississippi State players were reluctant to make excuses, but they couldn't help but wonder: Had they had a better chance of winning the year before, when the team was a little hungrier and went 24–1 during the regular season? If they had played in the tournament that year, win or lose, would the experience have helped them in 1963? Had McCarthy cracked their confidence with his elaborate praise of Loyola's victory over Tennessee Tech? Would they have been readier to play Loyola if they'd been able to practice without the distracting political buffoonery going on all around them? Bobby Shows said, "I think we played our game before we ever got there. Are we going or not? Yes you are. No you're not. Yes you are. No you're not. For all of us that was very emotional— emotionally draining."

Loyola's Hunter recalled, "We tried to play without incident for a while there, because of how they were portraying the game. You know, you didn't want a fight or anything like that. If the history hadn't been the same, if we had had the killer instinct right away, we probably could have started better. But those guys could play. They boxed out, they had guys who could handle the ball, they could shoot well, and they worked hard on defense. They probably played as good a game against us as anybody during the tournament."

The next night in the consolation game, Mississippi State earned back some self-respect. With Joe Dan Gold on the bench—a Saturday morning x-ray showed that he'd finished the Loyola game with a broken hand—they held off Bowling Green 65–60, even though Nate Thurmond pulled down 31 rebounds. Bowling Green was one of the two teams that had beaten Loyola in the regular season.

They flew home to Starkville on Sunday. As their plane approached the airport they could see a long line of cars and a crowd of about a thousand people. Someone wondered out loud, "Are they here to greet us, or to send us back?" But they knew the answer. "[W]ith plaudits from newfound Yankee friends ringing in their ears," reported the *Starkville Daily News*, the team received "a warm and happy reception from home folks in Oktibbeha County." From that day forward, as best the players could remember, not a single student, or newspaper article, or stranger at the doughnut shop ever said a negative word about their tournament adventure. Bobby Shows told a reporter, "Even though we lost, we came home as winners."

In July 1965, Richard Holmes, the foster son of a Starkville doctor, enrolled as the first black student at Mississippi State. Years later he would work as a staff physician at the MSU student health center. The front page of the *Clarion-Ledger* said, "No Incidents as MSU Registers First Negro—Attracts Little Attention at Enrollment Routine."

The Ramblers' win over Mississippi State set up an all-Illinois final in the Mideast regional: the independent upstarts from Loyola, ranked third by the AP, versus the Big Ten champions from the University of Illinois, ranked eighth. It was Saturday night, March 16. Illinois had "twin towers" in the frontcourt, Skip Thoren from Rockford, Illinois, and Bill Burwell from New York. Burwell was on the Boys High team that Harkness and DeWitt Clinton had defeated for the New York City championship in 1958. He and Thoren were both about 6-9 (accounts varied), but Loyola controlled the boards anyway, taking 65 rebounds to Illinois' 49. Hunter and Rouse took 34 between them, while Harkness put on a 33-point scoring show.

With 3:50 left in the game the Ramblers had a 28-point lead. A bugler in the Loyola section rose and played taps. The Illini narrowed the margin in garbage time, but no thanks to Ireland, who left his starters in the game until the last 70 seconds. Maybe he was trying to build his team's confidence. Maybe it was a thumb in the eye from a coach who was tired of living in the shadow of the Big Ten. Or maybe it was just force of habit. Harry Combes, the Illinois coach, walked off in a huff at the buzzer. Ireland had to chase him down to shake his hand. Now he could afford to be a good sport. He was going to the final four.

That night was the night of the busted bicycles, a postgame celebration that led Ireland to threaten that he would kick two players off the team and go to the final four with just seven. Chuck Wood, who was Egan's roommate and now sixth man on the team, remembered it this way:

"Egan's got a buddy who's a running back at Michigan State, went to St. Rita's. He invites us to a party, we go to the party, we have a good time at the party. At 2 or 3 o'clock in the morning, we're walking back to the hotel. They had a hotel management program on campus, that's where we were staying. And we end up in front of a girls' dorm. Coincidence, we didn't know where we were going. I don't know if there was a girl in the window or what. Anyhow they have two bike racks, and maybe a hundred bikes, in front of this dorm. So Egs says, why don't we take a bike back to the hotel? So I said sure. I go over—this one's chained. And this one's chained. He says shit, this one's chained too. He's pulling it off and the frame's coming off and the front wheel's lying there. So I'm pulling them off too. We're throwing them around, now we got maybe 30 girls sitting in the window, on the second floor, looking at us. Now there's cars parked there, and we start running across the top of the cars—for the girls, just to show off. Sure enough, a cop pulls up. Egs says, we better get goin'.

"We start walking and we go a hundred yards, cop comes over, pulls to the side. 'Hey boys, come over here. What's goin' on?' I'm not doin' any talkin', because I know Egan's the talker. He says 'What do you mean?' Cop says 'Well, we just got a call from the girls' dorm, apparently there's been a little problem over there.' Egan says 'Woo—

what are you talking about, what kind of problem?' 'Well, apparently some bikes have been damaged, and there were some people dancing on top of cars.' Egs says 'You know, there were four guys ahead of us, in trench coats just like ours, and we were trying to figure out what the hell they were doing.' So now the two cops get out of the car, they say, 'You stay here.' Egs says 'No problem.' They go into the dorm."

Egan, the son of a cop, a future defense lawyer, told Wood what would happen next. "Egs says to me, 'I've been through this. There were some other guys ahead of us. That's our story and we're sticking to it. They're gonna take us down to the station, they're gonna separate us, and they're gonna say that you rolled on me, that I rolled on you. Whatever you do, *stick with the story.*'

"The cops come back to the car and say 'We gotta take you down to the station.' And I'm thinking, oh shit. We get there, sure enough one of the cops takes me in one room, another cop takes Egan in another room. The cop asks me, 'What happened?' 'I don't know. I don't know what you're talking about, but we heard some commotion, there were a couple guys ahead of us, you know, and that's all I can tell you.' He walks out of the room, about five minutes later he comes back in. He says 'Well, Jack Egan just told us that you were damaging some of the bikes, and he couldn't stop you.' I thought that son of a bitch, he rolled! But I said, 'I don't know why he would ever say that, but that's not what happened.'

"And so they grilled us maybe 20 minutes, and then the cop says 'Your buddy wants to make a phone call.' Oh my God. I'm gonna lose my scholarship, my dad's gonna kill me, we could be on the front page of the *Trib*! But anyhow they brought us together, I guess because we stayed with the story—and they didn't push us real hard, they were campus cops, they probably deal with it all the time. They probably knew we were lying but they couldn't prove it, and the witnesses had said we were both the same size. Well, looking down maybe we did look the same size. But we said obviously we're not the same size. I'm 6-3, he's 5-10. So one of the cops says, 'Who you gonna call?' Egan makes the call, to Jerry Lyne." Lyne, the assistant coach, was easier on the players than Ireland and sometimes served as a sympathetic go-between. "Jerry's gonna come over and get us out. That's what we think.

"Who walks in? George. Oh no. He comes up, he pops me." Wood smacked an open hand to his face to illustrate. "He lets me have one. I say, 'We didn't do anything. Christ we didn't do nothin', we're innocent!' But he walked in, he didn't even ask, he walked right up and he just let me have it. Next morning the guys are all laughing because all I could have was juice through a straw. I go 'George, what the hell did you hit me for?' I knew Egan had convinced him that I was the bad influence, not him. I know that!"

Miller: "I'm rooming with Jerry on the road, Ireland knocks on the door and says, 'Oh, Jerry, I got a problem, what do I do?' He says Jack and Chuck broke some bikes. 'That damn Chuck Wood gets Jack into so much trouble, maybe I should just send Chuck home.' But not Jack! He immediately knew he had to do something, so who could he punish, it definitely wasn't going be Jack." But who was instigator? "Jack! Of course. It was always Jack."

The next morning, no one bothered to wake Egan and Wood. They were the last ones to get on the bus back to Chicago. Wood: "Nobody talks to us. George says 'You sit up here in front, don't you say a word.' The guys are in the back, they're laughing their asses off. We get back to the dorm, George says, 'See you tomorrow at practice.' All right, we go to practice, we're shooting around, George calls the guys together. Egs and I, we start walking over, he says, 'I don't want to talk to you guys, I want to talk to your teammates.' Egs says, 'You know what they're talking about: whether or not they're going to have us come with the team.' This is the final four the next week! Egan said, 'Who the hell's he shitting, he's not going anywhere without us. Fuck him, let's play horse.' So we play horse. He calls us back together and says, 'Well, the team has voted that you guys should go.'"

CHAPTER 24: LOUISVILLE
The Final Four

1963 was the 25th NCAA men's basketball tournament. For the second straight year the final four was held at Freedom Hall in Louisville. Three of the AP's top four teams were there: number-one Cincinnati, which had won the Midwest regional; number-two Duke, from the East; and number-three Loyola, from the Mideast. The fourth team was Oregon State, which had upset number-four Arizona State in the West regional. *Sports Illustrated*'s early prediction, two weeks before the final four, was that Duke and Cincinnati would play for the championship and Cincinnati would probably win it. As the final four began the magazine still liked Duke and Cincinnati but allowed that "Loyola, for all its undisciplined, madcap ways, has looked hotter than anybody in the regionals."

Loyola was slotted to play Duke in the semifinal. Like the Ramblers, the Blue Devils were a running team. After they beat St. Joe's to win the East regional, their coach Vic Bubas predicted that the game against Loyola would be a "basketball track meet." The Blue Devils were not then the basketball power they would become, but they had a higher profile than Loyola, having played the tournament in 1955 and again in 1960. They brought a 20-game win streak to Louisville and had two top-tier players: Jeff Mullins, 6-4, who would later be a three-time NBA all-star, and Art Heyman, 6-5, 1963's college player of the year according to both the AP and the U.S. Basketball Writers Association. Heyman was from Long Island. He and Harkness had played with and against each other on the playgrounds of New York. Harkness would be guarding him in the semifinal.

At that time the final four was just a two-day affair: two semifinal games on Friday night, then the consolation game and the final on Saturday night. The Loyola team flew by charter to Louisville on Thursday. Egan and Wood were on board. That night at the Sheraton, Mike Ireland recalled, his father had a visitor who brought him a gift from North Carolina coach Frank McGuire—a scouting report on Duke. "You didn't have the television you've got now, anyone who was that far away you just didn't see them. And so McGuire's assistant came up to the room and they went through the scouting report. That guy's name was Dean Smith."

His father and McGuire were friendly, Mike Ireland said, but there may have been more to it than friendship. Art Heyman had originally intended to attend North Carolina but switched to Duke at the last minute. In 1961, Heyman and a player he had known in New York, Larry Brown, came to blows during a North Carolina-Duke game and in the melee that followed Heyman had punched Frank McGuire in the groin. Mike Ireland said, "I think the rivalry between North Carolina and Duke was so great that McGuire was willing to help anybody beat Duke."

By game time on Friday night, Loyola was a slight favorite, thanks to their impressive victories over Mississippi State and Illinois. The game was a surprise nonetheless. Loyola led the whole way and at the half held a 44–31 advantage. Duke gained in the second half, and with about four and a half minutes left in the game, Heyman scored a basket that brought his team within three, 74–71.

And then, as had become their habit, Loyola went into another gear. Or they stayed in the same gear while their opponents flagged. This was the payoff for all the cross-country running and emphasis on conditioning. This was where Jerry Harkness's remarkable lung power came to the front. Miller scored from the side and then again on a drive. Hunter blocked a shot by Heyman and Harkness scored on the fast break. Loyola ran off ten quick points while Duke scored none. In his book *Fast Break Basketball*, John McLendon had called the fast break a "demoralizing" offensive attack, and this is what he meant. "It was all over for Duke and everyone knew it," wrote Roy Damer in the *Tribune*. "The crowd gasped in amazement and wonder at one of the most decisive spurts ever seen on a basketball court." By the time it was over Loyola had scored 20 points to Duke's 4. The final was 94–75.

It was a satisfying win for Les Hunter, who years later admitted to writer Ron Fimrite that he felt something extra playing all-white teams from the South. "I wanted to run it up on those guys. We weren't just beating players. We were beating a student body, a system, the Klan. We weren't just playing a team, we were playing an ideology." Hunter led Loyola with 29 points and 18 rebounds. He hit 11 of 20 shots from the floor.

Art Heyman had 29 points and 12 rebounds. He hit 11 of 30 shots from the floor. Though Heyman's team did not play in the final, he was later named the tournament's most outstanding player.

————————

As the clock wound down on the Duke game, the Loyola fans in the arena chanted "We want Cincinnati." The Bearcats had not yet earned a place in the finals—their game against Oregon State would follow—but everyone knew they were the team to beat. They may have been a surprise in 1961, and underappreciated in 1962, but this year they had been ranked number one all season long. On Friday, before the semifinal games, the U.S. Basketball Writers Association finally named Ed Jucker coach of the year. As fans and press poured into Louisville for the weekend, the city "belonged to Jucker's favored Bearcats," wrote John Underwood in *Sports Illustrated*. "A lapel was not stylish if it wasn't pinned with a 'Cincy' button....Jucker's boys peered out from glossy pictures in jewelry store windows. The handsome Jucker family (wife and four kids) smiled two columns wide from the pages of *The Courier-Journal* and the coach was revealed to be a 'chicken-and-ham' eater." Cincinnati was reaching for the record book: no team had ever won the NCAA tournament three years running. Jucker told Underwood, "we want to very badly."

The game set up as a confrontation between two diametrically opposed styles of play: offense versus defense, the highest-scoring team in the country against the team that allowed the fewest points; the fast, high-flying style of the playgrounds—a game that Ireland sometimes called "controlled chaos"—versus a methodical, low-risk, highly coached game that (in Underwood's words) "takes, as if by slow surgery, the joy of life from its opponents."

Some sportswriters said it was a confrontation between excellent defense and no defense, but that, Loyola players later insisted, was a misreading of the statistics. Loyola's opponents scored many points, but that was because Loyola scored many points, and every time they scored their opponents were handed the ball. But the Ramblers had held two running teams, Illinois and Duke, to 64 and 75 points respectively. Duke was the fourth highest-scoring team in the country. And a lot of Loyola's scoring came off steals, interceptions, and forced turnovers. How can you call that no defense?

It was certainly a contest between different coaching styles. Jucker's players called him Juck. He was a long sufferer. If a player took a "twister"—his name for a forced, low-percentage shot that required a lot of midair contortion—he would throw up his arms and cry out in pain. "What are you doing to me?" Ireland, whose players called him the Man, was a critic. He once told Les Hunter, "The next time I want you to take that shot, I'll send you a telegram."

Jucker was all about defense and preparation. He devoted 80 percent of practice time to defense. Usually one of his assistants, either Tay Baker or John Powless, would scout the opposition, then Baker would train the second team to run the opponents' offense so the first-stringers could practice against it. Larry Shingleton recalled that in one game—maybe against Texas Tech in the '61 regional—the starters took a big lead. When the substitutes came in, they played using the opponents' own offense. The opposing coach "went berserk," Shingleton said. "He said, 'They're running it better than we do!'"

Ireland also availed himself of the occasional scouting report; indeed, he claimed that he and his unpaid assistant, Nick Kladis, had scouted Cincinnati several times before the tournament. But Ireland never really followed through with the preparation, Harkness recalled. He'd start, saying, "This guy will go over here and pick, then they'll come around here, and there's a double pick over there...." But the strategizing would not last long. Ireland would lose his patience for it—or pretend to, in order to psyche his team up. According to Harkness, "He'd say 'Ahhhh,' and he'd throw the scouting report down on the floor. He said 'They'll never get a chance to get into that stuff, we'll press 'em all over the place.'"

It was freedom against discipline, fast against slow, new against old. And it was on television. It was not the first final to be televised nationally—that had been in 1954. And to say it was televised nationally is not to say it was seen everywhere. It was syndicated, seen only in the markets where stations chose to buy it. But 1963 was the first year of the NCAA's multiyear contract with Sports Network, Incorporated, a six-year deal that arguably launched the long-term symbiosis between television and the phenomenon that came to be known as March Madness. When that contract expired, NBC picked up the tournament and kept it through 1979, when Larry Bird's Indiana State team and Magic Johnson's Michigan State set a TV ratings record. Then the tournament went to CBS, where the late-round games remain today.

When viewers tuned in for the start of the game they saw something that had never been seen before. People all over the U.S. saw it, in rural areas as well as urban, in the South as well as in the West and Northeast, casual fans and players and coaches alike, as well as youngsters who were the players and coaches of the future. What they saw then is now taken for granted. The two best college basketball teams in the country formed up at center court for the opening tip. Seven of the ten players were black.

OVERTIME: LOUISVILLE, MARCH 23, 1963

The five-minute overtime period began with a center-court tip. George Wilson was jumping for Cincinnati, Vic Rouse for Loyola. For the third time that night, Rouse prevailed. He tipped toward the Loyola goal to Hunter, who turned instantly downcourt as though he knew what he would find there: Jerry Harkness breaking for the basket. Harkness gathered in the pass and laid it up. Two seconds, two points. Loyola led for the first time all night, 56–54.

Cincinnati brought the ball down and set up their offense. They took their time. Wilson set a pick for Thacker. Thacker shed his defender and Wilson turned to the basket. Thacker passed high to him and Wilson laid it in. 56–56.

Hunter missed a jumper from just inside the foul line. Wilson took the rebound and Cincinnati set up again. Under their basket, a pass from Thacker went off Wilson's hands and out of bounds. Loyola took the ball down but lost it out of bounds when one of the Bearcats deflected a pass from Miller to Rouse. Cincinnati tried a long pass downcourt and Miller intercepted. He dribbled down to the right side of the key, launched a 20-footer, and drained it. Loyola 58, Cincinnati 56.

Thacker missed a jump shot. Then Loyola had four tries in rapid succession: Miller missed a jumper. Rouse missed a tip. Another missed tip and then Rouse missed again. Finally Thacker took the rebound and *threw a bomb downcourt to Larry Shingleton, who scored an uncontested layup. 58–58.*

About 1:45 was left on the clock. Red Rush, the radio announcer, speculated that Loyola might now hold for the last shot. "Wouldn't that be a switch," he exclaimed. If they could keep the ball while the clock ticked down to the last few seconds, they could take the last shot without worrying about the consequences: if it goes in, the game is over; if it doesn't, the game is still tied and goes into a second overtime.

1:20 left. Miller had the ball in the Loyola backcourt. Yates came out and tried to make something happen. He slapped the ball away from Miller. Egan went for the loose ball and Shingleton tied him up. Jump ball.

Here was Shingleton's chance to redeem his missed free throw. If Cincinnati could control this tip, they would get to hold for the last shot. And they were a lot better at it than Loyola. It was what they practiced every day.

Egan and Shingleton stood opposite each other at center court. Both were 5-10. Miller and Thacker stood beside each other to the side. The ball went up. For years afterward, Bill Jauss of the Chicago Daily News *would say that Egan turned his "considerable backside" into Shingleton to keep him away from the ball. But Egan didn't think so. On the game film it looks like he simply timed his jump better. He tipped the ball back toward his own goal. Miller, who was standing on that side, had a step on Thacker and beat him to it. Loyola had the ball with 1:15 left. Still 58–58.*

Now Thacker tried to make something happen. He got his hand on a pass from Miller to Harkness, but Harkness came up with the ball. 50 seconds. Harkness was now being guarded by Ron Bonham, Cincinnati's weakest defender. He dribbled into the right corner, then passed outside. He started to back in on Bonham but then passed outside again.

"And this is a twist!" Red Rush chortled. "Cincinnati, the team that always holds the ball. They're seeing what it feels like now. How does it feel? We'll find out in about 23 seconds."

Loyola moved the ball around the backcourt. 15 seconds. "I guarantee you one thing," Rush promised. "They'll give it to Harkness when the time comes." Egan passed to Miller. Rouse came out to the backcourt and Miller passed to him. Red Rush started counting down. "Nine, eight..."

The rest happened in a flurry. Rouse passed back to Miller, who crossed behind him, then Rouse turned right and headed for the basket. Miller dribbled in and passed to Harkness, who was left of the free-throw line. "Harkness has got it. Here he goes!" He had a step on Bonham, but Bonham recovered and reached out a long left arm to smack Harkness's left wrist. Harkness was a few feet in from the left corner—about the same shot he'd taken to tie the game in regulation. He went up. Bonham's feet stayed on the floor. Wilson was in the paint under the basket. Rouse was arriving underneath from the right with Thacker at his side.

Harkness and I watched on the game film as he rose to the top of his jump...

and flipped the ball over to Hunter, who was by himself on the left edge of the foul line. "Jerry!" I asked. "Why didn't you take that shot?" It was a question he had answered many times. He didn't feel it. Bonham's slap to the wrist had discombobulated his rhythm.

Wilson went out to get Hunter, leaving Bonham underneath on the left side, Thacker and Rouse on the right. Hunter put up a ten-foot jumper.

"I've taken that shot in my mind's eye four thousand times...," he later told Sports Illustrated's Ron Fimrite. "And it's always the same."

The ball clanked off the rim, hit the backboard, and came down on the right side. But Hunter's longtime teammate Vic Rouse was waiting for it. He knew where to be. "I've played with Les a long time," Rouse told the press after the game. "So I was able to get into position." He shot up over Thacker and took the ball in two hands. He didn't tip it, he said. He was taking no chances. He banked it off the glass and into the hoop.

"I looked at the referee and waited for him to call something," Miller told reporters. "Then I looked at the clock and there was one second left." Thacker had his hands up to call time out, but spectators on the sideline were already spilling onto the court. "It's over, it's over," Red Rush exclaimed. 'We won. We won. We won. We won the ballgame!"

PART THREE:
POSTGAME

CHAPTER 25:

Dancing in the Streets

In Wilmington, Delaware, Ron Miller's uncles Matt and Cookie watched on TV with their families as Miller broke downcourt in the last seconds of regulation time. He took Hunter's outlet pass and pushed the ball on to Harkness. Harkness took the pass, went up...and the TV screen went dark. Matt Jr., Miller's three-year-old cousin, had pulled the plug. By the time they got the picture back, a commercial had come on. They didn't know what happened.

In Chicago, some people knew what happened before they saw it on TV. It was a big night for Chicago sports, and the city was not exactly gripped with Ramblers fever. Channel 7 was airing the finals of the Illinois state high school tournament. A Chicago team, Carver High, was playing for the championship after having lost it the year before in a heartbreaking one-point game. Meanwhile channel 11 had the Indiana state high school championship. The NCAA championship was tape-delayed so channel 9 could show the end of a Chicago Black Hawks hockey game. The only live coverage in town was Red Rush's radio call on WCFL. When it ended, according to a story that was bound to be told whether it happened or not, an enterprising student, or several, went out to earn some money for textbooks. On TV Loyola was still 15 points down. It wasn't hard to find a tavern full of people who would bet against them.

In the south suburbs, a 13-year-old boy named William C. Rhoden listened to the game on the radio. Forty years later, he wrote about it in the *New York Times*'s "Sports of the Times" column. Loyola was from Chicago and he was too. Loyola was Catholic and he attended a Catholic grammar school. "[S]o the Ramblers were not only the Vatican's team, they were my team," he wrote. He did not mention in his column that they were black and he was too. Later he told me that he hadn't noticed. He continued:

> I listened to the game on radio and was so crushed when they fell behind by 15 points that I turned off the broadcast to avoid hearing the dismal end. When my father told me that Loyola had won in overtime, I was convinced that a miracle had taken place. We watched the tape delay of the game. The snapshot I remember of it was the look of horror and disbelief on the face of George Wilson, one of Cincinnati's star players, as time expired. Wilson went to inbound the ball, but the game was over, and he dropped the ball and held his head between his hands as the final horn sounded.

> I've been hooked on the tournament and its relative democracy ever since.

As soon as the game was over, Loyola students spilled onto Sheridan Road and danced in a conga line. The *Tribune* estimated their number at "more than 400 students, about the capacity of the dormitory."

In the papers the next day, Loyola shared the spotlight with Carver High, which had won the state championship thanks to the storybook heroics of a sophomore guard who sat on the bench almost the entire game. With 15 seconds to go and downstate Centralia High leading 52–51, Anthony Smedley, all 5-7 of him, came off the bench, stole the ball from Centralia's all-state center, and drained a 20-foot two-hander to win the game. Later his coach explained, "I panicked. I just told him to go in and get the ball. He did it on his own....It was the smartest move of my life."

The Sunday *Tribune* ran the Carver and Loyola stories side by side on the front page of the sports section. Carver was on the left, but Loyola got first mention in the headline: "Loyola Rules the U.S., Carver the State!"

On Monday, the *Daily News* (which did not publish on Sundays) ran a Carver story on page one above the nameplate. Readers had to turn to the sports section to read about Loyola, but there too the high school tournament got the bigger splash.

Roy Damer's *Tribune* story on the NCAA final told an interesting statistical tale. In the last 13:56 of regulation time, Loyola had outscored Cincinnati 24–9: what seemed like a long, slow, and rather sloppy comeback looked on paper like a familiar Loyola spurt. The "undisciplined, madcap" Ramblers made only 3 errors in the game; the ball-control Bearcats made 16. Evidently, Loyola's pressing defense was better than expected. Most remarkable, the Bearcats had shot a respectable 48.9 percent from the field, while the Ramblers shot a pitiful 22.7. Or, to put it another way, Loyola had taken 84 shots to Cincinnati's 45. It wasn't because Loyola dominated the boards. Indeed, Cincinnati won the rebound battle 52–47. But Loyola was shooting and Cincinnati was not. After the intermission, according to an unofficial scorer,[29] Loyola took 48 or 49 shots, Cincinnati 17.

In the days and years and decades to follow, Cincinnati's coaches and players would insist that they did not stall. Their problem, they said, was foul trouble. Their tightly disciplined team fouled rarely; going into the tournament, they had fewer fouls than every team in the nation save one. But before the game Ireland had said, "I think we can make them foul," and he was right. Thacker, Yates, and Wilson each finished the game with four fouls. Fifty years later, virtually all the Cincinnati players I talked to were still complaining about the calls. They said the fouls prevented them from forcing the action and from playing their usual tight defense. They had no choice but to run their offense cautiously, trying to create high-percentage shots;

---

29   Your author, watching a hacked-up game film.

when they failed, they took the ball back out and tried again. But the Loyola players and many observers felt that they were too disciplined for their own good.

CHAPTER 26:
The Future of Basketball

The National Association of Basketball Coaches holds its annual convention at the final four. In the days when college basketball was done on a more modest scale, coaches would meet there and arrange their schedules for the following year. In 1963, about 750 of them were watching as Loyola demolished the all-white team from Duke and cracked the textbook game of Cincinnati. One of them was Morris "Bucky" Buckwalter, a young assistant at the University of Utah. Fifty years later he remembered the buzz among the coaches as they loitered in the stands after the games and when they went out for beers later. Some of them were inclined to dismiss what had just happened, he said. Others thought they had seen the future of basketball.

Buckwalter played his college ball at Utah. His teams reached the NCAA tournament twice, in 1955 and '56, both times losing to the eventual champions, the University of San Francisco team of Bill Russell and K.C. Jones. After graduating and serving a hitch in the Army, Buckwalter began a long and respected career as a basketball coach and exec. He led the way in bringing European talent into the NBA. As VP for basketball operations of the Portland Trailblazers, he was named the NBA executive of the year in 1991, when the Blazers posted a 63–19 regular season record. He was one of the heroes of

David Halberstam's basketball classic *The Breaks of the Game*, which credits him with opening doors for black players.

What Buckwalter saw in Louisville made a strong impression on the young coach. It wasn't just that most of the players in the final had been black. Or that the team with four black starters had embarrassed the white guys from Duke. Buckwalter realized that the game itself was changing. He was old enough to remember stories about coaches who would sit a player down for taking a jump shot. "A lot of coaches thought there was no way that you could control your body in the air," he told me.

"During that time, you have to remember, California and some other teams"—including Ed Jucker's, whose scheme was inspired by Pete Newell's at Cal—"really stressed the fundamentals of the game, correct passing, and it was all done horizontally. There wasn't any thought of jumping ability being an important asset." But when Buckwalter saw the 1963 championship, he felt that the game's axis had just been tilted 90 degrees. "With the shot blocking and the rebounding and the high-flying dunks, it was no longer a horizontal game; it had become vertical."

Another thing Buckwalter noticed was that Loyola's game was "definitely playground: do what you can do, do a little showtime. That was accepted with all the team members and they understood that that was part of their game. Coaches had been to the Chicago playgrounds and New York and D.C. and seen a lot of this stuff, but at that time they didn't see it translating into successful major college programs. After that final four I think there was a change of mind on that.

"Some of the old timers said this will never last, this is not the way basketball should be played, it was an aberration. I would say maybe half of the coaches had that attitude. And the other half said, wow. This is a whole new avenue that we can pursue." Less emphasis on technique and fundamentals, more appreciation for athletic skills and improvisation.

"Coaches are very practical people," Buckwalter told me. "If they see somebody who can help win games, that's what they want....I'll never forget watching coaches watch players. Coaches learn from players. If a player does something and it works out well, even though it's something the coach has never done or seen before, the next year it's in his playbook. That's how the game changes."

———————

Chances are good that Don Haskins was also in Louisville that weekend. He was in his second year as head coach at Texas Western College, now called the University of Texas-El Paso, or UTEP. They had played in the Midwest regional but lost in the first round to Texas, which then lost to Cincinnati.

Haskins did not need to be exposed to the idea of black ballplayers. Whatever conventions may have been observed in the rest of Texas, the rest of the South, and the rest of the country, those rules did not apply in the diverse border town of El Paso. Texas Western had been integrated since 1955. When Haskins took the head coaching job in 1961, the basketball team had four black players; his predecessor, Harold Davis, was already recruiting in New York. Hilton White, a legendary community coach in the South Bronx, had been stationed in El Paso as a serviceman and knew that young black kids could get a chance there.

But Haskins did have something to learn about the changes that black players were bringing to the game. In his autobiography (written with Dan Wetzel) he tells the story of Bobby Joe Hill, a Detroit kid who came to Texas Western in 1964. "He was the Allen Iverson of his time," Haskins wrote. "In the open court you could not stop him. If he was comin' right at ya', the quickest way he'd go around you was by whipping the ball behind his back going one way or the other. He'd just leave the defender flat-footed."

"This is where I had to learn a little about coaching."

Haskins was an old-school, defense-minded coach. He had played at Oklahoma A&M for one of the seminal coaches, the notoriously tough Hank Iba, and in fact Iba's son Moe was now his assistant at

Texas Western. Neither coach liked Hill's flashy style. They thought he was a hot dog. In Hill's first season at Texas Western, Haskins tried to make him over into a player Hank Iba would like: Play defense. No showboating. Dribble in front, nothing between the legs. Hill tried, but it didn't work for him. Fans started booing because they knew he could do better. "[H]e was tryin' to play the way I wanted him to play, which was the wrong way," Haskins wrote. "It hurt our team because I took away the things he could do. It was my fault."

> So before the 1966 season I called Bobby Joe into the office and I said, "I want you to get the ball down the floor the best way you know how, and I want you to play just like you've always played." He sat over my desk and he started grinnin'. I'll never forget what he said then: "Coach, everything is going to be OK now."

As most basketball fans know, Hill and Haskins made history that year by winning the NCAA championship with an all-black starting five, including a core of players who had come via Hilton White in New York. With Hill leading the scoring, they defeated an all-white Kentucky team coached by Adolph Rupp, who was famously slow to recruit black players. Haskins and Texas Western's championship were the subject of the 2006 Disney movie *Glory Road* and Haskins's tie-in autobiography of the same name. Their story—all black starters against all white; the rebellious young color-blind coach against the crusty old face of southern prejudice—was made for the movies, and their victory is seen by many as the watershed moment in the integration of college basketball.

The players who took part in the Loyola-Cincinnati final of 1963, three years before Texas Western's championship, watched *Glory Road* with special interest. Several of those I talked to had the same reaction:

Where's our movie?

———————

Perry Wallace was 15 in March 1963. Later in the year he would enter Pearl High School in Nashville. In 1967, he would cross the last racial frontier for college basketball players, as the first black player in the SEC. He did not see the Loyola-Cincinnati game on TV, but he didn't really need to. The black community in Nashville had been tracking the progress of their favorite sons, Hunter and Rouse, since they'd enrolled at Loyola. When the Ramblers reached the NCAA tournament the whole city was watching. Wallace knew it was big because it wasn't relegated to the back of the sports section, like most black sports stories. It was up front—"in what we used to call the white section of the sports page."

"It was the talk of the black town," Wallace remembered. He heard it from his coaches, from the ballplayers who hung around at Tennessee State, from older people in the neighborhood. "They kept up with it the way we're keeping up with events in Libya.[30] It was that mesmerizing and that level of heightened interest."

The interest was not limited to basketball fans, Wallace remembered. "You had three parallel conversations—you had sports fans, the general public, and then the kind of educated class who were vitally concerned about racial progress. They tracked athletes and others who attained some note because there was always some potential for leveraging it. And any time you had the races cooperating, it was a real victory and it deserved our attention."

For Wallace, who dreamed of going to college on a basketball scholarship, Loyola's success had a more particular meaning too. "Growing up in the segregated schools of Nashville, and in particular going to Pearl High, it was a powerful, powerful influence. Here were these guys who came from the world that I came from. I played on the same playgrounds they did. I grew up sort of under their aura. They looked like me. I played like them. We came up in the same system. It was ready-made role model stuff. Coaches really knew how to use it to inspire us. I always remembered stories about Hunter and Rouse and when they played in the South and then how they went up

---

30   We spoke in March 2011, in the midst of what came to be known as the "Arab Spring."

north to Chicago, which was kind of a dream that all of us had. And then when they won the national championship, of course this was huge. It really pumped up the hopes and dreams about going to a big college outside the South and playing major college ball. In terms of black culture and literature and lore, going up north, ever since the Underground Railroad, the North was always the land of hope. And in many respects it became kind of a mythical place where you could go and be free compared to the South."

As the 1963 final fed the dreams of youngsters, it also opened the eyes of those who controlled access to those dreams. "The prospect of integration was scary to many whites," Wallace said, "but some of the coaches and administrators were beginning to peep out and say, wow, what could we have done this year had we had a Hunter and a Rouse? Basically they were beginning to look at the spigot that had spewed out the Hunters and the Rouses and they were looking for more."

As it turned out Wallace did not go to college in the North. In his senior year at Pearl High he led his team to a 31–0 season and victory in Tennessee's first integrated state championship. He had become a college coach's dream—6-5, a prodigious leaper who could score and rebound, a high school All American, and valedictorian of his class to boot. He had about 80 college offers from all over the country (including from George Ireland at Loyola), but in the end he succumbed to the school on the white side of town. Vanderbilt chancellor Alexander Heard was eager to integrate the SEC and Perry Wallace was perfect for the job.

Vanderbilt recruited two black basketball players in 1966. The other one was Godfrey Dillard, a four-sport athlete from Visitation High School in Detroit. He was a little less perfect. Wallace and Dillard played together as freshmen, but then Dillard injured his knee before the start of their sophomore season and was "mysteriously" cut, Wallace said, when he came back as a junior. His style of play did not please Vanderbilt coach Roy Skinner—Dillard liked to rip it and run—but the real problem, according to Wallace and to Dillard himself, was that he was too much of a "Northern Negro": confident, aggressive, outspoken, political. In a word, uppity. He'd been a model citizen in high school—president of the student council in a mostly white Catholic school—but that was Detroit and this was Nashville. And it was 1968. Martin Luther King had been assassinated, provoking riots in several northern cities. At the Democratic National Convention in Chicago, protestors provoked a "police riot" that was broadcast nightly on television. In Mexico City, Tommie Smith and John Carlos shocked the sports world by raising black-gloved fists on the medal podium of the summer Olympics. Coach Skinner had told Dillard to turn down his political volume, but Dillard didn't listen. Perry Wallace, the native Nashvillian, understood better the delicate rules of southern race relations.

Not that Wallace had an easy time of it. He didn't meet another black player in the SEC until his senior year. He was cursed, called names, and spat on—at Mississippi State among other places. What he remembered most, though, was the indignity of the "nigger-ball" stereotype—the persistent notion that he and other black players were brute athletic talents incapable of thinking for or controlling themselves. They had no discipline. They couldn't play defense or be counted on under pressure. If they fell behind they would panic and scatter.

Since boyhood, Wallace had been captivated by the dunk. To him it had a certainty that was not available in everyday life. "When I first started watching basketball, I saw Wilt Chamberlain and Bill Russell dunking, and this was a fantastic inspiration to me—not just as an athlete, but it had a spiritual, Proustian effect. You know, I'd walk through these white communities, past these white houses and schools, and they had everything. We didn't seem to have anything. And we could be picked on at any time. In a world that was a lot of times not hopeful, not so certain, where you were powerless, these black athletes seemed to be powerful and strong and sure." A dunk could not be deflected or misconstrued. It was an act of will and control. To the young Wallace, it was "just magnificent." In the evening he would work on his dunk muscles while watching TV. "Squat after squat after squat, watching *Leave It to Beaver* and *Dragnet*—doing squats and practicing jumping." John McLendon was no longer coach at Tennessee State, but the gym there was still a gathering place for basketball players from the school and the neighborhood. When Wallace first showed up there, a 6-foot 2-inch 13-year-old kid, "I got on the floor and at one point I got the ball and I drove in and I dunked and these college guys went wild."

The dunk was banned from college basketball at the end of Wallace's freshman year at Vanderbilt. It was the end of Lew Alcindor's sophomore year at UCLA, his first year as a varsity player. The new rule was approved just three days after UCLA won the national championship. Some basketball people called it the Lew Alcindor rule. According to the *New York Times*, an NCAA spokesman said it was needed to prevent injuries and because there was no defense for the dunk. "The founders of the game, he said, intended the ball to be thrown through the hoop, not pushed." Perry Wallace remembered that some people saw it differently. "A lot of people ascribed it to the fear of these black players slam-dunking with these strongly symbolic moves."

Wallace developed an alternate move. "One of the things I used to do was to go up high above the rim and just drop the ball in." The dunk rule prohibited his hands from crossing the cylinder of airspace over the rim, but Wallace learned to drop the ball in without violating the cylinder. "It was a strategy on my part," Wallace said, especially useful when he had to play center against taller players. "Now when I did that, routinely, one of the fans, or one of the athletic supporters, would come up to me and this was the interpretation they had of my strategy: 'Boy, you got that ball, and, and you were all excited, and, and, and you just went up and you were gonna dunk the way you used to dunk, and then you remembered at the last minute and dropped the ball in.' Every game: 'Boy, I know what you were doing out there, you just forgot and you just, you just, you went wild for a minute, and then you caught yourself.' Now here I am, a valedictorian, I'm a major in the engineering school at Vanderbilt, in electrical engineering and engineering mathematics. I'm making As and Bs. 'Boy, you just lost your mind, you just went wild and then you just remembered at the last minute.' Every game! And this wasn't hatred at work. They liked me! This was the ultimate in stereotyping."

Wallace graduated with his engineering degree in 1970. He was drafted by the Philadelphia 76ers and flirted briefly with pro basketball before enrolling at Columbia University law school, which awarded him a J.D. in 1975. He worked as a trial attorney in the U.S. Department of Justice during the Carter and Reagan administrations. Since 1993 he has been a tenured professor of law at American University in Washington, D.C.

Godfrey Dillard transferred to Eastern Michigan and received a law degree from the University of Michigan in 1973. He took a master's in international affairs, worked for a time in the U.S. State Department, and had a role in the 2003 Supreme Court cases that upheld the University of Michigan's affirmative action admissions policy.

CHAPTER 27:
The Man

———

Jack Egan spoke at George Ireland's funeral. He said, "George didn't see color. He hated all of us the same."

Ireland died on September 14, 2001, just a few days after the terrorist attacks on the Pentagon and World Trade Center. He was 88. Jerry Harkness recalled being surprised that there weren't more people at the funeral. Flying was difficult in the few days after the attack, but Harkness took it as a comment on the deceased. When DePaul coach Ray Meyer died, five years later, 2,000 people came to the wake and a thousand came to the funeral mass, including coaches and players from all over the country. Ireland, by comparison, "was not well liked," Harkness told me.

Clarence Red's memory was completely different: there were plenty of people at the funeral, he said, and Ireland was a "fine man— a great man in my opinion." That's how it was with Ireland. The players served as his pallbearers. When they carried him out, a lot of mixed feelings and unanswered questions were left behind.

Clarence Red loved the guy. "He leaned on his players a lot. But he wanted you in shape, he wanted you to produce. He was just a tough man; he'd just as soon hit you as say something to you. But we all knew that, and all the players I knew respected him. I respected him. As a man I loved him, I sure did. I'll never forget him. He did a lot for me. And he did a lot for his other players as well."

It's sometimes said of Ireland, and of other coaches who defied the racial quotas of their day, that they were not race-relations pioneers, they were simply coaches who wanted to win. They had a color-blind eye for ability and they took advantage of an imbalance in the athletic market. But just a few days after winning the national championship, following a parade in downtown Chicago, Ireland reminded his audience that the final had been played at a place called Freedom Hall. "What could be a more appropriate place for Loyola to win, with four Negroes on its team?" In the years to come he would claim pioneer status for himself. And Clarence Red believed he deserved it: "He wanted to win, but he also wanted to open things up, bring communities together. As I grew to know him, and listen to him, I knew that was his dream and that was his goal. He was far ahead of his time. I can remember him saying to me, 'Clarence, there's no reason why the black athlete shouldn't participate in everything the white athlete is participating in.' He said, 'I'm gonna get as many black kids on this team as I can.'"

Art McZier, the first black player Ireland recruited, thought the coach was special. He remembered that on road trips to places like Kentucky, Ireland and the athletic director, Father Hartmann, would eat room service with him while the white players ate in the dining room downstairs. "I liked the guy and I respected the guy," McZier said. "I mean the man was tough love. A lot of people really didn't understand the coach, and it took me time to appreciate what he was trying to do. I remember my freshman year, I think it was about the second semester, he was just hard. I mean he didn't treat me unfairly, he was just hard. He was demanding. So I was gonna transfer. He came and talked to my mother, my mother said 'You're going back to school with Mr. Ireland.'...

"He was always there for me. If I had an issue or problem, whatever it was, I felt comfortable going to talk to him. And if he could make a positive impact on the problem, he would do it." McZier stayed in touch after he graduated. "In fact I would go see Coach Ireland every time I came home, up to the time he died. I can see him right now. Gert, his wife, was bedridden, and I'd go to hold her hand, talk to her for a while, come back, sit with Coach Ireland and talk. He'd always reminisce about the same things."

The players on Ireland's championship team were more ambivalent. Most of them remembered him as a distant, lonely figure. He wasn't the sort to hang around schmoozing after the game or after practice. Les Hunter said, "He never hung out with his assistant coach, Jerry Lyne. He'd go his way after the game, assistant went his way. It prompted Jerry to say in later years, he never could figure out how a guy could be so alone in the world. He had just his family— that's the only people he liked or respected was his family. Period."

"I probably liked him more than anyone," Egan said. "I think I really understood where he was coming from. He really did want to win. And he knew innately who else wanted to win, who was willing to do the things that have to be done in order to win.

"He had a hard time controlling his temper, and as a result certain guys would turn on him. And that was his main problem, I think, that he would lose players who had talent."

Egan also stayed in touch after he graduated. Occasionally he would scout a team for Ireland. After the coach retired, he called Egan over to help him go through some of his memorabilia. "I think he was lonely. I think he actually missed me at times."

Egan thought Ireland cared about players who could help him win, and didn't care much about those who couldn't. Rich Rochelle, the backup center, would have to agree. He was the tallest man on the team but one of the last players off the bench. His memory was that Ireland was simply a bully—afraid of his stars and abusive with his subs. "Once Ireland realized what he had, with his starting five, he started kicking me in particular, to a point where my self-confidence went down, my self-esteem suffered. He was just in my opinion a bad person."

In his first game as a varsity player, against one of Ireland's early-season patsies, Rochelle came off the bench and scored 13 points and took 9 rebounds. The next day, he remembered, Ireland called him into his office and cursed him out, instructing him that his role was basically to take up space. He was not to shoot, not even in warmups.

Rochelle said that after the championship, at the postseason banquet, Ireland would not allow the four reserves to sit at the same table with the starters. "We worked very hard with the starting five to get through that year. He made us sit with the freshman team. As though we did not do anything, we didn't count, we were unimportant." The next year, Rochelle said, Ireland had him kicked off campus for a disciplinary matter that he had concocted out of thin air. To Rochelle (who struck me 50 years later as intelligent, well-spoken, and extremely mild-mannered—the antithesis of a troublemaker), it seemed like a personal vendetta.

Why didn't Ireland just cut him? "I think I served his purpose by being the whipping boy. I think that when all else failed, I was an easy target, because of my nature. I was not a fighter, I wasn't an arguer, I took a lot...."

"Ireland was afraid to approach certain people. He was never gonna go and get in Vic Rouse's face, for example, because Vic would have laid him flat. He took it out on the bench players."

John Crnokrak, a senior on the 1961–62 team, thought that Ireland was insecure and fearful of criticizing his best players. He wanted to be perceived as tough, and he had certain messages that he wanted to put across, but he was afraid of alienating his starters so he sometimes delivered his message through a hapless scrub. (See the night of the busted bicycles, Chapter 23.) Crnokrak was a starter in his sophomore and junior years, but was pushed to the bench as a senior by the talented group of newcomers. Ireland named him cocaptain that year with another benched senior, Jerry Verwey. One day in practice, Crnokrak recalled, the younger guys were screwing up. Instead of correcting them, Ireland waited for Crnokrak to make a mistake—as he remembered it, he slipped and "traveled" running over a wet spot on the floor—and seized that moment to impart his coach's wisdom. "He tells the manager go downstairs to get this cowbell, puts it around my neck, and then he says, 'This guy is like the farmer whose cow gave him good milk, then he shit in it. You can't continue to make mistakes and travel and make bad passes and take crazy shots. And that goes for all you stars too!' You see what I'm saying? They would make mistakes and he would yell at me! He said to me, 'I've got these young black athletes that I don't want to lose, they've left me a couple times—packed their suitcases—but I've gotta get through to them and they can't take constructive criticism.' I said 'Well, so what are you telling *me*?' He said, 'You're the toughest kid I ever coached mentally, and I know you can take this.' I said, 'Hey coach, I got feelings too.'" Crnokrak's teammates later presented him with a memorial cowbell that he still keeps in his office.

Les Hunter recalled that Ireland complimented him once in his life—and that was when he was 40 years old. Otherwise, Hunter said, "It was all what he had done for me." Ireland liked to give the impression that he had rescued Hunter from a life of deprivation. "We would go from banquet to banquet and he would tell everybody I was raised by my grandmother. I wasn't, my mother and father just weren't home that day when he came. And I had two sisters who weren't home either, they were away at college. But from that day on, no matter what I told George Ireland, it was I was raised by my grandmother.

"I grew up in a nice home. We had four bedrooms and a formal dining room, formal living room, den, all of that. Lived in a big rock house. We had a lot for blacks living in the South. My folks were looked up to as pillars in the community. But Ireland would always make you think he took you out of some type of poverty and made you into somebody."

Nonetheless, Ireland and Hunter saw each other occasionally and passed some time together in later years. After Ireland retired, he lived in an assisted living home near his son Mike in Kansas City. That's where Hunter had wound up too; he had a barbecue place there. Ireland came in a couple times with Mike and gave Hunter an autographed picture to hang on the wall. In 1988 the NCAA final was played in Kansas City. Hunter and Ireland sat together at the game, and Hunter got an earful, a litany of coaches who had earned a place on Ireland's shitlist. "He never met a coach he liked. He didn't like Guy Lewis of Houston, he didn't like Lou Carnesecca at St. John's. Joe Lapchick [Carnesecca's predecessor at St. John's], he didn't like him, he didn't like Ed Hickey at Marquette. John Wooden is the only guy I ever heard him speak highly of. And Wooden liked him. They knew each other from way back when. He always considered John Wooden as his mentor."

Part of Ireland's antipathy may have been connected to his reputation for running up the high scores that first attracted notice to his championship team. He sometimes left his starters in longer than necessary. "He would flaunt the fact that he had some horses who could go get it, and he'd pour it on to these coaches, and I think they resented him for that," Hunter said. "So maybe that's why he ended up disliking so many of the other coaches, 'cause they were mad at him."

Shortly after Ireland arrived in Chicago, DePaul University vanished from the Loyola schedule, ending a natural rivalry between two Catholic basketball schools just a few miles apart. Reporters, players, and other observers assumed that there was some mysterious tension between Ireland and DePaul coach Ray Meyer, his old Notre Dame teammate. Given the timing and their respective reputations—the angry Irishman and the teddy bear—most assumed that Ireland was carrying the grudge. That impression was reinforced when Ireland left his job and announced that the DePaul series would be renewed. Meyer, for his part, showed up at Gert Ireland's funeral and then at George's, and he referred to George as a good friend on at least a couple of occasions. He told writers that Ireland called him in 1980 to commiserate after DePaul lost a big tournament game to UCLA:

"How do you feel?" he asked.

"Lousy, I said. "We lost the game."

"Well, I'll trade places with you," he said.

"What do you mean?"

"I just had a heart bypass."

"No, thanks, George, I don't want to trade."

Les Hunter once complained, "He was constantly talking about his own health. He'd talk more about his health to me than basketball."

Jerry Harkness thought Ireland was "different." He liked being controversial and he liked to be right. In Harkness's mind, it all went hand in hand with whatever pioneering Ireland may have been up to. "You had to be different, you had to be a guy like that, in order to break the rules," Harkness said. "You couldn't just be the norm, like a Ray Meyer, stay within the unwritten rules and just get two black ballplayers. Oh no, he was not like that! He's standing for no rules, no nothing. He had to find out what he could do, so it took him a while, but then he just got black ballplayers on top of black ballplayers. I think he was that type: Don't tell me what to do! And if they would get on him or something, that would make it even worse. They're not gonna get on me!"

"He didn't get along well with people," Harkness said. "But he was really good to me."

Art McZier said, "I don't think there were too many people that George liked. Period. But he used to tell people I was his favorite."

Egan said, "In the end, I have to say, he treated me very well."

"He really is a mystery man," Ron Miller said. "I got along fine with him."

———————————

In 1970 a new president took over at Loyola. He was Father Raymond
Baumhart, and he would remain in the post 23 years, the longest-
tenured president in the school's history. A 25-story dorm on prime
downtown Chicago real estate is named for him. He had joined the
faculty in 1962, having served in the Navy and received degrees from
Northwestern, Loyola, and a doctorate from Harvard. His specialty
was business ethics. He had played basketball in high school and enjoyed Loyola's championship run. He noticed how applications shot
up as a result of the publicity and he urged the school to capitalize
on it (and to hire Jerry Harkness as an admissions recruiter). But he
"didn't much admire" Ireland, he told me, and they didn't get along.

Ireland announced his resignation in the middle of the 1974–75
season. He revealed to the press that he had been hospitalized just before the season began and that he was suffering from cardiovascular
disease complicated by diabetes. According to the *Tribune* he decided
to hang it up after a 97–59 rout of Iowa Wesleyan. A "source close to
the university" said that Ireland looked bad after the game and had
griped at a referee's call when his team was ahead by 30 points. Ireland
was quoted saying that the team doctor then asked him if he wanted
to go on living. "Nobody had to tell me what to do," he said. "I saw
the handwriting on the wall."

In fact he had been pushed. Baumhart recalled that the health
issue was one of the ways he persuaded Ireland to step aside. Mike
Ireland told me, "I don't think he was ever ready to stop. I think he
would have gone to 105 if he could have." Baumhart, grateful for
Ireland's glory days, allowed him to remain as athletic director for a
couple of years.

Another issue Baumhart had in mind was Ireland's apparent
inability to deal with a new generation of black players. Baumhart
remembered talking about this with an informal committee of interested advisers, including Vic Rouse. In a remarkably short stretch
of time, the world had changed from *Guess Who's Coming to Dinner*
(1967) to *Superfly* (1972). Ireland's tough love and paternalism had

become square. And the market imbalance he had exploited in the early 60s was rapidly being corrected. According to a study published in the *Journal of Sport Behavior*, using a sample that included about 90 percent of major or Division I schools, between 1962 and 1975 the percentage of basketball teams with black players climbed from 45.2 to 92.4 percent; on integrated teams, the average number of blacks per team increased from 2.2 to 4.5; black players as a percentage of the total increased from 10.1 to 34.3 percent. Loyola, a rare opportunity for black players in 1960, was back where it had started—a little commuter school by the El tracks with a small, decrepit gym and an administration that was skeptical about special treatment for athletes. If Ireland was a social pioneer, he quickly became a victim of his own leadership. To make matters worse, Jerry Harkness recalled, somewhere along the way Ireland had alienated Walter November and the New York pipeline went dry.

All of this might have been forgiven had Ireland continued to win, but he didn't. He had a few good seasons after 1963. In '64 Loyola was 22–6 and went to the NCAA tournament again; they returned in 1966 (22–3) and 1968 (16–9). But after that they had only one winning season in six. Ireland left the job with a record of 321–255. Before Harkness came, he was 107–106. After Rouse, Hunter, Miller, and Egan left, he was 125–129.

He did not go quietly. Baumhart said he received "anonymous" letters that he was sure came from Ireland; they were addressed to Father "Bum-heart." According to others, Ireland undermined the efforts of his replacement, his former player and longtime assistant, Jerry Lyne.

Baumhart recalled a tableau that summed up his memory of Ireland. "There was a reunion in the gym, at a basketball game, like 20 years after we won the championship, and a number of the ballplayers from the national championship were there. And at five minutes before halftime, there was a loudspeaker announcement: will those players who are here from the 1963 national champions please gather

at the south end of the gym? So they could come out and be introduced together. They gathered, and George stood by himself....It was
so unmistakable. The players are chatting, glad to see one another
again, and there's George 30 feet away."

———————

Of course George Ireland's family has different memories. His
daughter Judy remembered a guy who was always buying ice cream
and bringing strays home for dinner; a fun-loving prankster who
kept candy in his pocket and chased his kids around the house with
shaving cream on his face. His grandson Brian Van Dyck remembered
a Pied Piper-type who built a basketball court in the backyard for the
neighborhood kids. Brian showed me the spot where his grandfather
would stand, about 35 feet out, hitting his old two-handed set shot
six or seven times in a row.

Ireland's son Mike remembered running into Bob Knight at the
airport in Salt Lake City. "I put my hand out and I said, 'Mike Ireland.' He said, 'How's your dad?' I mean just that quick, how's your
dad? This was back when we had phone booths in airports, and I said
'You got a minute?' So I went over and I dialed home and my dad
answered and I said, 'Here, somebody wants to talk with you.' Bobby
got on and they talked for about 10 or 12 minutes, then Bobby had
to go catch his airplane. And he said, 'You know, every clinic I give,
I mention your dad's name. When I was a coach at Army, I went to
one of his clinics and I picked up something from him that I use in
every one of my clinics.'"

(Father Baumhart told me, "After Ireland, we had a couple of
coaches, and I remember specifically insisting that as president I
would sit in on the final three fellows that the committee was recom-
mending. And one of the questions I always asked was, 'Who is your
role model?' And when this one guy said Bobby Knight, I said that's
it, I'm not going to approve him.")

Mike Ireland, an avid golfer, said he took his father out once but couldn't get him interested in the game. "I would love to have played golf with him when he was retired, but he had no interest in anything but basketball. When he was living down here in assisted living, I'd go in and he'd have all the papers, and it was always the sports page. All kind of articles that he cut out. I don't know what he did with them, but he was just cut-cut-cut-cut-cut-cut.

"He did get bitter, and some of the friendships dissolved, there's no doubt about it," Mike said.

Was it all ruined for him then? His son sighed heavily. "No, I mean he still liked to talk about it, a lot."

Here's the story that Mike Ireland left me with. He did not remember the opponent, but the circumstances match a 1954 game against Manhattan College.

"One thing I really remember, at the Chicago Stadium, I was on the bench, keeping score. Art Schalk was on the free-throw line, it was right at the end of the game, and Loyola was behind by one point. Art was a very steady ballplayer, he was the leader of the team that year. And he missed both free throws. And my dad got up and he went right out to the free-throw line, put his arm around him, and walked him all the way down the steps to the locker room with his arm around him. Because Art was suicidal at that point. I stood there and I watched that, I went, holy shit.

"So, there were some awful nice things he did."

CHAPTER 28:

Afterward

Babe McCarthy, who some only half-facetiously observed could have been governor of Mississippi if there had been an election in 1963, coached just two more seasons before he had to resign from Mississippi State. They were not good seasons—9–17 in 1963-64, 10–16 the year after that—but his real problem was extramarital. He had presented himself in Starkville as a Christian gentleman. Bobby Shows remembered that he and McCarthy worshipped together when Shows signed to play at Mississippi State, and that when the team was traveling the coach took them to church on Sundays. He didn't push it, Shows said. Most of his players were churchgoers anyway.

A few months after the scandal, McCarthy came back to the First Baptist Church of Starkville to ask for the congregation's forgiveness. Judy Shows, Bobby's sister-in-law, was there that day and was touched by his confession. Dr. Billy T. Nimmons, the associate pastor, remembered it as an extraordinary act of humility and courage. McCarthy had already left town and easily could have kept on going.

He coached at George Washington University for a year and then went to the New Orleans Buccaneers in the nascent ABA, which may have been an environment better suited to his worldly side. Pictures from those days show a paragon of late-60s style—high turtleneck, wide lapels, ankle boots, loud checks. Leland Mitchell, who played for him in New Orleans, remembered a coach who liked to have a drink with the boys and kept a pistol under his pillow. One night, Mitchell recalled, Babe had some fun with a couple of his players by setting off a firecracker and pretending to have shot himself in despair over losing two games in a row. He was the first coach in the ABA to win 200 games, the league's coach of the year in 1969 and 1974. In 1975, at age 51, he died from colon cancer a few hours after being inducted into the Mississippi Sports Hall of Fame.

Leland Mitchell was taken by the St. Louis Hawks in the second round of the 1963 NBA draft, but he didn't play in the NBA. In 1967–68 he played 78 games in the ABA for Babe McCarthy's New Orleans team. After returning to the Starkville area he prospered in real estate and construction. He suffered a spinal cord injury in 2001 and was paralyzed from the neck down.

Red Stroud also played briefly for McCarthy in New Orleans. He later coached high school ball. He died from leukemia in 2008.

Joe Dan Gold stayed at MSU after graduation; he was freshman basketball coach under McCarthy and took over as head coach when McCarthy left. He coached the Bulldogs for five seasons and was actively recruiting black players by his second or third year, he recalled. Having been on the well-known cloak-and-dagger team helped get him through some doors and into some kitchens, but Mississippi State was still a hard sell for black players and he never did succeed in signing any. He coached for a couple years at Paducah Community College in Kentucky, then for a year at Mercer University in Macon, Georgia. His 1973–74 team went 16–8 and nearly earned an invitation to the NIT, but by that time Gold's kids were starting school and he decided to get out of college coaching. He taught and coached in high school for a few years and wound up in school administration. He died in 2011 after a long illness. Jerry Harkness went to his funeral in Benton, Kentucky. Harkness was the man of the hour—a tall, well-dressed, personable black man in an otherwise all-white room. Near the casket was a large print of the famous handshake photo. Gold's widow told me she had dreamed Harkness would be there.

Bobby Shows coached high school basketball and became active in the Missouri Baptist Convention. In 2001 he founded Sports Crusaders, a ministry that runs Christian sports camps in several states. He retired in 2008.

Doug Hutton graduated in 1964 and stayed in Starkville to work as a basketball assistant while he completed a master's degree and postmaster's education credits. He then began a 32-year career as a high school teacher and baseball and basketball coach, including 16 years at his hometown high school in Clinton, Mississippi.

Aubrey Nichols attended law school at Ole Miss and received his degree in 1966. As of September 2012 he was still practicing in Columbus, Mississippi.

Jackie Wofford graduated from Mississippi State in 1965 and went back for a master's degree and a doctorate in education. He has been a high school teacher, coach, and counselor, a college history teacher, and a consultant to the Mississippi department of education. With his wife he operates a funeral home in Starkville.

Jimmy Wise, the student manager, graduated in 1963. He had been recruited as a player and had played a bit in his freshman year, but it quickly became apparent that he wasn't going to see much action. To stay with the team and keep his scholarship he became student manager. Babe McCarthy suited him up for the last game of his senior year, against Ole Miss, but it was a tight game (75–72) and he didn't get in. After a few years as a high school coach and teacher in Pontotoc, Mississippi, he went to work as a salesman and eventually general sales manager for a forest-products company. Retired since 2010, he still lives in Pontotoc, which is about 75 miles from Starkville. He's an active booster of Mississippi State athletics, owner of 8 season tickets for basketball and 14 for football.

Don Posey went to grad school and earned a degree in education but decided that teaching wasn't for him. He went into the insurance business, sold securities, then took a turn into government. He became the administrator of Oktibbeha County in 1996.

Dean Colvard served as president of Mississippi State for six years. In 1966 he was lured back to North Carolina to become the first chancellor of the UNC's new campus at Charlotte. Supporters in Mississippi tried to get him to stay by offering a $10,000 yearly salary supplement and a new Cadillac.

Ross Barnett's term as governor of Mississippi ended in 1964. He tried running again in 1967 but finished fourth in the Democratic primary. He died in 1987 at age 89. His *New York Times* obit quoted him saying, "Generally speaking, I'd do the same things again."

In 1971, Mississippi State signed its first black basketball players, Larry Fry and Jerry Jenkins. When the Bulldogs next reached the NCAA tournament, in 1991, four of their starters were black.

———————————

Ed Jucker lasted only two more years at Cincinnati. He resigned after the 1964–65 season, saying the pressure was too much for him and he wanted to spend time with his family. Later he admitted, "I just dropped out." Carl Bouldin, cocaptain of his 1960–61 team, thought he'd been run out, chased at least partly by the notion that he had lost the 1963 championship by stalling. In 1967 Jucker signed on with the NBA's Cincinnati Royals, who still had Oscar Robertson, but after two seasons there he was replaced by Bob Cousy. In 1972 he took the head coach job at Rollins College, a Division II liberal arts school in Florida—a lower pressure environment that evidently agreed with him. He coached there for five years and twice made the NCAA Division II tournament. He developed prostate cancer and died in 2002 at age 85.

Tay Baker, Jucker's longtime coaching partner, succeeded him as head coach at Cincinnati and led the Bearcats to a Missouri Valley Conference championship in 1965–66. In the NCAA Midwest regional that year, they lost to Texas Western, the "Glory Road" team, by two points. Baker remained as head coach for seven seasons, sat out a year, and then coached another six years at Xavier University, Cincinnati's crosstown rival.

Tom Thacker was drafted by the Cincinnati Royals in 1963 and played three years for them, a year for the Boston Celtics, and then three years in the ABA for the Indiana Pacers. In 1972 he injured his knee, retired from basketball, and returned to the University of Cincinnati for a master's degree. He worked for government programs and nonprofits, sold business forms and chemicals, taught and coached in public schools, and coached and did front-office work for a number of semipro teams. When we spoke in 2011 he was "retired from everything....All I do now is get up in the morning and play golf."

Carl Bouldin played professional baseball after college. A right-handed pitcher, he was signed by the Washington Senators in 1961 and played five seasons in the majors and Triple-A. He appeared in 27 major league games, compiling a record of 3–8. He hurt his arm and retired from baseball in 1965. He has been an investment adviser ever since.

Larry Shingleton majored in finance, earned a master's degree at UC, and made a career in business, eventually owning and running trucking companies in the Cincinnati area.

George Wilson won a gold medal in the 1964 Olympics as a member of the U.S. basketball team, which also included Bill Bradley, Walt Hazzard, and Jeff Mullins, among others. He was drafted by the Cincinnati Royals and played seven years for six different teams in the NBA, averaging 14.1 minutes, 5.4 points, and 5.2 rebounds per game. After basketball he taught in the Cincinnati public schools and worked with young people—but never as a coach or ref, he told me, because he believed that officials had too much influence over the outcome of games. We spoke in his "man cave," the memorabilia-stuffed basement of his home in Fairfield, Ohio, near Cincinnati. He said, "If the officials who refereed the Loyola game are still alive, I want somebody to give them a lie detector test."

Jerry Harkness graduated with a degree in sociology in spring 1963. After nearly flunking out as a freshman, he got the hang of being a student, and academic life became a little easier for him when he started concentrating in his major. He read books like William Foote Whyte's *Street Corner Society: The Social Structure of an Italian Slum*, which he could relate to. And he sought the help of teachers, who were impressed by his effort if not always by his brilliance. An adviser told him to take his time—concentrate on basketball and finish his coursework later—but Harkness took that as an insult; he was determined to graduate with his class.

He was drafted by the Knicks, but he didn't last long. He was too short to play forward in the NBA, and his outside shot wasn't good enough for guard. After playing in five games for a total of 59 minutes, he was cut. He took a job as a route salesman for Quaker Oats. The company transferred him back to Chicago and gave him a territory that included the Loyola neighborhood and villages on the North Shore, the affluent and nearly all-white suburbs north of Chicago. By this time he was married to Judy Carroll and they had a young daughter. They tried to rent an apartment on the North Side, not far from the campus where Harkness had lived for four years, but were turned away by a landlord who didn't want blacks in the building. They wound up living on the South Side.[31]

With four starters returning from their national championship team, Loyola was ranked tops in the country when the 1963–64 season started. But without Harkness the team never really jelled. Ireland groped for a fifth starter, trying Chuck Wood at first and then a couple of sophomores; by the end of the season he had settled on Jim Coleman, a black player from Chicago. The Ramblers lost six games in their regular season, but they were ranked eighth and earned a chance to defend their national title in the NCAA tournament.

Their second game in the tournament was against Michigan, ranked second in the country. Jack Egan remembered it well. In

---

31   That landlord's son, who had accepted Harkness's deposit for the apartment, was Jeremy Lazarus. In 2012 he called Harkness to apologize and invited Harkness to a dinner celebrating his induction as president of the American Medical Association.

practice the week before, Ireland was prepping Ron Miller to guard Michigan's star, Cazzie Russell, a Chicago native who would be named college player of the year in 1966 and would later win an NBA title with the New York Knicks. Though Miller at 6-2 was a better match physically for the 6-5 Russell, Egan thought he could do a better job and eventually persuaded Ireland to let him try. "I was so happy when he said OK, you can guard him. I'm just thinking, oh God. I know I'm gonna foul out but I really want to do a good job on him." Egan pressed Russell even when he didn't have the ball. "A lot of times guards hate that," he said. "You're making him go down the court with you in his face all the time and he doesn't even have the ball. It's troublesome, it's bothering. So that's what I'm doing to him, right from the git-go. And they call a time out, and instead of going to my huddle, I go to his huddle! He says, 'Get the hell out of here, what are you doing?' And so then he's trying to post me up, and I was getting help from the back—the other guys know that they're going to try to throw it over my head and stuff like that. Trying to do that with someone, especially when you're out-sized, I did enjoy that. It was just a fun, fun game."

Egan held Russell to four points in the first half but did eventually foul out. Loyola's shooting was cold and Michigan led by as many as ten at three different points in the game. They led 81–74 with 1:30 left, but in the next minute Loyola put on a 6–1 spurt. With 22 seconds left the score was 82–80.

"Michigan brought the ball up cautiously," wrote Roy Damer of the *Tribune.* "Then Jim Coleman, with a burst of third-effort speed, cut in front of Michigan's Bob Cantrell and batted the ball toward the basket. He dashed in to take possession and scored a layup, apparently tying the score."

But back at the site of the steal, the ref was signaling that Coleman had traveled. That was the end of the Ramblers' 1963–64 season. Ireland didn't complain. Perhaps he remembered the traveling call that hadn't been made on Ron Miller in the championship game a year ago.

After the game, Egan recalled, Cazzie Russell told a Chicago sportswriter that Egan was the dirtiest player he'd ever seen. A couple years later their paths crossed again. "I played in a tournament on the South Side. Cazzie Russell was a hero for the Knicks at the time. This is the park league, championship game, lot of good players. He knows some guys on our team, it was mostly black guys, and he comes over by our bench and someone goes to introduce him to me." Russell said curtly, "We've met."

Could one assume that Egan relished this moment? "Sure!" he exclaimed, laughing gleefully. "Better yet!"

———————

Egan, Hunter, and Harkness played in the North American Basketball League for a couple years, driving up to Michigan on weekends to earn a hundred bucks a game or so with the Twin City Sailors. (The twin cities were Benton Harbor and St. Joseph, Michigan.) Ron Miller joined them a few times, but he was pretty much done with basketball. He took an extra semester to finish his degree and then got a job as a production supervisor at Campbell's soup. He married a white girl from Mundelein College. They met when she asked him to sign a petition against the death penalty. She was JoAnn Ugolini, the daughter of Louis, an Italian carpenter, a union man, one of several people Miller remembered as the nicest guy he ever met. "I said 'This is going to be a problem,' when we started dating, and she said, 'No, come meet my parents.' Louie just shook my hand and said 'I've heard of you, you play basketball,' and that was all. He had one family member who was very upset. He said to Louie, 'We have to talk about this. You can't let her do this, you're going to ruin the family name.' Louie said 'What family name are you talking about? A generation ago we were sleeping with the shit of the sheep in Italy.'"

When Ireland heard about the couple's plans to marry, Miller recalled, the coach pulled him aside and asked, "'Are you sure you want to do this? I don't know if the climate is right.'" Miller said he was sure. "And then when he met her he said to her, 'You got a real winner. You couldn't get any better. I wish you guys all the luck.' That's the last thing he ever said about it."

JoAnn's father was the business agent for the carpenters' local. "He used to try to get more blacks into the union," Miller said. "The guys at the union hall said, 'Louie, you say all of that stuff, but how would you feel if your daughter married one?' And he said, 'My daughter has!'"

Ron and JoAnn lived for a time above Jerry and Judy on the South Side. JoAnn and Judy became friendly and marched together in 1966 when Martin Luther King led his fair-housing campaign in Chicago. "She was the more experienced marcher at that time," Judy recalled. "She could tell me things that you needed to do or not do."

Eventually Ron and JoAnn moved to California. Big American companies were trying to diversify their sales forces and Miller worked for a number of them, including U.S. Steel, Container Corporation of America, and Wells Fargo. He and JoAnn had two kids and adopted two more. One of the adopted kids was black, the son of two Chicago teenagers; the other was the son of a Vietnamese woman and an American serviceman. The couple divorced after about 15 years of marriage. Both remarried, Ron to Patty Jeffries, a white woman he met in a drugstore; they have one adopted mixed-race daughter. Miller wound up starting, running, and ultimately selling a company that processed credit card transactions. He said his partner in the business was an Indian guy who was born in Kenya. Miller lives in the Bay Area, close to JoAnn and many members of his large various family. When there's a new baby in the clan, he asks what color.

Egan went to Loyola law school, as planned. In his last year there, in need of money, he signed a contract to play as a defensive back for the Montreal Alouettes of the Canadian Football League. He spent the bonus money, finished his degree, went up to Montreal with a load of law books, and was back home taking the bar exam within a couple of weeks. He went to work for the Cook County State's Attorney's office, a well-worn training track for Chicago lawyers. To the surprise of no one who knew him, he then became a criminal defense lawyer. He was still practicing as this book went to press.

Vic Rouse, who impressed his teammates as the most serious student among them—a guy who was going somewhere—was by age 28 running his own planning and consulting firm. He earned four graduate degrees, including a doctorate in public administration from USC. He wound up in Washington writing and consulting on issues such as crime and minority business development. He died of a heart attack in 1999, at age 56.

Chuck Wood went back to his high school, St. Catherine's in Racine, Wisconsin, as a teacher (briefly), coach, and guidance counselor. He earned a master's degree in counseling and worked for about 25 years in various administrative jobs at a community technical college in Racine. He retired in 2004 and returned to St. Catherine's as an assistant coach and then athletic director.

John Crnokrak graduated in 1962 and played for a month with the college all-stars who toured as opponents of the Harlem Globetrotters. He was offered a tryout with the St. Louis Hawks of the NBA, but first he tried the American Football League, which had yet to merge with the NFL. He went to the Houston Oilers' training camp and stuck with the team into the exhibition season, then sustained a knee injury that ended his athletic career. After a few years as a high school teacher and coach, he moved into sales and marketing and eventually became president of a Wisconsin company that sold health and safety products. He retired in 2003 and since then has been writing books and consulting as an executive coach and motivational speaker. Though he did not play on Loyola's championship team, he has assumed the role of ringleader, organizing reunions and distributing phone numbers to keep everybody in touch.

Rich Rochelle stuck with the team for his three years of varsity eligibility. When it ended, he still needed a couple semesters of coursework to complete his degree. He finished one of those semesters, but when he tried to enroll for the second, he recalled, he was informed that George Ireland had blocked his enrollment on what Rochelle said was another imaginary disciplinary charge. He went to work as an insurance claims adjuster, got married, and 13 years later, with the prodding of his wife and the help of a sympathetic faculty member, he worked up the gumption to go back to Loyola and finish his degree. He then earned a master's from the University of Illinois and worked for nearly 30 years in the Evanston school system as a teacher, coach, and assistant principal.

Sometime in the late 90s, Rochelle said, George Ireland called after seeing an article about him in one of the local papers. "He said 'I just thought about how if it hadn't been for me and the things I did for you, you wouldn't have been able to do the things that you're doing today.' I said 'Excuse me, Mr. Ireland. I am where I am and I'm doing what I'm doing in spite of you. Had I had a father, you would be a dead man. Because no man should treat another man's child the way you treated me. I do not want you to ever call my phone again. Do not make another contact with this house.' And I hung up the phone." When we spoke, in the spring of 2012, Rochelle was retired and slowly reconnecting with his teammates and the university. He had just attended a Loyola basketball game for first time since 1964.

Les Hunter was drafted by the Detroit Pistons of the NBA, who then traded him to the Baltimore Bullets. He was not tall enough to play center in the NBA. After playing all through college with his back to the basket, he now had to turn around and play forward. He was cut from the Bullets in midseason. He returned to Chicago and finished his degree at Loyola while selling tires for BF Goodrich and playing weekends in Michigan, where he worked on learning the forward position. He had a brief tryout as a tight end with the Chicago Bears, but his football career ended with a broken collarbone. By this time he and his Nashville sweetheart Betty had married and settled in Chicago. When he completed his degree Hunter went to work at the Audy Home, a juvenile detention center on the South Side, as a casework supervisor.

When the American Basketball Association (ABA) formed in 1967, Hunter and Harkness and many other players got a second chance at a professional career. Hunter took some vacation time and went up to Minneapolis to try out for the Minnesota Muskies. That was the start of a six-year career in the ABA, where he became known as "Big Game." In addition to the Muskies, who later became the Miami Floridians, he played for the New York Nets, the Kentucky Colonels, and the Memphis Tams. He twice made the ABA all-star team and over 444 games averaged 12.8 points and 7.1 rebounds.

After basketball he went into the restaurant business, which landed him in Kansas City, Kansas. For about ten years he had a barbecue place there, Hunter's Smokehouse. Later he went into education, teaching disadvantaged youngsters and GED students. As of summer 2012 he and Betty were still living in the Kansas City area.

Jerry Harkness played for a year and a half as a reserve with the Indiana Pacers. He did well at the start of each season, he recalled, but as the games accumulated he felt his body giving out on him. One night in Minnesota he tried to shake and bake and threw his back out. That's when he decided to give it up.

But by then he had earned a place in the record books. On November 13, 1967, the Pacers were playing away against the Dallas Chaparrals. With two seconds left in the game, Charles Beasley of Dallas hit a jump shot from the corner to put his team ahead 118–116. While the Dallas players celebrated their victory, Indiana's Oliver Darden took the ball in. "He just handed it to me in bounds," Harkness recalled. "I took a dribble and pulled it back and let it go. I had no choice. I was just throwing toward the basket. Right before the buzzer, I'm not sure if I even got it off. Heaved it—a hook, to put some force behind it. It banked in. And I started pleading with the refs, because it was so close to the buzzer. I didn't know if they were going to count it." The ABA was only a month old at the time, and players were not yet habituated to its most important innovation, the three-point shot. For a moment Harkness and his teammates thought they'd tied the game. Then they realized they'd won the game. Some sources called the shot a 92-footer and the longest basket ever. (The regulation court is 94 feet long.) Harkness later recalled that Dallas officials measured and it was closer to 88 feet. In any case it was and remains the longest buzzer beater in the history of American professional basketball.[32]

When his playing days were over, Harkness worked as a fund-raiser for the United Way and as a weekend sportscaster and color announcer for Pacers games on WTHR, channel 13, which was then ABC's Indianapolis affiliate. He was on the air for about 12 years. "I was horrible at first, then got to be halfway decent. But then this guy comes in and he was telling me how bad I was, and I got nervous and I got sensitive, and then I wasn't any good. And then they let me go." Harkness became executive director of the Indianapolis chapter of 100 Black Men, a national organization dedicated to the mentoring and development of young blacks. Then he went into the athletic shoe and apparel business, franchising a couple of Athlete's Foot stores in Indianapolis and eventually going out on his own with an independent store in nearby Anderson. As this book went to press he was mostly retired from paying pursuits but still active with 100 Black Men. I was with him one afternoon when he took his basketball team, a busload of third and fourth graders, to the Pacers' arena downtown for an awards ceremony. On a wall display he showed them a bigger-than-life photo of their coach as a younger man.

Jerry and Judy were divorced after 27 years of marriage. He married Sarah Hawkins, a public schoolteacher. Judy did not remarry. She still lives in the Indianapolis area and works as a resource tutor at a Catholic grade school there. Their first daughter, Cynthia, died at age three of asthma. They have two other children who have grown up and done well. Harkness gave Judy a lot of credit for that. She'd been brought up in a good family and knew what to do.

But he was also inclined to see their kids' success as part of a plan, the same unfolding story that brought him to Louisville in 1963. It also brought him to Indianapolis, where he became a minor celebrity

---

32 The exact nature of Harkness's record is clouded by time and by the 1976 merger of the ABA with the NBA. Baron Davis of the Charlotte Hornets is credited with the "NBA record" for an 89-footer made at the end of the third quarter at Milwaukee in February of 2001. There's no photo or video of Harkness's shot so its distance can't be verified. At the very least it's an ABA record and the longest game-ending shot in either league.

and was able to earn enough money so Judy could stay home with the kids. And it got him that TV job, never mind the sour way it ended, and "with God's grace," he said, he sometimes brought the kids down to the studio. His daughter Julie watched intently while he performed in the bright light. His son Jerald was fascinated by the director in the control booth. Julie became a performer herself, a dancer with the Radio City Rockettes and later an actress and a reporter for the celebrity TV show *Made in Hollywood*. Jerald became a producer of documentary films; in 2008 he made *Game of Change* for the NCAA, about Mississippi State's defiant participation in the 1963 tournament. Both of them have families of their own now—four granddaughters who are all doing great too.

None of it would have happened if Harkness hadn't caught on with the Pacers. Which probably wouldn't have happened without the championship—without Hunter's growth spurt, or Rouse's determination, or Egan's indignation over the insult of a renewable scholarship. Harkness wouldn't even have played with those guys if it hadn't been for Walter November and George Ireland.

"It all started by me getting a chance at Loyola," he said.

Which is true as far as it goes. But the story reaches back farther than that—back to Jackie Robinson and Oscar Robertson, and to Holcombe Rucker and John McLendon and James Naismith himself, and to a thousand nameless coaches and players who saw basketball before color and changed the world by playing their game.

ACKNOWLEDGMENTS

I owe my first and humblest thanks to the many players, coaches, and observers who agreed to be interviewed for this book and then graciously endured the rude surprise of my ignorance and pestering. Most of them are named repeatedly in the text, but some are mentioned only in passing or not at all, including Eddie Bowen, Myles Dorch, Frank Hogan, William McKinnis, Joey Meyer, Ernie Morris, Clara Payne, Frank Perez, Butch Purcell, and some I have no doubt neglected. Sincere thanks to all of you for sharing your time and your memories. I hope I've done them justice.

I express the same humble gratitude to the writers and documentarians who covered parts of this story before me, particularly William Doyle, Milton Katz, Scott Ellsworth, Frank Fitzpatrick, Vincent Mallozzi, John C. Thomas, and Paul Attner; filmmakers Jerald Harkness and Robbie Coblentz; newspapermen Richard Dozer, Roy Damer, Dick Forbes, and Bill Jauss; and the elegant pros at *Sports Illustrated*, particularly Walter Bingham, Ray Cave, Ron Fimrite, John Underwood, and Alexander Wolff. I hope I have represented your work accurately and credited it amply.

I'm very grateful to the following for providing research materials, photographs, and miscellaneous assistance: at the Loyola University archives, Ashley Howdeshell, Kathy Young, and Rebecca Hyman; at the Loyola athletic department, Bill Behrns and Pat Schultz; at the Mississippi State library and archives, Rachel Cannady, Christine Fletcher, Ryan Semmes, and Michael Ballard; at the Mississippi State athletic department, Gregg Ellis; at the University of Cincinnati, Kevin Grace and Doug Mosley; at the NCAA, Gary Johnson and Ellen Summers; at the Memphis *Commercial Appeal*, Kyle Veazey; in Nashville, Tyler Bittner; and numerous unnameable librarians and media relations people who generously and patiently helped me without asking what I was up to or what was in it for them.

Thanks to Bob Roth and my colleagues at the *Chicago Reader* for giving to me and countless other writers the most important gift we could receive, the time and space we needed to find our voices. Thanks to Mike Curtis for encouragment at a crucial juncture, to Normand Saucier and Ed Belsheim for the gift that got me started, to David Larabell for helpful advice about how to tell this story, to David Carr and Tony Judge for network-sharing beyond the call of friendship, to Ted Williams for inspiration and encouragement, and to Mary Carolyn Mitchell for inspiration and logistical assistance. For literary advice, commiseration, and moral support, thanks to my comrades Dick Babcock, Jonathan Black, Steve Bogira, John Conroy, Jonathan Eig, Ted Fishman, Katie Hafner, Alex Kotlowitz, and Lee Sandlin.

Thanks to Doug Seibold and the staff at Agate Publishing for taking this project on, handling my text with care and sensitivity, turning it into this handsome book, and bringing it to market. It's been a pleasure working with you.

For technical support, thanks to the makers of Evernote, Page-Four, SoundTap, and Express Scribe.

For lodging, comfort, and companionship on the road, thanks to my brother and sister, Tom and Dana Lenehan; my cousins Dennis and Dan Lenehan and their wonderful wives Alex and Mary; Bob Wachter; Tim Nagler; Craig, Terry, Alicia, and Ryan Buksar; Sarah Harkness; Mary Frederickson and Clint Joiner; Dave Kehr; Toni Schlesinger; and my special friend Karen Koshner.

Finally, thanks to friends and colleagues who read the manuscript, or parts of it, and offered advice and comments: Mark Starr, John Conroy and Steve Bogira (again), Eli Tullis, and especially Mary Williams, my first and best reader for more than 30 years, who has supported me and this book in every sense of the word. To her and our children, Jack and Rose, I express my deepest thanks. I wouldn't have done it without you.

NOTES AND SOURCES

I have tried to cite published sources directly in the text whenever practical. I hope the notes below will cover the situations in which it wasn't so practical. My purpose here is not to annotate every last fact, but to acknowledge important sources and point readers and especially researchers to some that might be difficult to find otherwise. I've probably missed a few chances, for which I apologize in advance. I welcome queries and will do my best to post answers, protests, corrections, etc. on my website, MichaelLenehan.com.

I have not cited publicity sources such as university media guides or press releases. Media guides, which for most schools are readily available online, were an important source for historical schedules, records, scores, and so on. For rosters and records of teams, players, and coaches I also used these websites: basketball-reference.com, ncaa.org, hoopedia.nba.com, fanbase.com, and espn.com, among others.

A lot of my material comes from interviews. Most were conducted in person, some by telephone, and one (former Kansas coach Ted Owens) by email. I usually indicate interview material by saying a person "remembered," "recalled," "told me," or "said" it. I have edited most of the extended interview passages for clarity and flow. In those cases I reviewed the edited text with the subject whenever possible.

I consulted articles, game accounts, and box scores published in the *New York Times* (NYT), *Chicago Tribune* (CT), *Chicago Sun-Times* (CST), *Chicago Daily News* (CDN), *Chicago Defender* (CD), the *Clarion-Ledger* of Jackson, Mississippi (CL), *Jackson Daily News* (JDN), *Cincinnati Enquirer* (CE), *Cincinnati Post* (CP), and the New Orleans *Times-Picayune* (TP). Though I spent a lot of time blinking at microfilm, I inevitably favored newspapers whose online archives reach back beyond the 80s, particularly the *Tribune*, the *Defender*, and the *New York Times*. I probably missed some good stuff as a result.

The game action in the Prelude, Interlude, and Overtime sections is based mostly on an NCAA film that is not generally available. I borrowed an out-of-print DVD version from the Loyola athletic department. It's rather low-fi, chopped up, and poorly synced with play-by-play audio from WCFL's radio broadcast. I may have blown a call or two.

Two of the books I consulted deserve special mention: Chapter 17, on James Meredith and the uprising at Oxford, owes an enormous debt to William Doyle's *An American Insurrection: The Battle of Oxford, Mississippi, 1962* (Doubleday, 2001). This is a detailed, dramatic account that covers the political background, Meredith and his motives, his lawsuit and enrollment, and the armed insurrection that he provoked. It's especially good at creating a chronology, which unfolds at times almost minute by minute, out of myriad sources including eyewitnesses, news reports, and official investigations. I have helped myself to that chronology and to facts and ideas both big and small. I am grateful to Doyle for his reporting and I heartily recommend his book to anyone interested in this subject.

Much of the information on John McLendon (Chapter 9) came from or was confirmed by *Breaking Through: John B. McLendon, Basketball Legend and Civil Rights Pioneer* by Milton S. Katz (University of Arkansas Press, 2007), a rich and very readable biography of a fascinating character.

ENDNOTES

Chapter 1

Page 23: Loyola founding and history: *Born in Chicago: A History of Chicago's Jesuit University* by Ellen Skerrett, Loyola Press, 2008.

Page 24: Harlem Globetrotters: *Spinning the Globe: The Rise, Fall, and Return to Greatness of the Harlem Globetrotters* by Ben Green, Amistad/Harper Collins, 2005.

Page 24: Lenny Sachs: CT obituary, October 28, 1942; "Lenny Sachs: A Loyola Legend" by John C. Thomas, ramblermania.com/sachs.htm, retrieved November 2012; conversion to Catholicism, Loyola University Alumni Association of Chicago Year Book and Directory, 1943 Edition.

Page 25: Wooden-Ireland job offer: Mike Ireland, George's son, never heard this story. It comes from a disembodied magazine clip whose origin I am unable to trace. It is marked with no publication name and no date (the bane of researchers everywhere). The byline is Tony Kahn.

Page 25: Ireland wouldn't want Notre Dame job: "The King of the Hill Is No Patsy" by John Underwood, *Sports Illustrated*, March 9, 1964.

Page 26: *A Hard Road to Glory: Basketball: The African American Athlete in Basketball* by Arthur R. Ashe, Jr. with the assistance of Kip Branch, Ocania Chalk, and Francis Harris, Amistad, 1993. Ashe wrote a three-volume history on African-American athletes which was later reorganized into separate volumes on basketball, baseball, boxing, football, and track and field. The basketball volume consists of a few general essays and many lists, records, rosters, etc. For a long perspective on blacks' participation in basketball, see also *Elevating the Game: Black Men and Basketball* by Nelson George, Harper Collins, 1992. A valuable film about basketball at historically black schools is *Black Magic*, directed and produced by Dan Klores, ESPN Films in association with Shoot the Moon Productions, 2008.

Page 27: *Chicago Defender* stories on discrimination against black athletes: November 9, November 16, December 14, 1946; January 4, 1947.

Page 29: McZier's shot: CT February 16, 1958.

Chapter 2

Page 31: The Mississippi State part of this story has been the subject of several valuable works, including:

— "The 1963 Mississippi State University Basketball Controversy and the Repeal of the Unwritten Law: 'Something more than the game will be lost'" by Russell J. Henderson, *Journal of Southern History*, volume 63, number 4, November 1997. This is a well-annotated scholarly treatment, especially valuable for the social and political background.

— "The Defiant Ones" by Paul Attner, *The Sporting News 1995-96 College Basketball Yearbook*.

— "Ghosts of Mississippi" by Alexander Wolff, *Sports Illustrated*, March 10, 2003.

— *Game of Change*, a documentary film produced by the NCAA in association with Pathway Productions, 2008. Produced and directed by Jerald Harkness.

— *One Night in March*, a documentary film produced by Broadcast Media Group of Starkville, Mississippi, 2002. Producer Robbie C. Coblentz, coproducer Paul Jones.

— *Champions for Change: How the Mississippi State Bulldogs and Their Bold Coach Defied Segregation* by Kyle Veazey, History Press, 2012. Unavailable to me as I wrote, unfortunately, but an informative account by an accomplished reporter of the Babe McCarthy years at Mississippi State.

Page 31: Babe McCarthy: "Bouquets for Babe and His Bailey" by Dudley Doust, *Sports Illustrated*, February 23, 1959. Some info can also be found in Mississippi State's basketball media guide for 2010-11, which offers a narrative history of the program in addition to the usual stats and records. It was still available online as this book went to press.

Page 34: Evansville incident: Memphis *Commercial Appeal*, December 30, 1956; JDN December 29-31.

Page 34: "... the rule is as irrepealable as the law of gravitation": JDN January 1, 1957.

Chapter 3

Page 35: Oscar Robertson's ghostwritten autobiography is *The Big O: My Life, My Times, My Game*, originally published by Rodale Press in 2003, later republished by the University of Nebraska Press (which deserves thanks for keeping many valuable books about sports and society in print). *The Big O* owes a debt to *"But They Can't Beat Us": Oscar Robertson and the Crispus Attucks Tigers* by Randy Roberts, Sports Publishing Inc./Indiana Historical Society, 1999. An article on the connection between the two is "Unsportsmanlike Conduct" by Evan West, *Indianapolis Monthly*, March 2005.

Chapter 4

Page 41: Some info on St. Elizabeth is found in *Sweet Charlie, Dike, Cazzie, and Bobby Joe: High School Basketball in Illinois* by Taylor Bell, University of Illinois Press, 2004.

Page 42: The story of the University of San Francisco team is told in *The Dandy Dons: Bill Russell, K.C. Jones, Phil Woolpert, and One of College Basketball's Greatest and Most Innovative Teams by* James W. Johnson, University of Nebraska Press, 2009.

Page 43: The Georgia Tech-Pittsburgh game and its aftermath are described in *Benching Jim Crow: The Rise and Fall of the Color Line in Southern College Sports 1890-1980* by Charles H. Martin, University of Illinois Press, 2010. The New Orleans *Times-Picayune*'s game story was published on January 3, 1956.

Page 44: CD story on Loyola vs. Loyola: February 4, 1960.

Page 45: Correspondence between Father Hartmann and his superiors: Loyola University of Chicago Archives and Special Collections. Athletic department records, UA 1984.22. Box 1 Folder 4.

Chapter 5

Page 49: On New York and street basketball:

—*The City Game: Basketball from the Garden to the Playgrounds* by Pete Axthelm, originally published by Harper's Magazine Press in 1970, republished by Penguin in 1982 and Bison/University of Nebraska Press in 1999.

—*Asphalt Gods: An Oral History of the Rucker Tournament* by Vincent M. Mallozzi, Doubleday, 2003.

—*Pickup Artists: Street Basketball in America* by Lars Anderson and Chad Millman, Verso, 1998.

Page 52: I found very little in print about Mike Tynberg and even less about Walter November. Some sources spell the former name "Tyneberg." My spelling follows the most contemporary sources I could find, namely Howard Garfinkel's memory and an early Dick Schaap story in *Sports Illustrated*: "Basketball's Underground Railroad," February 4, 1957.

Page 58: The basketball scandals were well-covered in the *New York Times*. Two valuable books are *The Game They Played* by Stanley Cohen, Farrar, Straus and Giroux, 1977, and *Foul! The Connie Hawkins Story* by David Wolf, Holt, Rinehart and Winston, 1972. Wolf's book grew out of a *Life* magazine article (May 16, 1969) that's credited with helping Hawkins win his lawsuit against the NBA.

Chapter 6

Page 62: "McCarthy will resign...we'll march on the Capitol": "Bouquets for Babe and His Bailey" by Dudley Doust, *Sports Illustrated*, February 23, 1959.

Page 62: McCarthy's contract, Ole Miss game, rejection of NCAA bid: CL March 1, 1959.

Page 63: The documentary referred to here is *One Night in March* (see notes for Chapter 2 above).

Chapter 7

Page 66: On Ernie Carroll: "Kup's Column," CST September 15, 1988; "Minoso's mind cooks up days with a pal," by Dave Hoekstra, CST September 28, 1990.

Chapter 8

Page 71: *Cincinnati Power Basketball* by Ed Jucker, Prentice-Hall, 1962.

Page 72: "The Coach of Every Year" by Walter Bingham, *Sports Illustrated*, February 11, 1963.
Page 74: "We were completely ready....Two guys named Joe did it." CE December 18, 1960.
Page 75: After the Bradley game: *Bearcats! The Story of Basketball at the University of Cincinnati* by Kevin Grace, Greg Hand, et al, Harmony House Publishers, 1998.
Page 77: "Jucker Lauds Tom Thacker," CE February 1, 1961; a few days later: CE February 7, 1961.
Page 78: "[I]f Ed Jucker isn't named coach of the year, there is no justice": CP March 6, 1961.

Chapter 9
Page 80: John McLendon: Besides the Milton Katz biography cited above, I consulted an interview with McLendon published in *Untold Glory: African Americans in Pursuit of Freedom, Opportunity, and Achievement* by Alan Govenar, Harlem Moon/Broadway Books, 2007, and *Learning to Win: Sports, Education, and Social Change in Twentieth-Century North Carolina* by Pamela Grundy, University of North Carolina Press, 2001.
Page 81: *Fast Break Basketball: Fundamentals and Fine Points* by John B. McLendon, Jr., Parker Publishing, 1965.
Page 87: "Jim Crow Loses: The Secret Game" by Scott Ellsworth, *New York Times Magazine*, March 31, 1996. Ellsworth told the story behind the story in "The Secret Game: Defying the Color Line," *Duke Magazine*, September-October 1996. My account also includes details from Katz and the Govenar interview cited above.
Page 89: *The History of the National Basketball Tournaments for Black High Schools*, doctoral dissertation by Charles H. Thompson, Louisiana State University, 1980.

Chapter 10
Page 96: "Johnny Egan Remembers" by Bill Finger, *Chicago Reader*, March 23, 1979.
Page 98: Blockbusting: A summary article by Arnold R. Hirsch is published in *The Encyclopedia of Chicago* edited by James R. Grossman, Ann Durkin Keating, and Janice L. Reiff, University of Chicago Press, 2004. *Family Properties: Race, Real Estate, and the Exploitation of Black Urban America* by Beryl Satter, Metropolitan Books, 2009, is a detailed account by a Rutgers historian whose father, an attorney, represented exploited black families in Chicago.
Page 109: Proposal for freshman-varsity game: Loyola University of Chicago Archives and Special Collections. Athletic department records, UA 1984.22. Box 1 Folder 5.

Chapter 11
Page 112: "OSU eats little schools...": photo on p. 69 of *Bearcats!* See notes under Chapter 8 above.
Page 113: "That team is truly great" and more on 1961 NCAA regionals: "Ohio State All the Way" by Ray Cave, *Sports Illustrated*, March 27, 1961. On the final: Cave's "A Real Barn Burner in Kansas City," April 3, 1961.
Page 113: Governor's proclamation: CE March 28, 1961.
Page 114: "If we can hang in there in the first half, stay even with them, we'll win it": CE March 26, 1961.

Chapter 12
Page 119: Barnett and McCarthy on participating in 1961 tournament: JDN March 1, 1961.
Page 120: Lambert, Colvard, and McCarthy on participating in 1962 tournament: JDN March 1, 1962.

Chapter 13
No notes

Chapter 14
Page 142: 1962 tournament: "Cincinnati Is No. 1, No. 1, No. 1!" by Ray Cave, *Sports Illustrated*, April 2, 1962.

Chapter 15

Page 145: Sources differ slightly on Ireland's high school record. These numbers come from the story "Loyola Names George Ireland Basket Coach," CT March 22, 1951.
Page 145: Ireland's coaching style: *Loyola News*, October 9, 1958.
Page 149: New Orleans trip: CDN, CST, CT January 24, 1962.
Page 151: Ireland is in Africa: NYT September 20, 2001.

Chapter 16

Page 158: Jucker's complaint: CE March 5 and 6, 1962.
Page 159: "People said we were lucky...": "A Grudge Match for the National Title" by Ray Cave, *Sports Illustrated*, March 26, 1962.

Chapter 17

Page 161: I've already mentioned William Doyle's *An American Insurrection*. Other sources I consulted for this chapter include:
—*Mississippi: The Closed Society* by James W. Silver, Harcourt, Brace & World, 1966.
—*Three Years in Mississippi* by James Meredith, Indiana University Press, 1966.
—*Robert Kennedy and His Times* by Arthur M. Schlesinger, Jr., Houghton Mifflin, 1978.
—*The Camera Never Blinks: Adventures of a TV Journalist* by Dan Rather with Mickey Herskowitz, William Morrow, 1977.
—"The Mississippi Tragedy—What It All Means," *U.S. News & World Report*, October 15, 1962.
—"The States: Though the Heavens Fall," *Time*, October 12, 1962.
—"What Next in Mississippi?" by Robert Massie, *Saturday Evening Post*, November 11, 1962.
—NYT (many articles) and CT, October 1, 1962.
Page 163: Barnett in restaurant: "A Barnett Disturbance in Connecticut Recalled," NYT October 1, 1962.
Page 163: Barnett privately admitted that his legal theory of states' rights was bogus: *Saturday Evening Post*, see above.
Page 164: Transcripts of phone conversations between Barnett and the Kennedys are available online at americanradioworks.publicradio.org/features/prestapes/a1.html. Transcripts and audio recordings are available from the John F. Kennedy Presidential Library and Museum at microsites.jfklibrary.org/olemiss/confrontation.

Chapter 18

Page 182: First team to play five blacks: 2011-12 NCAA Men's Basketball Records, Playing Rules-History, Division I Basketball Firsts, retrieved July 2012 at fs.ncaa.org/Docs/stats/m_basketball_RB/2012/Rules.pdf; "Loyola recalls barrier-breaking moment long forgotten, ignored," by Lew Freedman, *Basketball Times*, February 2008, retrieved July 2012 at sportswriters.net/usbwa/awards/writing/2008/column.html.
Page 182: Biggest crowd ever: CT January 28, 1963.

Chapter 19

Page 186: Pablo Robertson's obit: *New York Amsterdam News*, June 30, 1990.
Page 190: "No nigger will ever set foot on this campus." *Cougars of Any Color: The Integration of University of Houston Athletics, 1964-1968* by Katherine E. Lopez, McFarland & Company, 2008.

Chapter 20

Page 195: Wade Walker says Mississippi State will not go to 1963 NCAA: "Scorecard," *Sports Illustrated*, February 18, 1963.
Page 195: Colvard's memoir: *Mixed Emotions: As Racial Barriers Fell—A University President Remembers* by Dean W. Colvard, Interstate Printers and Publishers, 1985. Also useful was a biography, *Dean W. Colvard: Quiet Leader* by Marion A. Ellis, University of North Carolina at Charlotte, 2004.

Page 198: Messages to Dean Colvard: Dean W. Colvard Papers (A79-39), University Archives, Mississippi State University Libraries.

Chapter 21
Page 210: "Nobody can beat a team like that": CT March 12, 1963.

Chapter 22
Page 211: Dean Colvard's account of the MSU escape appears in his memoir *Mixed Emotions*. See notes under Chapter 20 above.
Page 214: They were hearing rumors: "Ghosts of Mississippi" by Alexander Wolff, see notes under Chapter 2 above.

Chapter 23
Page 221: Doug Hutton on Miller's dunk: *Game of Change*, see notes for Chapter 2 above.

Chapter 24
Page 227: John Underwood provided *Sports Illustrated*'s usual exemplary coverage of the 1963 tournament: "Cincy Goes for a Third," March 11; "The Gunners Are After Cincy," March 25; "The Ramblers Wreck Cincy," April 1.
Page 229: "I wanted to run it up": *Sports Illustrated* again, "It Was More Than Just a Game" by Ron Fimrite, a lookback piece published November 18, 1987.

Chapter 25
Page 240: Anthony Smedley's heroics: CT March 24, 1963; coach's smartest move, CDN March 25.

Chapter 26
Page 245: Don Haskins autobiography: *Glory Road: My Story of the 1966 NCAA Basketball Championship and How One Team Triumphed Against the Odds and Changed America Forever* by Coach Don Haskins with Dan Wetzel, Hyperion, 2006. The Texas Western-Kentucky championship is also at the center of *And the Walls Came Tumbling Down: Kentucky, Texas Western, and the Game That Changed American Sports* by Frank Fitzpatrick, Simon & Schuster, 1999, published in paperback by Bison/University of Nebraska Press, 2000. Fitzpatrick, a longtime sportswriter, puts the famous game in a broader context of integration and social change.
Page 249: "Dillard Made Vanderbilt History" by Bill Traughber, Commodore History Corner, vucommodores.collegesports.com/sports/historycorner/spec-rel/122910aad.html, retrieved July 2012.

Chapter 27
Page 254: "What could be a more appropriate place..." CDN March 29, 1963.
Page 259: Ireland-Meyer conversation: *How March Became Madness: How the NCAA Tournament Became the Greatest Sporting Event in America* by Eddie Einhorn with Ron Rapoport, Triumph Books, 2005; also CT September 15, 2001.
Page 260: Ireland's resignation: CT January 21, 1975.
Page 261: *Racial Participation and Integration in Intercollegiate Basketball, 1958-1980* by Norman R. Yetman, Forrest J. Berghorn, and Floyd R Thomas, Jr., *Journal of Sport Behavior*, 5:1, March 1982.

Chapter 28
Page 268: Colvard offered a Cadillac: *Quiet Leader* by Marion Ellis, see notes for Chapter 20 above.
Page 268: MSU's first black recruits: *Across the Line: Profiles in Basketball Courage: Tales of the First Black Players in the ACC and the SEC* by Barry Jacobs, Lyons Press, 2008.

Page 268: Jucker after Cincinnati: "Ed Jucker Is Alive and Well and Winning in NCAA Division II" by Terry Dunham, *Cincinnati* magazine, April 1976.

Page 276: Harkness's long shot: nba.com/inside_stuff/at_the_buzzer_highlights.html; spursreport.com/forums/spurs-nba-fan-feedback/64426-tracking-longest-shot-nba-aba-history.html; both retrieved October 2012.

INDEX

——

*Notes: n = page reference is in footnote; pages A
—H are in the photo insert.*

Abernathy, Bill, *D*
Adams, John, 208
Alcindor, Lew (Kareem Abdul-Jabbar), 39,
    51, 250
Alumni Gym (Loyola), 25, 102, 182, 188,
    205, 208
American Basketball Association
    (ABA), 59, 265, 266, 269, 275, 276,
    277n
American Basketball League, 59
Anderton, Billy, *B*
Archibald, Nate ("Tiny"), 186
Army, U.S., 162, 165, 170-172
Axthelm, Pete, 49, 50, 176, 177, 177n

Baker, Tay, 113, 115, 159, 230, 268, *D*
Bards Room, Comiskey Park, 66
Barnett, Ross, 119, 121, 163-166, 168-
    170, 196, 197, 202, 268, *A*
Barnett, Ross, Jr., 171
Baumhart, Raymond, S.J., 260-262
Baylor, Elgin, 35, 39, 85
Beasley, Charles, 276
Berkshire, Jack, 121
Big Ten Conference, 38, 41, 100, 102,
    121, 140, 147, 182, 208, 223
Bilbo, Theodore G., 197n
Bird, Larry, 231
Birdsong, T.B., 170
Birmingham, Alabama, 172, 211
Blackburn, Tom, 105
Blasingame, Don, 32
blockbusting, 98
Bluitt, Ben, 26, 27
Board of Trustees of the Institutions
    of Higher Education of the State of
    Mississippi, 196, 197, 200-202, 213, 214

Bock, Charles, 37
Bonham, Ron, 20, 125, 126, 137, 140,
    142, 234, 235, *D*
Bonner, Will, 139
Bosley, Floyd, 108, 135, 146-148
Boston Celtics, 53, 63, 112, 269
Bouldin, Carl, 74, 76, 77, 113, 114, 137, 268,
    269
Bowen, Eddie, 177
Bowling Green State University (Ohio), 57,
    188, 189, 208, 222
Bowman, Nate, 206
Boyd, Edward, 88
Boynton v. Virginia, 148
Boys High School (New York), 57, 223
Bradley, Bill, 51, 269
Bradley University, 74-78, 141, 142, 159
Brinker, Stan, *B*
Brooklyn College, 86
Brown v Board of Education, 43n, 161
Brown, Gene, 42n
Brown, Larry, 228
Brown, Roger, 52, 53
Brownlee, Les, 28
Bryant, Kobe, 52n
Bubas, Vic, 227
Buckwalter, Morris ("Bucky"), 243, 244
Bunche, Ralph, 26
Burgess, Jack, 87n, 88
Burghardt, William, 81
Burwell, Bill, 223
Butts, Leon, 5, 43n
"Bye Bye Blackbird," 152

Calhoun, Jim, *D*
California Basketball Association, 42n
California, University of, at Berkeley (Cal),
    39
Cameron, Ben F., 163

Carlos, John, 249
Carnesecca, Lou, 258
Carroll, Ernie, 66
Carroll, Judy, 66, 99, 102, 270
Carver High School (Chicago), 239, 240, 241
Chamberlain, Wilt, 51, 61, 249
Chaney, Don, 191
Chicago Catholic League, 45, 99, 146, 187
Chicago Daily News, 28, 153, 234
Chicago Defender, 26, 27, 42, 44, 187, 284
Chicago Public League, 41
Chicago Stadium, 29, 41, 67, 102, 140, 180, 182, 263
Chmielewski, Bill, 155
Christopher Columbus High School (New York), 104
CIAA: Colored (now Central) Intercollegiate Athletic Association, 82, 85, 86
Cincinnati Gardens, 73, 75, 141
Cincinnati Power Basketball by Ed Jucker, 71, 73
Cincinnati Royals, 39, 137, 187, 268, 269
Cincinnati, University of, 35-40, 175, 182, 183, 189, 190, 205, 206, 227, 268
    1960-61 season, 71-78
    1961 NCAA tournament, 111-116
    1961-62 season, 137, 140-143
    1962 NCAA tournament, 157-160
    1963 NCAA tournament, 17-20, 123-128, 233-235, 241-244, 246
    number of black starters, 14, 40, 76, 140
City College of New York (CCNY), 49, 50, 58, 186
Clifton School (Nashville), 90
Clifton, Nat "Sweetwater," 149
Coleman, Jim, 270, 271
Columbia University, 58, 171, 251
Colvard, Dean W., 120, 121, 194-199, 202, 211-213, 268
Combes, Harry, 224
Comiskey, Charles, 66
Connaughton, Dan, 187, F
Connecticut, University of, 58
Cousy, Bob, 268
Crawford, Freddie, 68
Crispus Attucks High School (Indianapolis), 36, 37
Crnokrak, John, 135, 136, 256, 257, 274
Cullen, Hugh Roy, 189

Davis, Harold, 245
Davis. W.S., 90
Dayton, University of, 75, 77, 105-106, 141, 155-156
DeBusschere, Dave, 109
decoy team (Mississippi State), 212
Denver, University of, 33
DePaul University, 25, 74, 101, 253, 258

Detroit, University of, 26, 109, 148
DeWitt Clinton High School (New York), 55-57, 59, 65, 176, 177, 186, 223
Dierking, Connie, 76
Dierking, Fred, 76, 137, D
Dillard, Godfrey, 248, 249, 251
DiSalle, Michael, 113, 116
"district at large," NAIA, 83
Doyle, William, 162, 164, 165, 170-172, 284
Dozer, Richard, 29, 43, 147, 148, 178, 189
Drexel, Katharine, 149n
Drexler, Clyde, 191
Duke University, 20, 86-88, 100, 123, 175, 227-230, 243, 244
dunk, dunk rule, 249, 250
Durant, Kevin, 52n
DuSable High School (Chicago), 24

Egan, Jack (John, Johnny), 17, 107, 145, 146, 154, 156, 177-182, 185, 186, 188, 189, 201, 206-209, 218, 221, 224-226, 228, 261, 270-274, 278, F, H
    New Orleans trip, 152, 153
    1963 NCAA final, 20, 123-126, 234, 235
    relationship with Harkness, 102, 103
    relationship with Ireland, 253-255, 259
    youth, high school, recruitment, 96-102
Eisenhower, Dwight D., 162, 163
Ellsworth, Scott, 86-88
Elsasser, Larry, D
Entertainers Basketball Classic, 52n
Erving, Julius, 51
Evanston Township High School, 28
Evansville, University of, 33
Evers, Medgar, 162

fast break, 81, 91, 145, 210
Fast Break Basketball: Fundamentals and Fine Points by John B. McLendon, 81, 145, 229
Fette, Jack, 141
Five-Star basketball camps, 53
four corners, see stall, stalling
Frederick Douglass Junior High School (New York), 50
Freedom Hall (Louisville), 18, 157, 159, 227, 254
Freedom Riders, 149
freshman rule, NCAA, 28
Fry, Larry, 268

Gabcik, John, F
Gammel, J.D., B
Gant, Charlie, 41
Garfinkel, Howard, 52-54, 58, 105
Garrett, Bill, 38n
Gavin, Mike, 146, 148, 154-156, 175
Georgia Tech (Georgia Institute of Technology), 43, 202, 203
Glory Road (film), 246

Gold, Joe Dan, 117, 121, 193, 219, 222, 266, B, E
Gregory, Paul, 31
Grier, Bobby, 43n
Guilhard, Paul, 172
Gunter, Ray, 172
Gupton, William, 89

Haggerty, Tom, 24, 26-28
Hall of Fame, see Naismith Memorial Basketball Hall of Fame
Hampton Institute, 82, 83, 89
Hanson, Bob, 180
Harkness, Cynthia, 277
Harkness, Jerald, 278
Harkness, Jerry, 47, 65-69, 95, 96, 99, 107, 132-134, 145-148, 154, 156, 175-177, 188, 190, 205-208, 228, 231, 260, 261, 266, 270, 272, 275, 276-278, C, F
    against Mississippi State, 219-221
    New Orleans trip, 149-151, 153
    1963 NCAA final, 17-20, 123-127, 233-235, 239
    records and statistics, 109, 153, 148, 180, 207, 223, 276, 277
    relationship with Egan, 102, 103
    relationship with Ireland, 69, 253, 259
    youth, high school, recruitment, 54-60
Harkness, Julie, 278
Harkness, Sarah (Hawkins), 277
Harlem Globetrotters, 24, 59, 66, 178, 186
Hartke, Vance, 34
Hartmann, Cletus, S.J., 44-47, 254
Haskins, Don, 245, 246
Hatton, Vern, 29
Havlicek, John, 112, 114, 115, 121, 147, 148
Hawkins, Connie, 52, 53, 57, 59, 100
Hayes, Elvin, 191
Hazzard, Walt, 142, 269
Heidotting, Dale, D
Helms, Jesse, 162
Hemphill, Howard, B
Hester, Walter, 199
Heyman, Art, 227-229
Hickey, Ed, 258
Hicks, Art, 41, 58
High School Basketball Illustrated, 53
Hilbun, Ben, 33, 34, 62, 120
Hill, Bobby Joe, 245, 246
Hogan, Frank, 29, 106, 109
Hogue, Paul, 76, 77, 114, 115, 137, 140, 142, 158, 159, D
Holman, Nat, 49, 58
Holmes, Richard, 223
Hoosiers (film), 37
Houston, University of, 40, 100, 101, 189-191, 193
Howell, Bailey, 32, 61-63, 117, 121, 220

Hunter, Harold, 82
Hunter, Les (Leslie), 18, 106, 131, 134, 135, 145, 146, 154-156, 176-180, 183, 185, 188-190, 206-208, 218, 222, 223, 228, 229, 247, 248, 272, 275, 276, 278, F
    New Orleans trip, 152, 153
    1963 NCAA final, 123, 125-127, 228-230, 233, 235
    relationship with Ireland, 135, 136, 230, 255, 257-259
    youth, high school, recruitment, 89-93
Hutton, Doug, 121, 210, 219, 221, 267, B

Iba, Hank, 245, 246
Iba, Moe, 245
Idaho, College of, 36
Illinois, University of, 100, 140, 182, 183, 208, 223, 224, 228, 275
Indiana High School Athletic Association (IHSAA), 36
Indiana Pacers, 51, 269, 276-278
Indiana University, 37-38, 179
injunction against Mississippi State, 203, 211, 212, 214
Inniss, Warren, 27
Iowa, University of, 17, 59, 81, 100, 101
Iowa Wesleyan College, 260
Ireland, George, 17, 18, 23-29, 41-45, 95, 106, 123, 134, 146, 147, 149, 153-156, 178, 181, 182, 185, 187-189, 205, 209, 218, 219, 223, 224, 226, 228, 241, 248, 253-263, 270-272, 278, F, H
    college player and high school coach, 24, 25, 145
    hanging in effigy, 23, 188
    New Orleans trips, 43-44, 149-153
    number of black starters, 17, 135, 146, 154-156, 185
    race relations, 132, 149, 150, 254, 257, 259-261, 272, 273
    records, 145, 261
    recruiting, 18, 27, 28, 41-43, 54, 57, 60, 65, 79, 89, 92, 93, 102, 105, 106
    relationship with Egan, 226, 253, 255, 259
    relationship with Harkness, 68, 69, 253, 259
    relationship with Hunter, 135, 136, 257-259
    relationshsip with Rochelle, 151, 255, 256, 274, 275
    style of play, 145, 146, 230, 231
Ireland, Gert (Gertrude), 23, 25, 255, 258
Ireland, Judy (Van Dyck), 23, 262
Ireland, Mike, 25, 218, 228, 257, 258, 260, 263

Jackson Daily News, 34, 119, 120, 193, 194, 200-203, 212, 214
Jackson State University, 171

Jackson, Tony, 53, 58, 59
Jacobs, P.L., 80
Jacobson, Hank, 56
Jamaco Saints, 109
James, LeBron, 53
Jauss, Bill, 153, 207, 234
Jeffries, Patty, 273
Jenkins, Jerry, 268
Jesuits, 17, 23, 24n, 26, 35, 42, 43, 45-47, 67
Johnson, Dot, 213
Johnson, Earl, 187
Johnson, Magic (Earvin), 231
Johnson, Paul, 164, 170
Jones County Junior College (Mississippi),
    33
Jones, K.C., 42, 243
Jordan, John (Johnny), 25, 150
Jordan, Michael, 53
Jucker, Ed, 39, 40, 71-78, 111, 114, 116, 125,
    141-143, 157-160, 220, 229, 230, 244, 268,
    D, E, G
    early career, 71, 72
    number of black starters, 76, 77, 137
Junior Rose Bowl, 33

Kansas State University, 61, 112
Kansas, University of (KU), 35, 79, 89
Katz, Milton S., 80, 83, 85, 87n
Katzenbach, Nicholas, 167, 170
Kennedy, John F., 161, 163, 165-170
Kennedy, Robert, 163-167, 169
Kentucky, University of, 29, 32, 58, 61, 62, 85,
    113, 119, 121, 152n, 157, 158n, 165, 175, 194,
    220, 246, 254
Kerris, Jack, 205
King, Martin Luther, Jr., 99, 100, 249, 273
Kladis, Nick, 26, 231
Knight, Bob (Bobby), 112n, 121, 262
Komives, Butch (Howard), 188
Krause, Moose (Edward), 25
Ku Klux Klan, 36, 87, 165, 170, 172, 229
Kuehl, Fred, F

Lambert, Flavous (Butch), 120
Lapchick, Joe, 258
Lawson, B.W., 203, 211, 212
Lawson, Ronnie, 89, 91
Layne, Floyd, 186
Lazarus, Jeremy, 270n
Lee, Larry, B
Leo High School (Chicago), 187
Lewis, Guy, 101, 102, 191, 258
Little Rock, Arkansas, 162, 163, 165, 171
Lloyd, Earl, 82
Long Island University, 58, 104n
Loyola University Chicago, 54, 92, 93, 102,
    106, 132, 198, 243, 246-248, 258, 260, 261,
    270-272, 278
    admission of athletes, 45-47, 60

basketball through 1959, 23-29, 41-47
history, 23, 67, 260
1961-62 season, 145-156
1962-63 season, 175-183, 187-191, 205-208
1963 NCAA final, 17-20, 123-
    128, 233-235, 239-242, 244
1963 NCAA tournament, 208-210, 214,
    218-224, 227-231
number of black starters, 17, 140, 155, 156,
    185, 231
records and statistics, 26, 109, 205, 207,
    261
student life for black players, 65, 66,
    131-135
style of play, 18, 145, 146, 230, 231, 244
Loyola University of New Orleans, 43, 44,
    148
Lucas, Jerry, 112, 114, 116, 121, 147, 148, 159
Luchsinger, Dutch, 212, 213
Lyceum (University of Mississippi), 167,
    169, 171
Lyne, Jerry, 225, 226, 255, 261, F

Madison Square Garden, 24, 38, 39, 51, 57-
    60, 73, 105, 154
Maguire, James, S.J., 44, 46
Manhattan College, 58, 263
Manzke, Mary, 46
Marmion Military Academy (Illinois), 24,
    25
Marquette Park, 96, 99, 100, 185
Marquette University, 45, 50, 54, 148, 187, 258
Marshall High School (Chicago), 137, 139
Marshall, Thurgood, 162
McCarthy, Babe (James H.), 31-33, 62, 63,
    117-121, 172, 173, 193-196, 209-215, 218-220,
    222, 265-267, B
McCracken, Branch, 37, 38n, 179
McGill, Billy, 159
McGlocklin, Jon, 179
McGuire, Al, 49, 50, 54
McGuire, Dick, 49
McGuire, Frank, 54, 228
McKenna, Dennis, F
McKenna, George, 132-134, 176
McLendon, John B., 79-89, 91, 92, 145, 146,
    229, 250, 278
McZier, Art, 28, 29, 45, 65, 109, 145,
    152n, 254, 255, 259
Meredith, James, 161-169, 171, 196
Meyer, Ray, 25, 74, 101, 253, 258, 259
Miami, University of, 27
Michigan, University of, 38, 251, 270, 271
Michigan State University, 202, 212, 214, 217,
    224, 231
Milan High School (Indiana), 37
Miller, Ron, 95, 107, 108, 145-147, 154-156,
    175-177, 179, 180, 183, 188-190, 208, 221,
    226, 228, 259, 261, 271-273, C, F, H

New Orleans trip, 149-151
1963 NCAA final, 124-127, 233-235, 239
youth, high school, recruitment, 103-106
Mississippi Highway Patrol, 166, 169
Mississippi State University (College), 27, 31-34, 61-63, 117-121, 172, 173, 193-203, 208, 209, 211-215, 217-223, 228, 249, 265-268, 278
Mississippi, University of, at Oxford ("Ole Miss"), 31, 32, 62, 63, 161-165, 171, 172, 196-198, 267
Missouri Valley Conference (MVC), 74, 75, 77, 78, 111, 140-142, 189, 268
Mitchell, Leland, 117-119, 193, 210, 212, 213, 217, 219-222, 265, 266, B, C
Mitts, Billy, 199, 203, 211, 212
Mixed Emotions (Dean Colvard memoir), 195, 196
Mize, Sidney, 163
Molinas, Jack, 58, 59
Monroe, Earl, 51
Montgomery, Sonny, 198
Moore, Ernie, 206, 207
Morse, Art, 182
Mourning, Alonzo, 53
"Mr. Basketball" (Indiana), 36, 137, 179
Mullins, Jeff, 227, 269
Mundelein College, 132, 272

NAACP: National Association for the Advancement of Colored People, 162, 198
NAIA: National Association of Intercollegiate Athletics, 83-85, 91
NAIB: National Association of Intercollegiate Basketball, 83
Naismith Memorial Basketball Hall of Fame, 24, 32, 39, 50, 186
Naismith, James A., 80, 81, 83, 278
Nash, Cotton, 158
National Association of Basketball Coaches (NABC), 39, 157, 243
National Basketball Association (NBA), 51, 58, 59, 82, 149n, 277n
National Guard, 170, 171
National Guard, Mississippi, 166
National High School Basketball Tournament (National Negro Tournament), 41, 79, 83, 89
NCAA
   championships, 18, 35, 50, 85, 239, 241, 246, 278
   integration of, 82
   records, 18, 32, 182, 209
   rules, 38n, 45, 74, 118, 250
   tournament, 17, 24, 42n, 58, 61, 62, 73, 77, 79n, 82, 109, 112, 119-121, 142, 154, 157, 173, 183, 189, 193-196, 198, 199, 201, 202, 208, 209, 211, 214, 215, 227-231, 243, 247, 258, 261, 268, 270

televising of, 231, 239
Nevada, University of, 27
New York Knicks, 50-51, 68, 189, 270-272
New York University (NYU), 57-60, 105
Newell, Pete, 39, 244
Newsome, Manny, 147
Nichols, Aubrey, 213, 217, 218, 220, 267, B
Nimmons, Billy T., Dr., 265
NIT (National Invitational Tournament, National Intercollegiate Invitation Tournament), 24, 26, 27, 58, 74, 105, 154, 155, 189, 266
Noble, C.R. ("Dudy"), 27, 33
North American Basketball League, 272
North Carolina College for Negroes (North Carolina Central), 81-82, 86, 88, 89
North Carolina, University of, 51
Northwestern University, 28, 208
Notre Dame, University of, 24, 25, 91, 150, 208, 258
November, Walter, 53, 54, 57, 59, 60, 103, 105, 106, 155, 175, 176, 276, 278
Nowak, Paul, 25

O'Callaghan, J.J., S.J., 45
Ohio State University, 39, 111-116, 121, 143, 147, 148, 157-159, 206
100 Black Men, 277
Olajuwon, Hakeem, 191
Owens, Ted, 79, 89

Pallotta, Nick, 108
Parks, George, 87
Pearl High School (Nashville), 89, 91, 92, 95, 135, 218, 247, 248
Penn State University, 27
Perry, Hal, 42
Pettit, Bob, 61
Pittsburgh, University of, 43
Point-shaving scandal
   of 1951, 53, 58, 186
   of 1961, 53, 58, 59, 124
Pomerantz, Sandy, 76
Portland Trailblazers, 243
Portune, Robert, 71
Posey, Don, 172, 212, 217, 220, 221, 267, B, C
Powless, John, 230

Ransom, Samuel, 26
Rather, Dan, 167, 169
Rayl, Jimmy, 179
Reardon, Jim, 187, F
Red, Clarence, 42-44, 68, 92, 96, 109, 145, 148, 149, 253, 254
Reed, Willis, 51
Reis, Ron, D
Rhoden, William C., 240
Riddell, Tally D., 202
Roberts, M.M., 202

Robertson, Oscar, 35-40, 61, 71, 73, 75, 76, 78,
    111, 140, 268, 278
Robertson, Pablo, 132, 175-178, 182,
    185-187, 189, 207
Robeson, Paul, 26
Robinson, Jackie, 18, 26, 56, 57, 278
Rochelle, Rich, 108, 126, 187, 274,275, F
    New Orleans trip, 151, 152
    relationship with Ireland, 151, 255, 256,
    274, 275
Roggenburk, Garry, 155
Rossini, Lou, 57
Rouse, Vic (Victor), 17, 18, 20, 89, 91-93, 95,
    96, 106, 125, 126, 134, 135, 145-147, 152-156,
    206, 218, 222, 223, 233, 235, 247, 248, 256,
    260, 261, 274, 278, F, H
Rubin, Roy, 104, 105
Rucker, Holcombe, 50-52, 54, 278
Rucker Park, 51
Rucker tournament, 50-52, 177
Rupp, Adolph, 29, 85, 113, 119, 157, 193, 246
Rush, Red, 123, 125, 126, 234, 235, 239,
Russell, Bill, 35, 42, 178
Russell, Cazzie, 271, 272

Sachs, Lenny (Leonard), 24, 26, G
St. Catherine High School (Racine, WI),
    108, 274
St. Elizabeth High School (Chicago), 27,
    41, 42, 58, 67, 89, 99, 100, 149n
St. Ignatius College, 23, 67
St. Ignatius High School (Chicago), 67, 101
St. John's University, 49, 53, 54n, 58, 105,
    189, 258
St. Louis University, 74, 77, 78
St. Rita High School (Chicago), 99, 100,
    102, 208, 224
Samuel Gompers High School (New York),
    104
San Francisco, University of (USF), 35, 42,
    45, 243
Sanders, Tom "Satch", 53
Saperstein, Abe, 24n, 66
Schalk, Art, 263
Scheuerman, Sharm, 100, 101
Schoen, Harold, 155
Seattle University, 35, 85, 180
"Secret Game," 86-89
Seiden, Al, 53
Seton Hall University, 38, 58, 73, 75
Sheedy, Paul, 29
Shingleton, Larry, 75, 124, 126, 127, 137, 141,
    230, 234, 269, D
shot clock, 20, 220
Shows, Bobby, 117-119, 172, 193, 194, 217, 218,
    222, 223, 265, 267, B, C
Shows, Judy, 265

Siegfried, Larry, 112, 114, 115
Simmons, Jerry, 209, 212, B
Sizer, Tom, 76, D
Skinner, Roy, 248, 249
Smedley, Anthony, 240
Smith, Billy (Edward), 175-180, 183, 186, 187,
    189, 207
Smith, Dean, 220, 228
Smith, George, 38-40, 73, 115, 140
Smith, Tommie, 249
SMU (Southern Methodist University), 27
Snake Pit (Bradley fieldhouse), 74, 75, 77, 141
Sollazzo, Salvatore, 58
Southeastern Conference (SEC), 31, 32,61,
    62, 119, 120, 193-195, 202, 208, 211, 221,
    247-249
Southern Association of Colleges and
    Schools (SACS), 197
Sports Network, Incorporated, 231
stall, stalling, 20, 115, 123, 125, 126, 220, 241,
    268
Stallworth, Dave, 189, 205-207
Stroud, Red, 117, 193, 220, 221, 266, B
Sugar Bowl, 43
Supreme Court, U.S., 148, 161-163, 251

Taylor, Chuck, 85
Taylor, Fred, 111, 113, 147, 157
Tennessee State University (Tennessee
    A&I), 28, 79, 83-85, 89-92, 131, 145, 247,
    250
Tennessee Tech University, 208, 209, 222
Tennessee, University of, 32
Texas Southern University, 17, 40, 57
Texas Western College (now University of
    Texas-El Paso, or UTEP), 245, 246, 268
Thacker, Tom, 18, 19, 73-77, 115, 123-
    126, 137, 140, 142, 183, 190, 233-
    235, 241, 269, D, G, H
The Breaks of the Game by David
    Halberstam, 244
Thomas, John C., 207
Thoren, Skip, 223
three-point shot, 20, 206, 221, 276
Thurmond, Nate, 188, 189, 222
Trester, Arthur, 36
Triplett, Ajac, 178, 179
Twin City Sailors, 272
Tynberg, Mike, 52-54, 59

U.S. Basketball Writers Association
    (USBWA), 39, 228, 229
U.S. marshals, 164-171
UCLA (University of California at Los
    Angeles), 26, 57, 89, 91, 142, 157, 250, 258
Ugolini, JoAnn, 272, 273
Ugolini, Louis, 272, 273

unwritten rule (or unwritten law), Mississippi's, 33, 62, 193, 195, 197, 201, 259

Utah, University of, 112, 113, 159, 243

Van Arsdale, Dick and Tom, 179
Van Dyck, Brian, 262
Vanderbilt University, 248, 250
Verwey, Jerry, 256

Walker, Chet, 74, 158, 159
Walker, Edwin, 165
Walker, Wade, 195, 211, 214
Wallace, Perry, 247-251
Walsh, Donnie, 51
Ward, Jimmy, 200, 201, 202, 214
Wendell Phillips High School (Chicago), 24
Western Michigan University, 73, 147, 178, 179
White, Art, 27, 41, 89
White, Hilton, 245, 246

Wichita State University, 141, 142, 187, 189, 205-207
Wiesenhahn, Bob, 76, 77, 114, 115, 137, 190
Wilson, George, 20, 125-127, 137-142, 183, 233, 235, 240, 241, 269, D, G
Winter, Tex, 112
Wisconsin, University of, 28, 178
Wise, Jimmy, 194, 195, 209, 267, B
Wofford, Jackie, 210, 267, B
Wood, Chuck, 108, 135, 152, 179, 187, 190, 224, 226, 270, 274, F
Wooden, John, 25, 142, 258
Woolpert, Phil, 42
World War I, 24
World War II, 24, 26, 32, 50, 104, 138

Xavier High School (Cincinnati), 187
Xavier University of Louisiana, 109, 149, 150, 154, 158n, 175, 269

Yates, Tony, 75-77, 114, 115, 124-127, 137, 140, 158, 234, 241, D, G

ABOUT THE AUTHOR

Michael Lenehan is the former editor and executive editor of the *Chicago Reader* and a former contributing editor of the *Atlantic*. He grew up in Fair Lawn, New Jersey, and graduated from Notre Dame. He lives in Chicago with his wife, Mary Williams.